HUGH GWYETH

A ROUNDHEAD CAVALIER

HUGH GWYETH

A ROUNDHEAD CAVALIER

BY

BEULAH MARIE DIX

WILDSIDE PRESS

COPYRIGHT, 1899,
BY THE MACMILLAN COMPANY.

Set up and electrotyped March, 1899. Reprinted May, July, 1899.

CONTENTS

CHAPTER		PAGE
I.	Tidings out of the North	1
II.	How One set out to seek his Fortune	16
III.	The Road to Nottingham	34
IV.	To Horse and Away	49
V.	In and Out of the "Golden Ram"	66
VI.	The End of the Journey	81
VII.	How the World dealt by a Gentleman	95
VIII.	The Interposition of John Ridydale	113
IX.	The Way to War	132
X.	In the Trail of the Battle	152
XI.	Comrades in Arms	171
XII.	For the Honor of the Gwyeths	190
XIII.	In the Fields toward Osney Abbey	208
XIV.	Under the King's Displeasure	224
XV.	The Life of Edmund Burley	242
XVI.	Roundheads and Cavaliers	258
XVII.	The Stranger by the Way	274
XVIII.	The Call out of Kingsford	290
XIX.	The Riding of Arrow Water	307
XX.	Beneath the Roof of Everscombe	324
XXI.	The Fatherhood of Alan Gwyeth	340
XXII.	After the Victory	358

HUGH GWYETH

A ROUNDHEAD CAVALIER

CHAPTER I

TIDINGS OUT OF THE NORTH

Up in the tops of the tall elms that overshadowed the east wing of Everscombe manor house the ancient rooks were gravely wrangling. A faint morning breeze swept the green branches and, as the leaves stirred, the warm September sunlight smiting through fell in flakes of yellow on the dark flagstones of the terrace below. For a moment Hugh Gwyeth ceased to toss up and catch the ball in his hand, while he stood to count the yellow spots that shifted on the walk. Eight, nine, — but other thoughts so filled his head that there he lost count and once more took up his listless tramp.

Off to his left, where beyond the elms the lawn sloped down to the park, he could hear the calls of the boys at play, — his Oldesworth cousins and Aunt Rachel Millington's sons. The Millingtons had come to Everscombe a week before out of Worcestershire, where the king's men were up in arms and had plundered their house. Yet the young Millingtons were playing at ball with the

Oldesworth lads as if it were only a holiday. "Children!" Hugh muttered contemptuously and, conscious of his own newly completed sixteen years, threw an increased dignity into his step. He was a wiry lad, of a slender, youthful figure, but for all that he carried himself well and with little awkwardness. Neither was he ill-looking; though there was a reddish tinge to his close-cut hair it changed to gold when he came into the sunlight, and at all times there was in his blue eyes a steady, frank look that made those who liked him forget the freckles across the bridge of his nose and cheek bones, and the almost aggressive squareness of his chin.

Mouth and chin were even sullen now, as Hugh lingered a moment to glance up at the small diamond panes of the window of the east parlor. Within, Hugh's grandfather, Gilbert Oldesworth, the master of Everscombe, his sons, Nathaniel and Thomas, his daughter's husband, David Millington, and Roger Ingram, the lieutenant in Thomas Oldesworth's troop of horse, were conferring with men from Warwick on the raising of forces, the getting of arms, and all the means for defending that part of the county; and Peregrine, the eldest of the Oldesworth lads, was allowed to be of their counsels. Hugh turned away sharply and resumed his dreary tramp up and down the flagged terrace. "If I had been Uncle Nathaniel's son, they would have suffered me to be present as well as Peregrine," he muttered, pausing to dig the toe of his shoe into a crack between the flagstones. "'Tis not just. I am near a man, and they might treat me—"

He gave the ball an extra high toss and paced on slowly.

But, call as he would upon his injured dignity, he could not refrain from facing about at the end of the walk and retracing his steps till he was loitering once more beneath the window of the east parlor. He was not listening, he told himself, nor was he spying; there was no harm in walking on the east terrace of a morning, nor in lingering there to play at ball. So he stood slipping the ball from hand to hand, but his eyes were fixed on the little panes of the window above and his thoughts were busy on what was happening within. Would the people of the hamlets round about Everscombe, the farmers and ploughboys, who of a Sunday sat stolidly in the pews of the village church at Kingsford, would they truly resist their sovereign? The Oldesworths would head them, without doubt, but how many others scattered through the county and all through wide England were of the like mind? And what would come of it? Would there be war in the land, such wars as Hugh had read the Greeks and Romans had waged, such as the great German wars in which his own father had borne a part? And if there was a war and brave deeds to do and fame to win, would his grandfather and his uncles let him come and fight too, or would they still shut him out with the little boys, as they had shut him out to-day?

So he was thinking, when of a sudden the window at which he had been staring swung open, and Nathaniel Oldesworth, a mild-featured man of middle age, looked out upon him. Hugh flushed suddenly and kept his eyes on the ball he was still shifting from hand to hand. "You here, Hugh?" his uncle's voice reached him. "Take yourself off to your play."

"Ay, sir," Hugh answered, and sauntered away down the walk. He kept his chin up and his mouth was sulky, but in his boy's heart every fibre of awakening manhood was quivering at this last insult. Go play! when every moment was big with events, when war was bursting on the land, and there was work for every man to do, he was bidden to content himself with a ball!

He went slowly down the steps at the south end of the terrace and bearing off from the stables struck through the long grass toward the orchard. He walked with eyes on the ground, too deeply buried in his own resentful thoughts to heed whither he was going, but he realized when he entered the orchard, for the sunlight that had been all about him since he quitted the terrace went out; he saw the earth was no longer grassy but bald and brown, and he trod on a hard green apple that rolled under his foot.

A second small apple suddenly plumped to the ground before him, and a girl's voice called, "Hugh, Hugh."

The boy looked up. Just above his head, through the branches of the great apple tree, he saw the face of Lois Campion, the orphan niece of Nathaniel Oldesworth's wife. "Are you hunting for snails?" she asked, while her dark eyes laughed. "Prithee, give over now, like a good lad, and help me hence. I have sat here half the morning for lack of an arm to aid me."

She had slipped down the branches to the fork of the tree so that she could rest her hands on Hugh's shoulders, and as they came thus face to face her tone changed: "Why, Hugh, what has gone wrong?"

"Nothing," he answered shortly, swinging her down to the ground.

"You look as though you had eaten a very sour apple," said Lois. "Try these. There are sweet tastes in them, if you chew long enough." She had seated herself at the foot of the tree with her head resting against the gnarled gray trunk.

"It's not apples I want," Hugh replied gruffly, and then the troubled look in the girl's eyes made him sit down beside her with a thought of saying something to make amends for his surliness; only words did not come easily, for his mind could run on nothing but his own discontent.

"I think I know," Lois spoke gently and put her hand on his arm. "'Tis because of Cousin Peregrine."

Hugh shook off her hand and dropped down full length on the ground with his forehead pressing upon his arms; he felt it would be the crowning humiliation of the morning if the girl should see the look on his face at the mere mention of his trouble.

For a time there was silence, except for the thud of a falling apple and the soft rustle of leaves in the light wind; it was one of Lois's best comrade qualities, Hugh realized vaguely now, that she knew when to hold her peace. It was he himself that renewed the conversation, when he felt assured that he had himself too well in hand to let any childish breaking be audible in his voice: "I wish my father had lived."

"I wish my parents had, too," Lois answered quietly.

"I did not wish it, when I spoke, because I loved them, I fear," Hugh went on, digging up the scant blades of grass about him with one hand; "I do love them, but I did not think of it so, then. But I thought how, when a lad hath a father alive, things are made easy for him,—no, not easy; I do not mean skulking at home,—but he is helped to do a man's part. Now there was a good friend of mine, there at Warwick school, Frank Pleydall; I've spoke of him to you. I was home with him once for the holidays, to a great house in Worcestershire, where his father, Sir William Pleydall, lives. And Frank had his own horses and dogs, and the servants did his bidding, and—and his father is very fond of him." Hugh paused a moment, then gave words to the grievance nearest his heart: "And Peregrine, now, because he is Uncle Nathaniel's son, he is to have a cornetcy in Uncle Thomas's troop, and he will have a new horse,—I do not begrudge it to Peregrine, but they might try me and see what I can do."

"But, Hugh," Lois ventured, "you are younger than Peregrine."

"Only two years and a half," Hugh raised himself on one elbow, "and do but feel the thick of my right arm there. And at Warwick school when they taught us sword-play I learnt enough to worst Master Peregrine, I am sure. And I can stick to my saddle as well as he, though I never have anything to ride but a plough horse. And I have not even that now," he went on, with an effort at a laugh, "since all have been taken to mount Uncle Thomas's troop. But Peregrine will have a horse and a sword of his own and go to the wars. Do you understand what 'tis I mean, Lois?"

"Yes," Lois replied with a downward look and a quiver of the mouth. "You will think 'tis girl's folly in me, but I have felt what you mean when I have seen Martha and Anne have new gowns, and I must wear my old frock still."

There was another long silence, broken this time by Lois. "Hugh," she half whispered, "I believe we are very wicked and ungrateful to our kinsfolk."

"I do not believe so," the boy answered doggedly; "they have given us nothing but food and clothes, and one craves other things besides."

Lois nodded without speaking, then fetched a breath like a sob. "Lois!" Hugh cried in honest alarm; he had never seen her thus before, "don't cry. I am ashamed I bore myself so unmanly to hurt you. Don't cry." He took her hand in his, and tried to think of something comforting to say.

Lois bit her lips and made not another sound till she could answer with only a slight tremble: "What you spoke of, made me feel lonely."

"I am sorry I spoke so," Hugh said contritely, still holding her hand. "Shall we go look for apples now?"

The girl shook her head: "Prithee, do not put

me off, Hugh, and do not reproach yourself; I am not sorry that you spoke so. You are the only one to whom I can talk of such things, here at Everscombe."

"And you are the only one I have been able to talk to of anything that touches me nearly, these two years since my mother died. — Do you know, Lois, I sometimes think you look like her. She had brown hair like yours, for she was a true Oldesworth and dark. Now I am a Gwyeth, and so I come rightly by my red hair."

"You shall not slander it so," Lois interrupted.

"Aunt Delia calls it red. I care not for the color, but I'd like to let it grow." Hugh ran his fingers through his cropped hair.

"Would you turn Cavalier?" Lois asked half seriously.

"Most gentlemen wear their hair long; even my grandfather and Uncle Nathaniel, for all they hold to Parliament."

"Master Thomas Oldesworth has cut his close; he says all soldiers do so in Germany."

"My father did not," Hugh answered quickly. "And he had more experience in the German wars than ever Uncle Tom will have."

"Tell me about him again, Hugh, if you will," Lois begged.

The boy slipped down till he rested on his elbow once more. "There is not much I can tell," he began, but his face was eager with interest in the old story. "I remember little of those times, but my mother was ever telling me of him. His name was Alan Gwyeth; 'tis a Welsh name, and he had Welsh blood in him. They put him to school, but he ran away to follow the wars in the Low Countries. Later he was here in Warwickshire to raise men who'd adventure for the German wars, and he met my mother, and they loved each other, so they married. My grandfather and Uncle Nathaniel did not like my father, so he left the kingdom straightway, and she went with him on his campaigns in Germany. I was born there; I think I can remember it, just a bit. A porcelain stove with tiles, and the story of Moses upon them; and a woman with flaxen hair who took care of me; and my father, I am sure I remember him, a very tall man with reddish hair and blue eyes, who carried me on his shoulder." Hugh's look strayed beyond the girl and he was silent a time. "Then it all ended and we came home to England. I remember the ship and I was sick; and then the great coach we rode in from Bristol; and how big Everscombe looked and lonesome, and my mother cried."

"And—and your father?" Lois asked timidly.

"He died," Hugh answered softly. "My mother never told me how, but it must have been in battle, for he was a very brave soldier, she said. And he was the tenderest and kindest man that ever lived, and far too good for her, she said, but I do not believe that. And just before she died she told me I must try always to be like him, a true-hearted gentleman and a gallant soldier.—I am glad I look like him, and then, sometimes," Hugh's tone grew more dubious, "but usually 'tis when I have done wrong, Aunt Delia says I am my father over again."

"Aunt Delia has a sharp tongue," said Lois with a sigh.

"I know it well," Hugh answered ruefully.

"But still, she has a kind heart," the girl was amending charitably, when from across the orchard came a shrill call of "Hugh," which ended in a high-pitched howl.

Lois rose and peering under her hand gazed out into the sunlight of the level grass beyond the apple trees. "'Tis Sam Oldesworth," she said, and as she spoke a boy of thirteen or fourteen years broke headlong into the shade of the orchard.

"Where have you been, Hugh?" he panted. "Have you my ball safe? I've looked everywhere for you."

"For the ball? There 'tis," Hugh replied.

"Nay, not for that. There's something up at the house for you."

"What is it?" Hugh came to his feet at a jump, while his thoughts sped bewilderingly to swords, horses, and commissions.

"Guess," replied Sam.

Hugh turned his back and walked away toward the manor house at a dignified pace; it would not do to let a young sprig like Sam know his curiosity and eagerness. But Lois, having no such scruples, teased her cousin with questions till the boy, bubbling over with the importance of the news, admitted: "Well, the post from the north has come, and there is something for Hugh in the east parlor."

"A letter?" Hugh queried with momentary disappointment in his tone. But though a letter was not as good as a commission it was something he had never had before in his life, so he quickened his step and with high expectations entered the east wing and passed through the small hall to the parlor.

The door stood open, and opposite the sunlight from the window, still flung wide, lay in a clear rectangle upon the dark floor. About the heavy oak table in the centre of the room, in speech of the news brought from the north by the freshly arrived letters, sat or stood in knots of two or three the grave-faced men of the conference. At the head of the table, where the sunlight fell upon his long white hair, sat Master Gilbert Oldesworth, an erect man with keen eyes and alert gestures, in spite of his seventy years. Hugh also caught sight of Peregrine and noted, with a certain satisfaction, that this fortunate cousin sat at the foot of the table and seemed to have small share in the business in hand. But next moment he had enough to do to give heed to his own concerns, for Nathaniel Oldesworth called him by name and he must enter to receive his letter. He felt his cheeks burn with the consciousness that strangers had their eyes on him and that he must appear to them a mere dishevelled, awkward schoolboy; he grew angry with himself for his folly, and his face burned even more. Scarcely daring to raise his eyes, he caught up the letter his uncle held out to him and slipped back again into the hall.

Sam pounced upon him at once. "What is it?" he demanded, and Lois's eyes asked the same question.

Hugh forgot the hot embarrassment and misery of a moment before, as he turned the letter in his hand. "I don't know the writing," he said, prolonging the pleasure while he examined the superscription; then he tore open the paper, and the first sight of the sheet of big sprawling black letters was enough. "Ah, but I do know!" he cried. "'Tis from Frank Pleydall, Lois."

"Your school friend?"

"Yes. I have not heard from him these six months, since he left the school. Doctor Masham, the master, said the queen was a Babylonish woman, and when Sir William heard of that he came to the school in a great rage and called Doctor Masham a canting Puritan and a hoary-headed traitor, — truly, the Doctor is but little older and not a bit more white headed than Sir William himself. And he took Frank away, and — I was right sorry to lose him."

"But you have found him again now," said Lois. "Come, Sam." She coaxed the youngster, still reluctant and lingering, out upon the terrace, and Hugh, happy in being alone, set himself down at once on the stairway that led from the hall to the upper story. It was hard to find a secluded place in Everscombe those days, what with the men from Thomas Oldesworth's troop quartered in the old west wing, and the Millingtons and other refugee kinsfolk in the main part of the house. So in the fear that a noisy cousin or two might come to interrupt him, Hugh settled himself hastily and began his letter: —

GOOD HUGH:

It has come to my remembrance that it is many days since you have had news of me, so at a venture I send this letter to your grandfather's house, though the roads are so beset and the post so delayed it is doubtful if it ever reach you. I am here at Nottingham with my father. He commands a notable troop of horse, drawn out of our own county, and many of them men bred on our own lands, proper stout fellows, that will make the rebels to skip, I promise you. My father is colonel, and some of my cousins and uncles and neighboring gentlemen hold commissions, and I think I shall prevail upon my father to bestow one on me, though he maintains I be over-young, which is all folly. The king's standard was raised here week before last, and we all nigh split our throats with cheering. The town is full of soldiers and gentlemen from all over the kingdom, and many from following the wars abroad, and more coming every day. I have seen his Majesty the king,— God bless him! He rode through the street and he hath a noble face and is most gracious and kingly. I do not see how men can have the wickedness to take up arms against him. I have also seen his nephew, Prince Rupert, the famous German soldier, who they say shall have a great command in the war. My father has had speech with him and he commended our troop most graciously. It has been the most memorable time of all my life, and, best of all, I shall never go back to school now, but go to the wars. I would you might be with us, Hugh, for it is the only life for gentlemen of spirit. Heaven keep you well, and if this reaches you, write me in reply.

                Your loving friend to serve you,
                              FRANCIS PLEYDALL.

NOTTINGHAM, Sept. 5, 1642.

    I misremembered to tell you. Among the soldiers come from Germany is a certain Alan Gwyeth, a man of some forty years, with hair reddish gold like yours. It is an odd name and I thought perhaps he might be some kinsman of yours. We met with him the day the standard was raised, and I would have questioned him myself, but my father said I was over-forward and I had to hold my peace. Did your father leave any brothers or cousins in Germany? This man is a notable soldier and has got him a colonelcy under the Prince.
                                                F. P.

Hugh sat staring at the paper and saw the black letters and the words but found no meaning in them. Across the dim hall he could see through the open door the strip of greensward that ran across the front of Everscombe, part black with the shadow of the east wing and part dazzling bright with the noon sun. He fixed his gaze upon the clean line where the shade gave way to vivid light, till the sunny greenness blurred before his eyes; he felt the roughness of the paper, as he creased and recreased it with nervous fingers, but he could not think; he could only feel that something vast and portentous was coming into his life.

A noise of tramping feet and a burst of voices roused him. The conference ended, the men came slowly from the east parlor, and lingered speaking together, then scattered, some with Nathaniel Oldesworth into the main part of the house, some with Thomas Oldesworth out upon the terrace. Master Gilbert Oldesworth was not among them, Hugh noted, and on a sudden impulse he half ran across the hall and entered the east parlor, closing the door behind him.

Master Oldesworth looked up from the paper over which he had been poring. "You would speak with me, Hugh?" he asked, with a touch of displeasure in his tone.

"If I may. 'Tis important," Hugh stammered. "Will you look at this letter? No, not all, just this place, sir."

Hugh stood at his grandfather's side, griping the edge of the table so he saw the blood leave his fingers. In the elms outside the open window the rooks still scolded, and over in the corner of the room the great clock ticked loudly, but there was no other sound till Hugh had counted thrice sixty of its noisy ticks. Then the boy drew a quick breath, and, dreading what he might find, raised his eyes to his grandfather's face. But he saw no sign there for several moments, not till Master Oldesworth had laid down Frank Pleydall's letter, and then Hugh perceived there was something akin to pity in the old man's eyes.

"Well, Hugh, and what would you know?" he asked.

"That man, Alan Gwyeth, is he —" Hugh felt and knew what the answer would be before Master Oldesworth spoke the words slowly: "Yes, Hugh, 'tis your father."

CHAPTER II

HOW ONE SET OUT TO SEEK HIS FORTUNE

"You must have known at last, but I had not thought it would be so soon," Master Oldesworth went on. " 'Twas folly ever to have kept it from you."

In a blind way Hugh had groped for a chair and sat down with his elbow on the table and his forehead pressing hard upon his hand. His face was toward the window and he was aware of the brightness flooding in through it, but he could see clearly only his grandfather's thin, clean-shaven lips and searching eyes. "Tell me," he found voice to say at last, "I want to know all. My father—he has been alive all these years? You knew?"

Master Oldesworth nodded.

"You deceived me?" Hugh's voice rose shrill and uncontrollable. "You knew you were deceiving me? You had no right, 'twas wickedness, 'twas—"

"It was your mother's wish."

The burst of angry words was choked in Hugh's throat; with a little shudder of the shoulders he dropped his head upon his folded arms. "Will you tell me wherefore, sir?" he asked in a dull tone.

"Because of the never-dying folly of woman," Master Oldesworth replied, with a sudden fierce harshness of tone that made Hugh lift his head. He felt that, if the revelation of the letter had not made every other happening of that day commonplace, he would have been surprised at the sudden lack of control that made his grandfather's sallow cheeks flush and his thin lips move. But in a moment Master Oldesworth was as calm of demeanor as before and his voice was quite colorless when he resumed: "Hear the truth at last, Hugh, and you, too, will have reason to curse the folly of womankind. She, your mother, my best-beloved daughter, was most wilful, even from a child. Though you have none of her look I have noted in you something of her rash temper. Her own impulse and desire must always be her guides, and well they guided her. For there came a swashbuckling captain of horse out of Germany, with a brisk tongue and an insolent bearing, for which that mad girl put all her love on him, worthless hackster though he was."

"'Tis my father whom you speak of so?" Hugh cried, with an involuntary clinching of the hands.

"Your mother's work again!" said Master Oldesworth with a flicker of a smile, that was half sad and half contemptuous. "She fled away from her father's house to marry this swaggering rascal; she followed him into Germany; and there she found true all her kinsmen had told her of his worthlessness and wickedness. So she took her child and gladly came back to us again."

"She never uttered word of this to me," Hugh maintained doggedly.

"I urged her to," Master Oldesworth continued, "but, with the weakness of her sex, before six months were out she had forgot his unworthiness and baseness. She remembered only that she loved him and she blamed herself that she had left him; indeed, she would have returned if she had been assured he would receive her back. But I forbade her hold communication with him while she dwelt beneath my roof, and he himself did not care to seek her out, though she long looked for him. When he did not come she was the more convinced the fault was hers, and, since she had robbed her son of his father, as she phrased it, she would at least give him a true and noble conception of that father to cherish. Perhaps she held it compensation for the wrong she thought she had worked Alan Gwyeth that she sketched him unto you a paragon of all virtues. And partly for that he was dead to her, and partly for that she would not have the shame of her flight, as she called her most happy deliverance, be known to you, she gave him out to you as dead. 'Twas ill done, but I suffered her to rule you as she would; I had ever a weak fondness for her."

With a sudden jarring noise Hugh thrust back his chair and stumbling to the window stood so Master Oldesworth could not see his face. His poor mother, his poor mother! Because he knew in his heart she had done ill to him with her weak deceptions he loved her and pitied her all the more, and his eyes smarted with repressed tears that he could not see her nor tell her that it all mattered little, the agony this disillusionment was costing him; he knew she had meant it kindly and he thanked her for it.

He was still staring out between the elms at the sloping lawn, where, he remembered as if it had happened years back, he had played that very morning like a boy, when his grandfather's dry tones reached him: "This man would seem to have roistered through life without thought of her. Of late I did not know myself whether he were dead or living, but it seems he is sailing on the high waves of royal favor and has found himself fitting comradeship among the profligates and traitors of King Charles's camp."

Hugh swept his hand across his eyes and faced about squarely. His father a profligate who had abandoned his mother! Who dared say it or believe it? His mother's face as she had looked before she died came back to him. A true-hearted gentleman and a gallant soldier, like his father, — like his father.

"And you never suspected anything of the truth ere this?" Master Oldesworth pursued.

"Once, months back, Aunt Delia told me a story somewhat like this," Hugh's voice came low but so firm it surprised him, "but I held it only some of her spitefulness and I did not believe it."

Master Oldesworth looked up with a curious expression. "Do you believe it now?" he asked.

"No," Hugh answered honestly, then quickly added, "I crave your pardon, sir, but I cannot believe it."

"Have back this letter of yours," Master Oldesworth said, rising, and as Hugh came up to him he put his hand on the boy's shoulder. "You have a loyal heart, Hugh Gwyeth," he said dryly, "and 'tis no shame of yours you have such a father."

"I am not ashamed of him, sir," Hugh replied stoutly.

"You are your mother over again," said the old man, in a tone that held something of vexation and something of amusement, yet more of kindliness than he was accustomed to show his orphan grandson.

Hugh was in no mood to note this, however, but, delaying only to take his precious letter, left the east parlor at a brisk step that verged upon a run. Once in the open air, where he was freed from the restraint of his grandfather's presence, he leaped down the low terrace and, hallooing at the top of his lungs, raced full speed across the lawn. But when the shadow of the tall oaks on the border of the park fell upon him the noisiness of his joy somewhat abated. He rambled on more slowly with a happy under-consciousness of the dusky green of the old trees about him and the shimmer of the stray sunbeams; he wondered that the dull, familiar park seemed so joyous and beautiful a place.

Not till he had crossed the grassy roadway that led to the manor house, and plunged into the thicker growth of trees, did he come again to the power of framing connected thoughts. Little by little he let his pace slacken, till at length he flung himself down in the shade of a beech tree and pulling out Frank's letter read the last sentences aloud. His father was alive, an officer in the king's army, at Nottingham, only the width of two counties away. Hugh clasped his hands behind his head and lying back gazed up unwinkingly at the cloudless blue sky; in his heart there was no room for any feeling save that of pure happiness, of which the bright day seemed a mere reflection. For he neither remembered nor heeded the words his grandfather had spoken of Alan Gwyeth; he only knew that a few score miles away the tall man with reddish hair and blue eyes, who used to carry him upon his shoulder, was alive and waiting for him.

The resolve formed in these hours of reflection he told to Lois Campion, when, late in the afternoon, he crashed his way out to the edge of the park with the briskness of one who has made up his mind. The girl was playing at shuttlecock with Martha Oldesworth, but at sight of Hugh she quickly laid aside her battledoor and came to him where he was lingering for her beneath the oaks. "Where have you been?" she cried. "We missed you at dinner, and Peregrine, who was honey-tongued as ever, said you were sulking. But I knew 'twas some witchery in that letter."

Hugh laughed excitedly. "Witchery? Ay, 'twas that indeed, Lois. Can you believe it? My father is alive, at the king's camp; and I have determined to go to him."

With that he made her sit down beside him and told her all, so confidently and happily she dared not venture more than one objection: "But 'tis a long way to Nottingham, Hugh."

"I can walk it. Take no heed to the way, Lois, but think of the end."

"When shall you go?" she asked, playing absently with some acorns she had gathered in her hand.

"To-morrow night."

"So soon?" The acorns fell neglected to the ground.

"Nay, 'tis delaying over-long. I would set out this very night, but I suppose I should take some time for preparation."

"And you must run from home by night?" she repeated sadly.

"Like Dick Whittington. I wonder if I have such good fortune as he."

"How happy your father will be to see you!" Lois continued.

"'Twill be naught but happiness for us all," Hugh ran on boisterously. "Ah, must you go, Lois?"

"I must finish my game with Martha," the girl answered steadily. Hugh saw, however, that she did not go near Martha but walked away to the house, and he was vexed because she did not care enough about his departure to stay to talk with him.

It was well for Hugh the day was nearly spent, if his plans were to be kept secret; for he longed to speak of them, and, now Lois would not listen, there was no one in whom he could safely confide. Moreover, Sam Oldesworth was so curious about the letter that it was a perilously great temptation to hint to him just a little, especially when the two boys were preparing for bed. Since the

Millingtons had come to Everscombe Sam and Hugh had been obliged to sleep together, an arrangement never acceptable to the older boy and this night even dangerous. Fortunately he realized his weakness enough to reply shortly to all his companion's eager questions, however gladly he would have told something of his secret, till Sam at last grumbled himself to sleep. But Hugh turned on his side and for hours lay staring into the dark of the chamber, planning for his journey and sometimes wondering where he would be in the blackness of the next night.

In the morning, when he first woke and lay gazing at the familiar room, it gave him a feeling of surprisingly keen regret to tell himself that this was his last day at Everscombe. Perhaps it was the outward aspect of the day that made him feel so depressed, for a slow, drizzling rain was falling and the sky was thick with gray clouds.

All the morning Hugh avoided his cousins, and even Lois, against whom the resentment of the previous afternoon still lasted, and prowled restlessly about the house to pay farewell visits to the rooms that he had known. Thus his Aunt Delia found him, loitering upon the garret stairs, and sharply bade him go about his business, so Hugh, his sensitive dignity a-quiver, drew back to his chamber, where he pretended to choose equipments for his journey. In reality it was a simple matter; he would wear his stuff jacket and breeches, — he owned no other suit of clothes, — and his one pair of stout shoes. He did not trouble himself about clean linen, but he took pains to see that his pistol was in order; it was an old one that had belonged to Peregrine, before he received a case of new ones in keeping with his position as cornet in the Parliament's army. Peregrine's old riding boots had also fallen to Hugh's share; they were a trifle too big and were ill patched, but there was something trooper-like about them that made him sorry when he realized that he could not take them with him. He reluctantly dropped them back into the wardrobe, and then, the sight of them reminding him he had yet to bid farewell to his friends the horses, he spattered out through the rain to the stables.

The stones of the stable yard were slippery and wet; at the trough in the centre three horses, with their coats steaming, were drinking, while the man at their heads, one of Tom Oldesworth's newly levied troopers, joked noisily with a little knot of his comrades. Inside the big dark stable a great kicking and stamping of horses was rumblingly audible above the loud talk of the men at work. Hugh loitered into the confusion and, making his way through the main building, entered the quieter wing, where were the old family horses with whom he had acquaintance. But when he stepped through the connecting door he perceived that even here others were before him; standing with hands behind him and legs somewhat wide, as befitted a veteran horse-soldier, was Tom Oldesworth, a close-shaven, firm-mouthed man of thirty, in talk with his lieutenant, Roger Ingram. Near by stood Peregrine Oldesworth, a heavy-featured, dark lad, who was bearing his part in the conversation quite like a man. Whatever the matter was, they seemed too merry over it for any business of the troop, so Hugh thought it no harm to saunter over to them.

"Looking for a commission, eh, Hugh?" Tom Oldesworth broke off his talk to ask jestingly.

"Not under you, sir," Hugh retorted, rather sharply.

Oldesworth laughed and patted his head. "Never mind, my Roundhead," he said cheerfully, as Hugh ducked out of his reach, "your turn'll come soon. No doubt Peregrine will get a ball through his brains ere the winter be over, and then I promise you his place."

"Then you think the war will last till winter?" questioned Ingram.

"Till winter? I tell you, Roger, we're happy if we have a satisfactory peace in the land two full years hence."

"You're out there, Captain. These gallants of the king's will stand to fight here no better than they stood against the Scots. They'll be beat to cover ere snow fall—"

"Pshaw!" replied Oldesworth, convincingly. "Look you here, Roger." Thereupon the two fell to discussing the king's resources and those of Parliament, and comparing the merits of commanders, and quoting the opinions of leaders, till Hugh tired of it all and strolled away.

He passed slowly down the line of stalls, caressing the soft muzzles of the kindly horses, and lingered a time to admire the big black charger that belonged to Captain Oldesworth. In the next stall stood a clean-limbed bay, which thrust out its head as if expecting notice; Hugh hesitated, then began stroking the velvety nose, when

Peregrine swaggered up to him with a grand, " Don't worry that horse of mine, Hugh."

" I was not worrying him," Hugh answered hotly. " But you can be sure I'll never touch him again." He turned and walked away toward the open door.

" Oh, you can touch him now and then," Peregrine replied, as he followed after him out into the courtyard, where the rain had somewhat abated. " But he's too brave a beast for you youngsters to be meddling with all the time. You'd spoil his temper." Then, as Hugh still kept a sulky silence, his cousin asked abruptly, " What's amiss with you to-day ? "

" Nothing."

" You've not been friendly of late. I believe you are jealous that I have a commission."

" I do not want your commission," Hugh replied, and to show he spoke the truth he forced a laugh and tried to say carelessly, as he might have said a month before, " Tell you what I do want, though: a new flint for my pistol. Will you not give me one, Peregrine ? "

" Are you going to shoot Cavaliers ? " the elder boy asked, as he halted to fumble in his pockets.

" Maybe."

Peregrine drew out three bits of flint, turned them in his hand, then gave the least perfect to Hugh. " I took it from my new pistol this morning," he explained. " 'Tis good enough for any service you'll need of it."

Hugh bit his lip, but with a muttered word of thanks took the flint.

" I was furbishing up my weapons this morning," Peregrine went on. "We go on real service next week; we determined on it yesterday at the conference."

"I thought Uncle Tom said the troop would not be in fit condition to serve for a fortnight."

"Not all the troop. But Uncle Tom, and I, and Lieutenant Ingram, are to take some thirty men that are in trim and go into Staffordshire to see what can be done among the godly people thereabouts."

"Good luck to you, Peregrine," Hugh forced himself to say, then shook off his companion and, passing from the stable yard, trudged away through the wet grass, with the old jealous pang worrying him as savagely as ever. But soon he told himself that his father would probably give him a horse and good weapons too, and, being a colonel in the king's army, would very likely let him go to the wars with him, perhaps even give him a commission; and, thinking still of his father, by the time he returned to the house he had quite forgotten Peregrine.

The rain had nearly ceased; there seemed even a prospect of a clear sunset, and with the lightening of the weather Hugh cast aside the heavy feeling of half-regretful parting which had weighed on him all day and grew impatient for darkness, when he could set out on his journey. But the night came slowly, as any other night, with a rift of watery sunset in the west and mottled yellow clouds, that fading gave place to the long, gray twilight, which deepened imperceptibly.

Hugh started early to his room, which was in the east wing, so he went by the staircase from the little hall. Halfway up, as he strode two steps at a time, he almost stumbled over a slight figure that caught at his arm. "Lois!" he cried.

The girl rose to her feet. "Why are you angry with me, Hugh?" she asked, and though he could not see her face he knew by her voice she was almost sobbing.

"Why did you run away from me yesterday?" he replied, feeling foolish and without excuse.

"No matter. I have forgot. But I wanted to have speech with you."

"You waited here to bid me farewell? 'Twas good of you, Lois," Hugh blurted out. "I am sorry I was so rough to you about yesterday."

"Then we'll part still friends?" Lois said eagerly. "And here is something you are to take with you."

"Your five shillings?" Hugh broke out, as she pressed the coins into his hand. "Nay, Lois, I cannot."

"You must; 'twill be a long journey, and you have little money, I know. And I shall never have need of such a hoard. Prithee, take it, Hugh, else I shall think you still are angry because I left you yesterday. But truly, 'twas only that I could not bear the thought of your going." She was crying now in good earnest, and Hugh tried awkwardly to soothe her and whisper her some comfort: he wished she were a boy and could go with him, perhaps even now he could come back some time and fetch her; he never would forget what a good friend she had been to him; and much more he was saying, when Martha's voice came from below in the dusk of the hall: "Lois."

"I must go," the girl whispered. "Farewell, Hugh."

"Farewell, Lois."

"God keep you, dear, always."

He heard her go slowly down the stairs and wished she had stayed with him longer; he might have said more cheering things. Then he heard the footsteps of the two girls die away in the hall, and he went on to his room.

He had placed his pistol on a chair beneath his cloak and hat, and had just lain down in his undergarments and stockings beneath the coverings, when Sam came in full of conversation, which Hugh's short replies quickly silenced. But after the boy had lain down Hugh remembered that this was the last night they would sleep together, and, repenting his shortness, he said gently: "Good night, Sam."

"What's wrong with you?" asked his cousin, which made Hugh feel foolish and answer curtly, "Nothing."

Then there was a long silence in the dark chamber, till at length Sam was breathing deep and evenly. He was well asleep, Hugh assured himself, so, slipping quietly from the bed, he quickly drew on his outer clothes, put on cloak and hat, and tucked the pistol in his belt. He was just taking his shoes in his hand, when Sam stirred and asked drowsily: "What are you doing now?"

"I saw Martha's battledoor out o' doors," Hugh

mumbled. "I must fetch it or the dew will spoil it."

Sam gave a sleepy sigh, then buried his head in the pillow again, and Hugh, waiting for no more, stole out of the room into the darkness of the corridor that was so thick it seemed tangible. He scuffed cautiously to the stairs and with his hand on the railing groped his way down. As he went he grew more accustomed to the blackness, and so, treading carefully, came without stumbling or noise to the outer door. He worked back the bolt, cautiously and slowly, and with a nervous start at each faint creak, till at last he could push the door open far enough to slip through. The grass felt cold beneath his stockinged feet; the night wind came damp and chilly against his face. With a shiver that was not all from cold he drew the door to, more quickly than he had thought, for the metal work jarred harshly.

With a feeling that the whole household must be aroused he ran noiselessly across the terrace, and, pausing only to draw on his shoes, struck briskly through the wet grass toward the park. At its outskirts he halted and, glancing back, took a last look at Everscombe, black and silent under the stars. Only in one window, that of his grandfather's chamber in the main building, was a candle burning, and the thought of the habitable room in which it shone made the night seem darker and lonelier. Hugh looked quickly away, and calling up his resolution plunged in among the trees.

He had meant to go through to the highway by a footpath, but the woods were blacker than he had thought for; again and again he missed the track, till at last, finding himself on the beaten roadway from the manor house, he decided the quicker course was to follow it. He had covered perhaps half the distance and was trudging along with his head bent to look to his footsteps, when from the thicket just before him came a voice: "Stand, there!"

Hugh stopped where he was, half frightened for the instant, then half inclined to run, when an erect figure stepping from beneath a neighboring tree barred his path. By the long cloak and the staff on which the man leaned Hugh guessed it was his grandfather, even before Master Oldesworth spoke again: "So you are leaving us, Hugh Gwyeth?"

"Yes, sir," Hugh replied defiantly.

"So I had judged. You are bound for the near park gate?"

Hugh nodded.

"You must bear with my company that far."

So side by side they passed down the dark roadway, till presently the trees thinned and the starlight reached them. Then Hugh glanced up at his companion's face but found it fixed in so stern an expression that he did not care to look again.

"You are going to your father?" Master Oldesworth queried after a time.

"Yes, sir," Hugh replied. The defiance had gone from his tone now.

At length the dimly seen roadway ran between two huge dark pillars, half hidden by the trees; it was the park gate, Hugh saw, and beyond was the king's highway. Involuntarily he slackened his pace, and his grandfather halted too, and stood by one of the pillars, resting both hands upon the top of his staff. "Then you have the grace to hesitate a moment," the old man spoke, "before you leave those who have sheltered you?"

Hugh dared not trust his voice to reply, and after a moment Master Oldesworth continued slowly: "It is your mother over again. We reared her and cared for her, and she left us for Alan Gwyeth; and you — Have you not had a home here?"

"Yes, sir," Hugh answered meekly. He knew well that the grievances which were so true when he told them to Lois would be nothing in his grandfather's sight.

"And what has this father for whom you leave us done for you?" Master Oldesworth pursued. "You cannot answer? He broke your mother's heart and deserted you —"

"He is my father," Hugh replied.

"Go to him, then, as your mother did before you. But mark you this, Hugh Gwyeth: I received her back when Alan Gwyeth wearied of her, but I shall never receive you back. Go now, and you go for all time."

"I shall never ask you to take me back." Hugh tried to speak stoutly, but his voice faltered in an ignoble manner.

"Now consider well," his grandfather continued. "When you pass the gate it will be to me as if you had never lived. Be not rash, Hugh," he went on more gently. "Come back with me to the house; this folly of yours shall never be known, and I shall look to your welfare as I always have. But if you choose to go to that place of perdition, the king's camp, and to that evil man, Alan Gwyeth, I forget you are my daughter's son. Now make your choice between that man and me."

CHAPTER III

THE ROAD TO NOTTINGHAM

Over in the marsh beyond the dim highway the frogs were piping their lonesome note; the shrilling call of autumnal insects sounded from the wayside; of a sudden the waste darkness reëchoed with solitary noises. All came clearly to Hugh's ear in the hush that followed his grandfather's words, and with them something that was akin to fright laid hold on him. Outside the park gate the world looked vast and black; he felt himself weak in his youthfulness, so even the butt of his pistol for which he groped did not strengthen his courage. He looked to his grandfather and involuntarily made a step toward him, but Master Oldesworth still stood with his hands upon the top of his staff and watched him but made no sign. With a stinging sense of rebuff Hugh drew back and held himself quiet, while he strove to think clearly and so make his resolution without prejudice. But all the time he felt that invisible hands were surely haling him back to Everscombe and with his whole will he struggled against them. "Will it be ended past question when I go out at the gateway?" he cried, almost before his thought had framed the words.

He did not even wait for an assent, but as he spoke stepped out beyond the pillars of the gate into the rough highway. There he faced about suddenly. "Grandfather," he cried, "I— I am grateful for all you have done for me. Prithee, forgive me." The words died away then, for he saw Master Oldesworth had turned and was walking slowly toward Everscombe, nor did he once look back.

For an instant it was borne in on Hugh to run after his grandfather, to implore pardon, to beg to be taken back and suffered to live the old dull life at the manor house; then the impulse left him and he was more ashamed of it than of his previous wavering. Still he lingered by the gate, straining his eyes into the dusk of the park till long after he had lost sight of Master Oldesworth. Once more he became aware of the sad piping of frogs in the marsh, and he listened stupidly, while heavier and heavier he felt the weight of loneliness press upon him. For he now realized that his decision had indeed been irrevocable; for all time he was cut off from his kinsfolk and his only home.

When at last he turned slowly from the gateway there was no hopefulness in his step nor did he lift his eyes from the ground, unless to glance up at the familiar trees of the park that he should not see again. But at length, through the branches before him, he beheld Charles's Wain shining clear and the bright Pole Star that seemed to point him northward to the king and to his father. At that Hugh straightened his drooping shoulders resolutely and in good earnest set forth upon his journey.

The new moon had long been set, but the stars were bright and the way amid the trees was plain to follow. A pleasant freshness of the early fall was in the faint night breeze and yet a lurking chill, that made Hugh glad to draw his cloak closer and trudge on more briskly. It was not long after midnight when he reached the first cottage on the outskirts of the village of Kingsford; he had passed the cheery little timbered dwelling many a time, but now, muffled in the night, it seemed unfamiliar. As his feet crunched the gravel of the road before the cottage he heard the house dog bark within, and a sudden feeling of being shut out came over him. The dark houses, as he hurried by them, had the awesome blankness of sleeping faces; even in the woods he had not been so lonely as here in Kingsford, where human beings were within call.

But as he drew to the end of the straggling village he slackened his pace. The road, ascending slightly here, skirted the churchyard, where he could see the light streak that marked the pathway, and the huddled stones, blacker against the turf. For a moment he rested his arms upon the lich wall and stood gazing across the graves at the dense bulk of the little Norman church, with its side porch overshadowed by a dark yew tree and its square tower cleanly outlined against the starry sky. In the chancel of the church his mother lay buried. She would have approved what he was doing, he told himself; she would gladly have returned to Alan Gwyeth. With every fibre of his resolution newly braced he once more took up his march, down the gentle slope and across the one-arched bridge that spanned the river Arrow. There, with the sound of the hurrying water in his ears, he paused and took a final glance at the tower of Kingsford church, and as he passed on wondered vaguely if he should ever set eyes on it again, and when, and how.

Beyond Kingsford the road ran once more through woods with now and again a space of open land or a retired farmhouse. Hugh gave little heed to the country round him, however; he noted only that he had firm road beneath his feet, the cool morning wind in his face, and the stars overhead to light him. But the wind grew chilly and faint with approaching dawn; the stars paled; from far away across the cleared fields a cock crowed and another answered him. When Hugh entered the village next beyond Kingsford, the sky was fading to a dull leaden color and he shivered with the cold of breaking day. Already people were beginning to stir; he met laborers going afield and from roadside barns heard men shouting to cattle, and the bark of dogs. About the little inn there were some signs of life, so he entered and bought bread of a tousled-headed woman. Coming out of the house he saw the eastern sky was breaking into billows of pink, and a little later the cold yellow sun burst forth.

Hugh munched his bread as he tramped along, and the food and the daylight heartened him wonderfully. When the sun got higher he slung his cloak over one shoulder, whistled for company, and almost felt it in his heart to run when he came to an especially even bit of road. For he was his own man now, out in the world, with his pistol at his side, his five shillings and odd pence in his pocket, and his face set toward Nottingham.

Something before noon he trudged into the great town of Warwick and made his way to a tavern he knew from his school days. That time was now a good four months past, so he felt entitled to put a bit of swagger into his gait and rather hoped that in his new freedom he might meet with some of his former schoolfellows. But he kept a wary eye out for his old master, Doctor Masham, who, he suspected, might apprehend him on the spot for a runaway and pack him off to Everscombe; so he drew a breath of relief when he reached the tavern in safety. There he bought him sixpence worth of bread and meat, and, too hungry to give great heed to the varied company in which he found himself, spared expense by eating in the common room.

As his hunger abated he became aware of an exceeding stiffness in the muscles of his legs which made him almost wince when he rose again. He hobbled as far as the door, where a bench in the sun proved so tempting that he sat down to rest him just a moment before starting out. Not only did his legs ache but he found his eyelids heavy and his head dull, and he was possessed of a great desire to yawn and stretch himself. He finally lay down with his head on his arms and would have given himself up to thoughts of Nottingham, only an endless line of swaying trees and dark farmhouses kept sliding before his eyes.

The next thing he knew some one shook him, and he heard the voice of one of the drawers saying, "Now then, master, dost mean to pay us for the use o' that bench?"

Hugh blinked his eyes open and sat up stiffly; one or two idlers stood gazing at him with amused faces, but for the rest the inn porch was deserted, and the sunlight had climbed above the windows of the second story. "Why, what's the time?" he cried, broad awake as he perceived that.

"Mid-afternoon and long past," said the drawer, whereat Hugh jumped to his feet and walked away, so vexed at his sluggishness that for the first half-mile he scarcely heeded the soreness of his legs.

After that his gait grew slower and more halting, but he set his teeth and pulled himself along, as if it were an enemy he held by the collar; he had made up his mind to sleep some six or eight miles out of Warwick at a hamlet that marked the furthest limit of his school rambles, and his plan should not be altered because he had foolishly slept away precious time. The sun set and left him toiling along the highway; the twilight darkened; and the crescent of the moon was riding low among the stars, when Hugh dragged his tired feet over the threshold of the inn for which he aimed. The house was about closing and there was little welcome for this belated traveller, but from sheer weariness the boy was past resenting uncivil usage. He ate thankfully what was given him, stumbled away to his chamber, and, almost before he had flung off his dusty clothes, was sound asleep.

When he woke the mid-morning sun was streaming through the window full in his face, but there was a sharpness in the air of the little chamber that made him pull the blankets up to his chin. The poor inn bed seemed far more comfortable than any he had slept upon at Everscombe; it took an inordinate amount of resolution to rise from it, and an equal courage to drag his shoes on to his swollen feet. But he had already lost the bracing early hours of the day and he must waste no more time in coddling himself, so he took the road at once, as briskly as his limbs would bear him.

Sore and stiff as he still was from yesterday's long march, he made slow progress; it was close on midday when, passing through the town of Coventry, he entered upon the old Roman road, the Fosse, which he was to follow. The sight of the straight way stretching endlessly northeast discouraged him at first, but after a short rest he pulled himself together and, hobbling on, half forgot the pain in his heels in the exhilaration of going forward. It was new country he was now passing through, for he was no traveller; Everscombe to Warwick had been his usual round, save for that one trip into Worcestershire with Frank Pleydall. Since the last year, when Peregrine had been up to London with his father, Hugh had fretted at the narrow range of his journeyings and felt aggrieved at having made his German travels so young that he could cudgel up only scant recollections of them. But now Peregrine might go to London or Staffordshire or whither he pleased; Hugh felt no jealousy, for he

THE ROAD TO NOTTINGHAM

knew it was far pleasanter to be an independent traveller, bound to Nottingham and a soldier father.

Thus, though he no longer had any wish to run, he contrived to jog along quite cheerily till mid-afternoon. Then the low-lying clouds darkened and a soft rain, striking chilly against Hugh's face, made him glad to pull his cloak up to his eyes. The fields and cottages looked gray through the downpour, and then all he saw was the broad puddles of the roadway, as of necessity he bent his head against the storm. At each step he could hear the water oozing in his shoes, his stockings were clammy wet, and his hat brim flapped cold against his forehead; but as the afternoon waned he lost these single sensations, and only knew that from head to foot he was soaked and numb and weary. Still he plodded on, because he must hold out till he reached an inn, but it was at a heavy mechanical pace, while he counted the steps and wondered drearily if the march would never end.

Twilight was turning to night when he splashed at last into a considerable village and stumbled into the first inn to which he came. There was a brisk fire in the common room and but one other guest, so Hugh was free to slip into the chimney corner and dry his dripping clothes while he ate his supper. For civility's sake he began talking to his companion, from whom he learned that he was now over the boundary and into Leicestershire. The knowledge gave him a childish homesick pang; Everscombe seemed to have fallen hopelessly far behind him and Nottingham was still distant the length of a county. With no further care to eat he thrust aside his trencher and dragged himself off to bed.

In his waking moments he heard the rain plashing softly on the thatch of the shed beneath his window, and with the morning light he found the sky still gray and the storm still beating down. He put out one hand to his coat, flung on the stool beside his pallet, and felt that it was not half dried from yesterday's soaking. Then for a time he rested quiet again, while he wondered in half-shamed fashion if he might not lie by a day till the storm was over. But when he reckoned up his store of money, he saw he could not afford to lose so many hours; it was yet more than two days' march to Nottingham, and he had not full three shillings to keep him on the way. He wondered at the speed with which money went, for he was new to ordering such matters; hitherto he had been sure of his three meals a day and bed at night, and looked upon stray sixpences as valuable only for the apples and tops into which they might be turned. He put that last recollection out of his head as speedily as possible, ashamed of his scarcely ended childhood, and, accepting the responsibilities of the manhood he had claimed for himself, got up and dragged on his damp clothes.

After breakfasting he wrapped his sodden cloak about him and plunged resolutely out into the rain. The heavy mud stayed him with clogging his shoes, but he was now somewhat seasoned for the march and managed to keep up a pace that, though not of the fastest, was steady. So he came at length through the afternoon drizzle to the town of Leicester, which he loyally told himself was not the half as fine as his own old Warwick. But none the less he made his lodging there that night, and he went to bed hopefully; for the western clouds were showing a faint yellow streak that promised better weather on the morrow.

Sure enough, when morning came the rain had ceased to fall, and though the air was still heavy with mist there seemed a prospect the sun might yet break through. Hugh took the highway in gay spirits, and plodding along at a stouter pace than on the day before congratulated himself on covering such a deal of ground. But by noon he came to a less flattering estimate of himself; for, talking with an idler at a small tavern he had entered to buy his dinner, he discovered he was now following the Fosse not to Nottingham but to Newark. Thereat Hugh faced about to retrace his steps, too vexed at his own stupidity to allow himself to stop for dinner. His informant called after him some direction about a cross-way to the Nottingham road, which he scarcely heeded at the moment; but afterward, when he was out of the village, he remembered, and striking across the fields came into a narrow road full of ruts and great puddles.

At first Hugh splashed along recklessly, but presently, when a streak of sunlight crept through the trees and turned the puddles bright, he let his pace slacken and little by little brought himself back to a more contented mood. After all, he could make up by steady walking what he had lost, and in any case Nottingham was now less than two days' journey distant. He began whistling for content, then stopped, as a rustling in the bushes ahead caught his ear. He saw the branches crackle outward, and two men, bursting through, came swinging down the roadway to meet him.

Recovering from his first surprise, Hugh prepared to give them the usual traveller's good day, but on second glance kept to his side of the road and walked more rapidly. One of the fellows was thick-set and well tanned, and chewed a straw as he trudged; the other, a younger man, clad like a field laborer, was taller and hulking, with a bearded, low-browed face. As they came abreast he bade Hugh a surly good even and on the word, almost before the boy could reply, gave a grip at his collar. Hugh dodged back and pulled out his pistol, while the thought flashed through his head that running was impossible in this mire, — and then it was not befitting his father's son. Next instant the tall man sprang upon him and Hugh, thrusting the pistol into his face, pulled the trigger, then felt the weapon knocked out of his hand and found himself grappling with his big antagonist. The man's fingers pressed into his throat, he knew; and he remembered afterward how a smooch of red flecked the fellow's beard, as he dashed his fist against his mouth. Then he was griping the other about the neck, hammering up at that stained face, and he heard the fellow bawl, "Devil and all! Why don't 'ee come in and help me, Jock?" Another gruff voice retorted, "If thou canst not handle a younker like that, thou deservest to have bloody

THE ROAD TO NOTTINGHAM

teeth." Then of a sudden Hugh found himself twisted over so he saw the sky above him all shot with black, and he felt a bursting pain in his forehead. Thrusting up his hands gropingly, he went down full length in the mud without strength enough in him to move, even when the tall man knelt over him and, with one hand on his throat, rifled his pockets.

"Here, have back your pistol, master," he heard the gruff voice say, and he dimly saw the well tanned man, with a grin on his face, fling the pistol down in the mud beside him. Then the two walked off at their old swinging pace, and Hugh dragged himself up on his elbow and lay staring uncomprehendingly at his bleeding knuckles. After a time he got painfully to his feet and in mechanical fashion reckoned up the damages; they had taken his cloak and cleaned his pockets of money and of everything but the creased letter from Frank Pleydall and a loose bit of string. They had left him nothing but the torn and well-muddied clothes he wore and the pistol, that now was all befouled with mire. As Hugh picked it up all the hot anger of the actual conflict swept over him again, and with some wild idea of making the robbers restore their plunder he staggered a few steps down the road. Then strength failed him, and dropping down by the roadside he sat with his aching head in his hands. The world was a brutal place, he reflected with dumb resentment; even if a man had courage enough he did not always have the muscle to defend his own, not even with a pistol to back him.

It did not better matters to sit there and whimper, so after a time he rose and, still rather dazed with his drubbing, went unsteadily on his way. At the first brook he halted to wash his wounded hands and cleanse the pistol, which he dried upon his coat as well as he could. The rest of the afternoon he marched slowly because of the dizziness in his head, and so the twilight had overtaken him before he reached the main road and a village that lay upon it.

Close by the wayside stood a tavern, where candles were lighted and food would be cooking, but Hugh only gave one wistful look and passed on. He made his supper of a drink of water from the public well, and, falling in speech there with some loiterers, he found he was now into the shire of Nottingham and not above ten miles from the town. His heart jumped at the news, but next moment he was telling himself he could not tramp those miles in the dark and he grew sober as he realized unwillingly that he must sleep in the open. Till mid-evening he lingered in the village street, then, drawing reluctantly away from the sight of the few candles that still shone in cottages, passed on to the outskirts of the hamlet. After a cautious reconnoissance he crept through a hedge into a field, where he had dimly made out in the darkness a stack of straw, in the lee of which he snuggled down. The straw rustled with startling loudness at his least movement, and the earth beneath him was so damp his teeth chattered in his head. The strangeness of the place kept him many moments awake, but he held his eyes shut that he might not have sight of the lowering sky. Little by little he forgot it

THE ROAD TO NOTTINGHAM

all and fell to thinking of the last time he had lain in the open, when he and Sam Oldesworth had stolen out for a frolic to lie the night in Everscombe Park. How Sam would have marvelled at this night's doings! And Lois, only Lois would have pitied him, like a girl.

Then he knew there had been a long space in which Lois and all other remembrances left him, and he found himself shivering in the midst of wet straw with gray morning light all around him. He crawled to his feet and making his way to the highroad slowly set forth again. He was keenly hungry with his twenty-four hours of fasting and stiff with the dampness of his lodging, but he cheered himself with the thought that before night he would be in Nottingham. He would have enough to eat then, and a bed to sleep in, and decent clothes once more; but he put aside these creature comforts at the thought that he would see his father before he slept again. He wondered what his father would say, and he planned what he would tell him, and how he would make light of his long walk and the hunger and the cold.

His heart fairly jumped within him when at last, in the mid-afternoon, he saw from a hill a great congregation of houses and steeples, which he knew must be Nottingham. He started down the hill on the run, though his knees were smiting together with his long fast. He thought he could keep up the pace clear to the gates of the town, but a troublesome stone got into his shoe, so presently he had to pause and sit down under a hedge to look to it. As he was pulling on the shoe again a man passing by bade him good day, and Hugh, seeing there were houses within call, so he need not fear a second assault, entered into talk with him: "Yonder's Nottingham, is it not?"

"O' course," answered the other, proportioning his courtesy to the state of Hugh's jacket.

"How do you like having a king lie so near?" Hugh laughed for the sheer happiness that was in him.

"Ill enough," growled the other, "wi' his swaggering ruffians breaking our fields and kissing our wenches. Praise Heaven they be gone now."

"Gone?" Hugh echoed blankly.

"Ay, his Majesty and the whole crew of his rakehelly followers went packing westward three days back."

CHAPTER IV

TO HORSE AND AWAY

IF Hugh Gwyeth had been a few years older he might perhaps have cursed his ill fortune; if he had been a few years younger he would assuredly have put his head down on his knees and wept; as it was, being neither man nor child, he blinked his eyelids rapidly and forced a weak grin, then asked: " There's a road that runs west from Nottingham, is there not, friend? Perhaps then there is some cross-way from here by which I may reach it?"

The man delayed long enough to give full information about a path, a stile, a meadow, and an ancient right of way, which Hugh checked off mechanically. But after the man had passed on he still sat a time staring at the distant roofs of Nottingham and blinking fast.

At length he got to his feet and started down the hillside by the path the man had shown him, slowly, for all the spring had gone out of his gait now, and his knees felt weak and shook so that more than once he had to pause to rest. During such a halt a sickening fear seized him: suppose after all he should never reach his father? There was no danger of his dying of starvation yet, for he had had food as late as the previous morning;

but what if strength failed him and he fell down in the fields or lonely woods and slowly perished there? That fear still staying with him, he made his night's resting-place under a hedge, almost within hail of a farmhouse. He lay down early in the twilight, too exhausted to make the day's march longer, but he could not sleep for very hunger. In the first hours of his waking the dim light in the distant farmhouse gave him company, but after that he had only the stars. He lay huddled in a heap for warmth and stared up into the sky at Charles's Wain and the North Star, that were shining clear as on the night when he quitted Everscombe.

He lost sight of the stars at last, slept, and woke in white moonlight, then slept and woke again, and, finding the chilly dawn breaking, rose and plodded painfully out into the highway. The farmhouse in the gray morning did not bear out the hospitable promise of its candle of the night before; so, sick with hunger though he was, Hugh went by it without so much as asking for a drink of water. But a few rods farther on, when he caught sight of some apple trees, he crawled through the hedge and helped himself, then hurried away guiltily and tramped the next quarter mile so fearful of apprehension that he durst not taste the plunder. When he did so he found that the apples were half sour and hard, so he could scarcely swallow a mouthful, and that little sickened him. When he resumed his walk he felt dizzier and weaker even than before.

About eleven of the morning he passed through a small village, where he met people coming to their midday meal. He loitered along slowly and rested a time by a well in the centre of the place; it was in his mind to go boldly to some cottage and ask for food, but he could not decide which house looked least inhospitable. While he was still debating, the shameful realization of what he was doing came over him; he jumped up and, pulling his battered felt hat over his face, walked away with something of his old dignified step. But once outside the village his pace slackened, as he told himself unsparingly that begging befitted a gentleman far better than stealing, and he must now do one or the other.

It was several hours later that a third resource occurred to him: he might trade something for food, his pistol, perhaps. He examined it carefully and decided that, though it looked a trifle rusty, it might serve. In the expectation of getting food for it at the next town he labored on more hopefully, but the next village seemed never to come, for his knees were now fairly knocking together and his halts grew more frequent and prolonged. Once, when he had to cross a small stream, he found himself too unsure of foot to keep the stepping-stones, so he must splash into the water up to his knees. A branch sent his hat into the stream, and, without heart enough left even to struggle after it, he let it drift away.

The sun was nearly set when at last he came to scattered houses, which he judged must be on the outskirts of a considerable town. At the thought of food he stumbled forward more rapidly, with his pistol in his hand ready for the barter, but he saw no possible purchaser till he came to a small inn. There he found a knot of men gathered about a side door, so, after a moment's hesitation, he ventured into the courtyard. Country fellows they proved to be, idling and smoking on the inn porch; one, who took the deference of his comrades as a matter of course, had the look of a small farmer; another seemed a smith; the rest were of the ordinary breed of tavern frequenters. Hugh paused by a horseblock, and, looking them over, found little encouragement in their appearance, yet he was trying to frame a proper greeting with which to go up to them, when a tapster bustled out on the porch and, getting sight of him, hailed him roughly, " Now then, what brings you here? "

Hugh hesitated over to the porch; he had forgot what he had meant to say and for a moment no words came to him; then, realizing it was now or never, he managed to stammer: " I have a pistol here. Maybe some one of you would — wish to buy it." As he spoke he held out the pistol, but the farmer, the great man of the crew, shoved it aside and, pulling fiercely at his pipe, wheezed out something about vagabonds and the stocks. The blacksmith, however, took the pistol carelessly, turned it over, and laughed. " How many men hast killed wi' this, sirrah? " he asked in a big voice, and passed the pistol to his neighbor, who grinned and offered a ha'penny for it.

Hugh gazed helplessly at the ring of mocking faces, then let his eyes drop to the ground, and with the blood tingling in his cheeks waited their pleasure. He would gladly have seized upon his pistol and flung away from them, but he felt too faint and hungry to walk a rod, and before he could get food he must make this sale. But at last, with slow sickening disappointment, he realized they had no notion of purchasing, but were making sport of him. "If you will not buy —" he blurted out with weak anger.

"What is going on here?" a pleasantly drawling voice struck in.

Turning sharply Hugh almost brushed against a man who had approached from the direction of the stables, a gentleman, by his dress and easy bearing. "Will you not suffer me to see, friends?" he drawled slowly, and reaching out his hand took the pistol from the man who held it.

Gazing up at him hopefully Hugh saw that the newcomer was not above two or three and twenty years of age, with long dark hair and a slight mustache, under which Hugh fancied he saw his mouth twitch as he looked the pistol over. Then the gentleman glanced up and showed a pair of humorous brown eyes, which, as he surveyed Hugh, suddenly grew grave. "Here, I've need of a pistol," he said, and held out a piece of money.

It was a crown piece, Hugh saw, that would buy unlimited bread, and meat, too; but, as his fingers were closing over it, the remembrance of the twitch in the purchaser's lips and the laugh in his eyes recurred to him, and of a sudden he understood that a pistol which thieves themselves would not deprive him of could not be worth even a ha'penny. He had no right to take money for it, he knew, and in his disappointment he grew angry at his own stupidity, and angry at the brown-haired gentleman for offering him charity, and angry at the other men who looked on and thought him a beggar and worse. " After all, I'll not sell it," he muttered sullenly. " Perhaps — 'tis not in good condition."

" 'Tis a serviceable weapon," replied the other.

" It's worthless," Hugh maintained doggedly. " Give it back to me."

" But I've taken a fancy to it."

" Keep it, then," Hugh retorted, fiercely, so his voice might not break, and elbowing his way through the group of men walked off. He could smell the food cooking inside the tavern, and hunger gnawed him so savagely that even the thought that he had refused charity and had not deceived any one into buying a worthless pistol could not keep a lump from gathering in his throat. His step wavered and he had to halt an instant to lean against the gate-post: out beyond the street looked lonely and chill in the misty twilight. Just then he heard the click of spurs upon the stones of the courtyard, and some one took him by the shoulder. Even before he heard the drawl he knew it was the young gentleman. " Look you here, sir, I cannot take your pistol as a gift."

More than one rough speech came to Hugh's lips, but he did not utter a word, only shook off the grasp on his shoulder and without looking up made a step forward. Then his knees seemed to give way, the ground suddenly came nearer, and, pride, resentment, and all, he pitched down on the stones at the gentleman's feet.

The other bent over him quickly, and this time

Hugh had neither strength nor will to shake him
off. "What's wrong with you, lad?" There
was almost no drawl in the speaker's voice,
"Hurt? Tired? Hungry?"

Hugh nodded dumbly.

"Well, well! That's easier remedied than a
broken leg. Up with you, now." Hugh found
himself upon his feet again, and, with the young
man's hand beneath his elbow, stumbled obediently back across the courtyard and through the
little group about the door, who made way for
them. Within they turned up a staircase, and
now he heard the man beside him asking:
"You'll not refuse to take supper with me, perchance? When gentlemen meet on the road—"

"You've no need to make it easy unto me,"
Hugh gulped out brokenly. "If some one did
not help me I doubt if I could tramp many days
more, and — I'd liefer take help from you."

Indeed, utter weariness and hunger had for the
moment made an end of Hugh's dignity as effec-
tually as if he had cast it quite away at the inn
gate. He suffered the stranger to lead him
into a room and seat him in a big chair by the
fire, where he drank what was given him and
swallowed down some mutton broth, sparingly,
at first, as he was told. He troubled himself
neither to think nor to speak, but he noted that
the dark inn chamber seemed like home, the fire
felt warm, and the candles twinkled dazzlingly.
He found, too, that the brown-haired gentleman
had a kind, elder-brotherly way with him, and
that in private life he dispensed with his drawl,
though his voice lost none of its pleasant tone.

"Well, you feel almost your own man again now, do you not?" his host queried at last.

Hugh essayed a smile in reply.

"Wait an hour or so and, if soft answers still have power with tavern women, we'll have a good supper then,—I take it you'll be ready for it. And now it seems time for ceremonious introductions. My name is Richard Strangwayes."

"And my name is Hugh Gwyeth. My father is Colonel Alan Gwyeth of the king's army." Hugh spoke slowly as if he liked to linger over the words; it was the first time he had ever claimed his father.

"And you are bound for the king's camp?" asked Strangwayes, sitting down on the opposite side of the fireplace.

Hugh explained very briefly that he had left home to join his father and had had a hard march, to which Strangwayes listened with sympathetic eyes, though when he took up the conversation again his tone was light. "We are headed for the same place, then, Master Gwyeth, for I am wearing out my horse to reach his Majesty's army. I am going to join my uncle, Sir William Pleydall—"

Hugh felt he could have hugged the man, he seemed suddenly to have come so very near. "Why, I know Sir William," he cried, "I was at school with his son. I've a letter from him here." Pulling out Frank's worn letter he passed it to Strangwayes, who stared at him an instant, then hastily scanned the sheet. When he handed it back Hugh noted a change in his manner; he had been kind before with the kindness of one stranger to another, but now he seemed to have taken to himself a permanent right to befriend Hugh. He came across the hearth and shook hands with the boy. "I'm right glad we chanced to meet, Hugh," he said warmly. "We'll journey the rest of the way together. Oh, yes, I can procure you a horse."

Hugh ventured some weak objection, rather shamefacedly, for he knew he hoped Strangwayes would thrust it aside, and he felt only satisfaction when the young man did so. "Leave you to come on alone? Folly! I only lend you the horse; your father will settle the matter with me. I'll charge him Jew's interest, if 'twill content you. Do you think I mean to leave my cousin Frank's comrade to fray out his clothes and his body along the road?"

Afterwards, when they were eating supper together and the maid who served them had quitted the room, Strangwayes suddenly looked up and asked quizzically, "You are well assured there is no Spanish blood in you?"

Hugh was quite sure; why had Master Strangwayes asked? What were Spaniards like, anyway? Strangwayes drawled on disjointedly for a quarter of an hour, while his eyes laughed in a provoking way: Spaniards were fierce fighters, and their women were pretty, and they liked gold, and they were proud as the devil, and they were very cruel, and they had a deal of dignity, and they grew oranges in their country. "Dream it out to-night, Hugh," he advised, as they rose from the table; but Hugh disobeyed flagrantly, for the instant he was laid in a Christian bed once more he was sound asleep.

He woke in broad daylight, and, having assured himself that the bed was real, so Richard Strangwayes could not have been a dream, dozed contentedly again, and woke with a start to rise and dress with the unsettled feeling of one who has slept long enough to lose count of time. When he went downstairs he judged by the sunlight that flooded the courtyard that it must be near noon, and his guess was verified by the tapster, who was vastly more respectful than he had been on the preceding evening. Those loitering about the courtyard, too, eyed him curiously but no longer mocked him. The only relic of last night's dismal scene which he found was a rusted pistol that lay near the post of the outer gate. After a hasty glance about to make sure none were looking, Hugh snatched it up and, hiding it beneath his coat, sauntered nonchalantly out of the courtyard. Just across the road was a sluggish muddy ditch, and into this he dropped the pistol that had once been Peregrine Oldesworth's. Even as he did so he felt a quick pang of regret, for he realized he had trusted in the worthless weapon as he never could trust again in the truest sword or the surest musket.

A bit saddened and a bit shamed at such a feeling, he retraced his steps to the gateway, where he came face to face with Strangwayes, very martial indeed with his big hat and riding-boots, who trotted up on a long-legged white horse. By the bridle he led a despondent-looking gray, which halted with the greatest readiness, as Strangwayes reined in his own steed and addressed Hugh: "What do you think of this high-tempered charger? Unless appearances are arrant liars, he is the prettiest bit of horse-flesh within two league of here. His Majesty, — Heaven bless him and requite it to his followers! — has carried away every well-seeming thing that goes o' four legs. Here, sirrah hostler, give the beasts a bite. We'll do the like service to ourselves, Hugh, and then the word is, 'To horse and away.'"

"I am ready," Hugh answered. "But I fear I have made you to lose time —"

"Time spent in horse-dealing is never lost," Strangwayes replied sententiously; "especially when the rascal who owns the horse has likewise a winsome daughter. Now come to dinner."

It was during this meal that a new care burdened Hugh. Now that he was no longer half starved and near desperate he had time to take heed to minor matters, and he was keenly aware of the holes in his stockings and the rents in his breeches and jacket. It seemed Strangwayes had guessed something of his thought, for, as they rose from the table, he spoke out with a half embarrassment: "Look you here, Hugh, I meant — to lend you money to get you fresh clothes, but, faith, the gray there cost a penny more than I thought, and, as we've no wish to starve again, methinks you must be content to let your new coat ride away on his back."

"'Tis no great matter," Hugh forced himself to say. "If you be willing to take the road with such a vagrant-looking fellow as I."

Strangwayes suggested, however, that they do what they could, so the tapster was bribed and the chambermaid cajoled, till out of the inn stores Hugh was furnished with a cap and a pair of boothose, and a good part of the hedge mud was brushed off the rest of his apparel. So when at last he rode out from the inn on the gray horse Hugh felt himself a very passable Cavalier, for his covered head greatly increased his self-respect, and the boothose in most hypocritical fashion concealed the torn stockings. But had he been quite out at elbow he felt he would have shone in the borrowed light of Strangwayes' completeness, and would have been content with that or anything he might owe to his new friend.

That night they slept within the borders of Staffordshire, and, sparing their horses, took the road late next morning beneath a lowering sky. They were headed for Shrewsbury, Hugh learned, whither the king was marching by a northern road; they would keep to the south, however, in the hope of speedily overtaking a scouting party led by one Butler, an old friend of Strangwayes, whom the reports of tavern-keepers placed less than four and twenty hours ahead of them. If the horses held out, they doubtless would come up with him in the course of a twelvemonth, Strangwayes announced dolorously, after a morning spent in flogging his beast along the heavy road. It was impossible to mend the pace, so they forgot it at last in talk, for after his days of non-intercourse Hugh was but too happy to tell some one his thoughts and plans; and he felt Strangwayes was as safe a confessor as a man could have. So he related his early life, much in detail, and the intimate reasons of his present quest, and all he knew of his father. At that Strangwayes' dark eyebrows went up amazingly and came down in a twist above his nose. "Name of Heaven!" he ejaculated, turning in his saddle to face Hugh, "do you mean to tell me you are tracing over the kingdom after a father who has not set eyes on you for twelve years? What think you the man will say to you or do with you?"

Hugh paused blankly, assailed with sudden queer doubts, as Strangwayes thus harked back to his grandfather's hints. But next instant the older man laughed off his surprise and plunged headlong into a tale that soon ended Hugh's discomfort. "Confidence for confidence, Hugh. Would you hear something of myself? If they ever put me in a chap-book they can say I was the unhappy third son of a worthy knight of Lincolnshire. They put me to school at a tender age, — pass over that; no doubt you can guess what it means. No, I did not run from school; mine has been a sober and industrious life, fit for all youth to take instruction by. When I was sixteen I betook myself to Oxford, for my father was too loyal a gentleman to trust even so poor a piece of goods as a third son among the Puritans of Cambridge. There at Oxford I improved my hours to best advantage and learned to play famously at bowls, and would have become a past master at tennis, had not the Scots war broke out. Sir William Pleydall procured me a lieutenancy —"

"And you have been to war once already?" asked Hugh, suffering the gray to slacken the pace to his natural amble. "Tell me of your battles, I pray you, Master Strangwayes."

"If you'll clip my title to Dick," replied the other. "It sounds more natural. Truth to tell, I was in but one battle, Hugh, and that was the fierce and bloodless battle of Wilterswick, here in this same pleasant Staffordshire. You remember, doubtless, when the king went against the Scots, how loath our excellent yokels were to follow after. Rank Puritans, the most of the levies were, and worked off their warlike energies pulling down communion rails and hunting parsons out of their parishes. We had a choice lot of such spirits in our troop, and, to put a leaven to the whole lump, the captain was an Irishman, ergo, a Catholic. A proper black fellow he was, Dennis Butler; the same one at whose mess-table we may chance to sit to-morrow night. This Butler and I took ourselves to rest one wet night at Wilterswick, and, faith, we waked to the hunt's up of a big stone crashing in at our casement and found our trusty followers crowding the street before the inn, clamoring to hang the captain for a Papist. At their head was a venomous, two-legged viper, Constant-In-Business Emry,—he was rightly named,—a starveling of a fellow,—I'd swear he began life a tailor. Butler had rated him a day or two before, so he was in earnest, and, truth, the rest of them looked it. So Denny Butler, being a gentleman of resources, gathered himself into his clothes and left by the rear door."

"And you?" Hugh cried out, "I hold your captain went like a coward."

"Nay, nay, we'd agreed to it; I knew they'd not hurt me. So I slipped on my shirt and breeches, and went down to speak unto them.

They threw stones and other things, and roared somewhat, but at last I made myself heard; then I talked to them like a preacher and a father, and tripped up Constant-In-Business Emry on a theological point, and demonstrated that I was a good Church of England man, like all my ancestors before me. By that they were tolerably subdued, so I called for a Book of Common Prayers and read them morning service, then down we all knelt in the mud of the courtyard and I prayed over them. You never know how hard you can pray till you're put to it. By that Butler was well away, so I went back to my chamber and finished dressing. I ruined a serviceable pair of velvet breeches kneeling in that mud, and the lesson of that is to go rough clad when you go to war. And that was the end of my military glory, for the king struck a truce with the Scots, I lost my commission, and, as I would have no more of the university, my father packed me off to London to take chambers in the Middle Temple. He held the Puritans should not have a monopoly of lawyers, 'fight the devil with his own weapons,' as 'twere. But I confess the only court I followed was the king's court and I learned far more of dancing and sonneteering than of the precepts of worthy Sir Edward Coke. Then my father, — Heaven rest him! — died, and left me an annuity. I have no liking for annuities; they encourage a man in the sordid practice of living within his means. I sold mine out of hand, and, with a droll streak of prudence, as rare as strange, committed a round sum to Sir William Pleydall to hold in trust for me, then set out with the rest to see the world. I went to the

Low Countries and served a time as a gentleman volunteer, and then to France, where I learned some handy tricks at fencing."

"You're a great swordsman?" Hugh queried with bated breath. "Did you ever fight a duel?"

"On my honor, yes," the other replied with a smile. "No earlier than last April I crossed swords with a certain Vicomte de Saint Ambroix. The manner of it? Do you think of challenging any one, Master Hugh? Why, monsieur the vicomte chose to speak some scurvy untruths of English-women in my company, so I did but go up to him and strike him across the mouth, saying, 'Monsieur, I do myself the honor of telling you that you lie in your throat.' Which was a great waste of words. But we fought and he was hurt somewhat in the shoulder. No, I have no scars, but I got then a piteous gaping wound in a crimson satin doublet of mine, which has never healed, as flesh and blood heals in time. That was the last adventure, fortunately, for here comes what shall abridge my story." Strangwayes pointed before him where the dusky roofs of a straggling village showed among the wet trees.

"But how came you home, Dick?" Hugh coaxed.

"Simply told. I heard there was work for men of enterprise, and I judged my loyal uncle would have turned my pounds and shillings into troopers and muskets, and would gladly give me a commission in exchange. So I spent what surplus money I had,—'tis the surest way to cheat thieves,—and took ship for King's Lynn. I paid a swift visit to my elder brother in Lincolnshire; he is for the Parliament,— Heaven and my father's spirit forgive him! So I mounted and faced me westward to the king, and here I am now, and here we are."

The two horses clinked across the cobbles of the courtyard of the village inn, a hostler ran up officiously, and the host himself came puffing out to greet the guests. "Well, friend, what news on the road?" cried Strangwayes, swinging out of his saddle. "Has a troop of Cavaliers passed through here?"

The host gazed from one to the other, then up at the sky, then back at the travellers. "Be you king's men?" he finally asked, with mild curiosity.

"Sure, I trust we all be honest people," Strangwayes answered dryly.

"Well, well, that may be as it may be; I say naught; only 'tis good hap for you, you lie in a snug haven to-night."

"Why, what mean you? Are there hobgoblins farther on?" Strangwayes' voice dropped to a ridiculous quaver that made Hugh smile.

"Worse nor hobgoblins, master," replied the host. "Have ye not heard, then? They do say a stout band of Puritan rogues are plundering the country, yonder toward the west of us."

CHAPTER V

IN AND OUT OF THE "GOLDEN RAM"

Though the dawn of another day had broken, slate-colored clouds still hid the sun and a mist like a fine rain hung in the air; even the white horse and the gray, standing saddled and ready in the inn yard, touched noses as if they vowed the weather bad. Hugh slapped their flanks and settled their damp manes, while he waited for Strangwayes to pay the reckoning to the mildly curious host, but the process proved so long that at last he mounted into the saddle and ambled slowly out into the highway. Turning the gray horse's nose to the west he paced forward, with his heart a-jump at the thought that yonder in the mist before him real danger that tested men's courage might be lurking.

A gay clatter of hoofs on the uneven roadway made him turn just as Strangwayes came abreast of him. At once Hugh blurted out what was uppermost in his thoughts: "Do you think, Dick, the host spoke true? Are there enemies before us? What think you?"

"I think there be two whose words are not to be over-trusted: a woman when she will have a boon of you, and a tavern-keeper when he will have you to tarry in his lodgings."

"Then you believe the host's talk of Roundheads—"

"Mere words to frighten children. It troubles me not the half as much as his showing me just now that Butler must have borne more northward. Well, let the Irish rogue go hang! We'll push on as we are and reach Shrewsbury,—some day.—Come up, you crows' meat!" This to the white horse, whose nose was at its knees.

"To-day will be but as yesterday, then, without any danger?" asked Hugh, a thought relieved, yet with room for a feeling of grievous disappointment at being cheated of his looked-for adventure.

Strangwayes' telltale eyes laughed immoderately, though he kept his mouth grave: "You'll have all the adventures you need, after you reach the king's army. Still, as I have an honest liking for you, mayhap, if you're a good lad, I'll find you one ere we come thither."

Then they fell to speaking of all they would do, when once they were enrolled among his Majesty's followers, and, what with talking and urging on their laggard horses, they kept themselves employed till past noon. "We'll bait here," Strangwayes announced, as rounding a curve they got sight of a tiny hamlet half concealed beneath a hill. "Then we'll make a long stage this afternoon and sleep the night well within the borders of Shropshire."

At that cheering thought they put the horses to their best pace and clattered through the village street quite gallantly, though there were none to admire them, save a flock of geese, and a foolish-looking girl, who seemed the whole population of the little place. Thus they came to the farther end of the hamlet, where, a bit retired from the neighboring cottages, stood a shabby inn, before which hung a sign-board bearing a faded yellow sheep. "Golden Ram!" Strangwayes translated it. "Mutton would suit me as well!"

They rattled into the little inn yard, ducking down in their saddles to save their heads from the bar across the low gateway, and drew rein just in time to avoid riding down a flurried serving-maid. Strangwayes almost fell out of his saddle, so promptly he dismounted to reassure her. "You're not harmed, my lass?" he asked anxiously, slipping one arm about her as if he expected her to faint, though, from her fine fresh color, that did not seem likely. Hugh had already seen something of his friend's civilities to barmaids, so he kept to his saddle and felt rather foolish, when suddenly the host, a scrawny man with a lantern face, appeared in the doorway. At sight of him Strangwayes, in his turn, looked a bit foolish, and stepping away from the maid began briskly, "Well, friend, what can you give us to dinner?" There he paused dumfounded, and stared, then cried out: "Heaven keep us! If it be not my constant friend Emry, as busy as ever! Verily, 'tis a true saying that the Lord will not see the righteous forsaken."

"Lieutenant Strangwayes was always a merry gentleman," Constant-In-Business Emry replied, with a rather dubious countenance.

"Tut, tut! You're all mistaken, my man. I abominate merriment as much as I do ale. Which calls it to my mind I am uncommon dry and thirsty. Jump down, Hugh. We'll have experience of a Puritan tavern."

"Ay, men must eat," sighed Emry. "Though my calling may smack of the carnal taint, yet 'tis not all ungodly, since — "

"Don't trouble yourself for that," Strangwayes replied. "Faith, I never thought to surprise you in so honest a calling."

With that he led the way into the inn, where he and Hugh dined together in an upper chamber. The food was none of the best, Hugh privately thought, but Strangwayes praised it mightily to the maid who served them, the same they had encountered in the courtyard. She was a stepdaughter of Emry, who had married her mother, the now deceased hostess of the "Golden Ram," so she told Strangwayes, and added much more touching Emry, who seemed the same old Puritan malcontent of Wilterswick. Soon the talk turned from him to gayer matters, for the girl was freshfaced and black-eyed, so Strangwayes gave more heed to her than to his meat and drink. Hugh, feeling more foolish and out of place than ever, choked down his food quickly, then left the room, and, as he closed the door, heard a suppressed squeak: "Don't 'ee, sir. An thou kiss me again I'll scream."

Hugh stamped downstairs and stood glowering out into the courtyard, where the mist was now dribbling down in a slow rain. He watched the grayish streaks it made across the black openings of the sheds opposite the inn porch, and athwart the gaping door of the stable at his right. A wretched chilly day it was, and — why need Dick

Strangwayes play the fool because a wench had red cheeks? When he heard his friend's step he did not even turn his head, and then Strangwayes came up alongside him, and clapping one arm about his shoulders said in a low tone, "Jealous of a tavern maid, or I'll hang myself!" Then he walked off laughing and disappeared into the stable.

But when Strangwayes came out again some time later the laughter had gone from his face, and in its stead was a troubled, angry look that made Hugh forget his petty vexation and run down from the porch to meet him. "What has happened, Dick?" he begged.

"Why, nothing," replied Strangwayes, and took hold of his arm, so they paced up and down the courtyard together, "and yet everything is amiss. The white horse has gone lame."

"Is that all?"

"Enough. Unless you fancy walking ten miles through the mud and rain to the next village. I do not."

"You can ride my horse. That is, he's yours, of course."

"Or you might carry me," Strangwayes answered soberly. "No, Hugh, neither you nor I will walk that ten miles nor the half of it, dragging a hobbled horse behind us."

"Well, at worst," Hugh tried to speak cheerfully, "we shall but lose a few hours."

"Ay, is that all? Tell me this, Hugh: why did a sound horse go lame in the mere course of dinner?"

"Then it's possible 'twas done with forethought?" Hugh cried. "Perchance they mean —"

"Hush, hush, you fire-eater!" Strangwayes interrupted hastily. "If 'twas the inn people lamed the horse they did it only to stay us here, that they might profit by our tarrying. Or to hinder us in our journey, for this knave Emry has no love unto me."

Yet Strangwayes, Hugh took note when they returned to the house, was merry as ever in his talk with the lean-visaged Emry. He ordered a chamber for the night, and then, free to go and come as he pleased, went sauntering into every corner of the hostelry, from the common room to the sheds and stable. About twilight the journey ended in the kitchen, where, finding Emry's stepdaughter at work, Strangwayes seated himself on a table and entered into ardent conversation with her about butter-making.

Left to himself, Hugh sat down on the settle and, poking the fire vigorously, watched the embers die down and then flare up again, while the light waned or reddened throughout the room. Bits of the smoky ceiling and black walls started into sudden radiance, or the fire gleam was given back by a copper kettle or pewter plate, and once the sudden blaze lit up the two who were by the table. Strangwayes' face was half shadowed by his long hair, so only his clean-cut chin and confident mouth showed vividly; but the girl's face, with drooping eyelids and sober lips that now were silent, was very clear to see.

Hugh turned once more to the embers and paid the others no further heed, till Strangwayes came to his side with the noisy announcement that, the kitchen being a very delectable place, they would eat supper there. So the maid lit candles and fetched them food, though she kept silent, even to Strangwayes' gayest nonsense. At the last she brought wine, as he bade, and filling a glass held it out to him. Hugh, glancing up, left eating to stare at the girl's white face, and Strangwayes of a sudden caught hold of her arm. "What's wrong with you, wench?" he asked abruptly.

At that the wine went slopping to the floor. "Don't 'ee tell, sir," the girl murmured, under her breath, "father'd kill me, if he knew. But there be Roundhead troopers,—they come hither to-night."

A side glance from Strangwayes checked the exclamation that was on the tip of Hugh's tongue. The girl went on softly: "Father said: 'He is a swaggering child of Satan, this Papist Strangwayes. A shall not go out of the "Golden Ram" till he goes strapped to another man's saddle-bow.'"

Strangwayes' nostrils contracted, but he said nothing, merely whistled between his teeth. "A merry fellow your father is," he broke silence at length; "he does not deserve to have so good a lass for his daughter. Here's a half-crown to pay for the good wine your floor will scarce appreciate, and here's a kiss for yourself. And prithee fetch me more drink."

As the girl turned away, Hugh, for all his hot excitement, found wit enough to say softly: "For the host's talk of Roundheads 'twas mere words to frighten children."

"My boy," Strangwayes replied, "if you do not hold your tongue as to that, I'll put you on the sound horse and pack you off to the next village." Then his face turned cheery as ever, as the maid came back with the glass of wine, which he sipped slowly, questioning her softly meantime: "What hour will these people come, do you know?"

"About mid-evening, I heard father say."

"How many?"

"Only five or six. A grand officer and some common men. They were here yesternight and before that."

"Are there any men in the inn save your worthy, busy father and his groom?"

"No others. But they are keeping watch of the inn gate and the stairs to the upper story."

Strangwayes drained off the last of the wine, then rose. "Tell me one thing," he asked, "is there any way from the upper floor into the stable?"

"Through the loft above the kitchen."

"It may chance your father and his man will be here in the kitchen the next hour; then, if you love me, lass, keep up a great clattering of your pans. Here, Hugh, take a brace of candles and off with you to bed."

Hugh went slowly into the common room, where sat Emry, to all appearances wrapped in pious meditations, and passed firmly up the stairs. How the little flames of the candles flickered, he observed, and how light and eager he felt; yet there was a kind of foolish trembling in his knees.

Scarcely within the chamber Strangwayes rejoined him. "Are you satisfied with this brave adventure, my man?" was his greeting.

Hugh nodded. "I know you'll bring us through safe, Dick."

"Humph! To do that we need but to slip out at a window of the inn. I've a better plan, Hugh, if you'll come in with me. We cannot bear off our noble white steed and our fleet gray, for to ride hence is the surest means to fall foul of these Roundheads. Then say we lurk here and, turn and turn about, possess ourselves of two of their horses."

"That's your plan?" Hugh repeated amazedly. "Why, yes, of course I'll follow, if you bid. But you must tell me what to do."

"First, here are the brace of pistols from my holsters," Strangwayes answered; "you are to take one of them. I grieve I cannot make two of my rapier, but 'tis impossible. Now, note you, we go to bed —"

"What do you mean?" Hugh cried.

"No, no, no, don't pull off your coat yet. To the mind of Constant-in-the-Devil's-Work Emry we take ourselves to bed, for we blow out our candles, save this one, which I cut down till it will burn not above half an hour. And I set it where the light will smite through the window. Now tread softly and follow me."

Outside the chamber the corridor was very dark and still, so that the least creak of a board was appallingly loud, but there was no other noise, save the faint sound of a girl's singing in the kitchen below. Down the corridor they passed what seemed immeasurable lengths, till Hugh's knees ached with the slow step, step, to a point where he felt for sheer nervousness he must stamp or shout or do something foolish. Then he heard the faint squeak of a door, as Strangwayes, a black figure in the dusk, swung it gently ajar, and he stepped cautiously into a loft, where a square of fainter darkness at the left showed a window was cut. After a moment he found it lighter here than in the corridor, so, groping with more confidence, he was presently at Strangwayes' heels. Right below he heard the muffled voice still singing words that were undistinguishable. "That's a rare wench," Strangwayes just breathed. "And here's the hole into the stable loft. Count sixty ere you follow, or you'll be putting your heels through my skull."

A long sixty it was, but Hugh counted ten more to be certain, then, crawling through a low window that bruised his head, hung an instant by his hands, while he wondered how far it was to fall. Just there Strangwayes put his arms about him and rolled him over into a pile of hay. "Not above a foot to drop, Hugh," he whispered, with a suppressed chuckle, "but an inch is as bad as a mile in the dark. For the rest of the way I am sure; I used my eyes this afternoon."

They quickly slid down from the hay-loft to the floor of the barn, and as they went Hugh found time, perilous though the moment was, to feel half shamed that Strangwayes was taking such care of him, as if he were a little boy. The lighter square of the opening guided them to the stable door, where Strangwayes caught Hugh's arm. "Briskly now; they may be spying from the gate. But softly."

Hugh fairly held his breath in the three quick paces across the corner of the courtyard till he found the grateful, pitchy darkness of a shed around him. He smelt the freshness of new litter, heard it rustle about his ankles, and then Strangwayes pulled him down beside him amidst trusses of straw. "You understand, Hugh," he whispered, "if we stayed in the stable these knaves of troopers might mistake us for hay, when they came to feed their horses, and the mistake would grieve us all. Now here in the shed we can lie close till they leave the stable under guard of a man or two, and then we will follow the fundamental maxim of warfare and supply ourselves from the enemy. Unless they come first to rouse us in our beds. Look you, Hugh, yonder, that little light, is our chamber. There, it has gone out," he added presently. "Now, when next we see a light in that room, we'll know they have gone thither and discovered our removal, and we must be up and doing."

Then for a long time there was silence betwixt them, while Hugh thought of many things and felt the brave pistol under his coat. He tried to make out a single star in the misty night that was around them, and he strained his ears with listening for hoof-beats, till he wearied of it and put his head down on his arms. Presently Strangwayes took him in the ribs with his elbow. "Hugh," he whispered in an odd, half-jesting voice, "have you courage?"

"In truth, I was wondering," Hugh blurted out. Strangwayes put his arm about him as they lay, and once more many moments ran by.

V IN AND OUT OF THE "GOLDEN RAM" 77

Then suddenly Strangwayes whispered sharply, "Hark!"

Hugh raised his head, and he, too, caught, far off upon the highway, the thud, thud of swiftly approaching horses, that slackened in speed but grew louder and louder. He felt his heart thump shamefully, and, reaching out his hand, griped Strangwayes' coat. Then the hoofs sounded right upon them, and there came shouts of men and the clatter of horses across the inn yard. Through the misty darkness shone a sudden light, against which Hugh could see outlined the top of the straw-pile. He saw, too, Strangwayes, with his bare head uplifted, peer out through an armful of the loose straw he held up before him, and he heard him whisper: "Six men, Hugh. Two are officers, I judge. One of them has passed into the inn. The rest are heading into the stable."

Hugh pulled himself up on his knees and gazed out. There were torches in the inn yard that made a half circle of light about the stable door, but left the rest black as ever. Men were leading horses into the stable, and calling and swearing to each other, so they could be heard even after the great door swallowed them up. The house itself was silent as before, but a moment later, and, even as he gazed, from the farther window in the upper story a faint light streamed out. "Curse them! They need not have gone prowling so soon," Strangwayes rapped out between his teeth. "We must make a dash for it. They are only five against two."

Both were now on their feet among the straw,

and Strangwayes had made a step to the opening of the shed, when Hugh caught his arm. "Wait, wait, Dick," he panted, the words instinctively saying themselves, "that's but a small chance. Nay, I am not afraid; 'tis only I have a better way. With my ragged clothes, — I'll slip my cap under my jacket, — they'll think me a stable-boy. Let me go first into the stable. Perhaps I can get a couple of horses out into the court. Yes, I am going."

Strangwayes gave a glance at the lighted window. "If you're beset, call. God speed!" he whispered, and Hugh ran out from the shed.

For a moment his eyes were dazzled with the sudden light about him, then he blinked it away and went forward. He seemed scarcely to feel the solid ground beneath him, nor to hear his own step, for the pounding of the blood in his temples. Yet there was no fear nor any feeling within him, only he saw the opened door to the lighted stable, and he stepped in boldly.

There he halted and of a sudden griped at the side of the door to hold himself erect. For just before him, saddled, bridled, and all, stood two horses, a black and a bay, which he had last caressed in the stable of Everscombe Manor. Beside the bay loitered a stalwart young officer, who at his step glanced up and showed the face of Peregrine Oldesworth. "Hugh!" he cried amazedly, and the troopers, unsaddling the horses at the farther end of the stable, looked up at the cry.

Hugh felt his nerves tingle, but with a calmness that seemed no part of him he walked into the stable. "Good even, Cousin Peregrine," he said quietly, though his voice shook a trifle. "May I lead out the horses to water?" His hands closed on the reins of the bay and the black.

"What are you doing here?" Peregrine asked astonishedly.

"What I can," Hugh replied, with growing confidence.

"You've come down in the world, Master Runaway," said Peregrine, and by his look Hugh knew he was not sorry that his proud cousin should groom his horse. That triumphant look strengthening him mightily, he deliberately faced the horses about and led them the few steps to the door. "I'm down, Cousin Peregrine," he said, with a quick laugh, "but maybe I'll be up in the saddle again."

"What are you about with the horses?" Peregrine cried, with a first realization that all was not well. "Halt, there!"

For answer Hugh gave a cry of "Dick!" and jerking at the bits brought the two horses into the courtyard on the run. The beasts were plunging and wrenching at their bridles, behind him he heard the stamp of men rushing across the stable,—all in a second,—then a dark figure had sprung out from the shelter of the shed. "Look to yourself, Hugh!" Strangwayes shouted, and helter-skelter Hugh made a spring for the back of the bay horse. He got the reins in his hand anyhow and his leg across the saddle, then, griping the pommel and the horse's mane, clung for his life as the frightened animal dashed for the gate. Men were shouting and running, he heard the thud of another horse behind him, the crack of a pistol, then, as he galloped past the inn, a casement suddenly swung open. A bar of light dazzled in his eyes, and for the fraction of an instant he saw the face of Thomas Oldesworth, as he leaned out, pistol in hand. He heard the report of the shot, and then he flung himself forward in the saddle to save his head from the bar at the gate.

Now he was out on the highway, the bay plunging and leaping beneath him, and groping wildly he got one foot into the stirrup. Just then the black horse with its bareheaded rider came abreast of him, passed him, and Hugh galloped blindly at its heels. Well in the rear he heard the beat of other horse-hoofs, but he had both feet in the stirrups now and the reins in his hands, so he turned boldly into the fields behind the black horse. There was a dark wall, he remembered, that he jumped recklessly, and a stretch of rough ground, where he must hold his reins taut. There the black slackened pace somewhat and Hugh galloped up breathless. "We'll give them the slip yet, will we not?" he cried, and then he heard Strangwayes breathing in quick painful gasps, and saw he sat drooping forward in his saddle. "Dick, Dick," he almost screamed, "sure, you're not — "

"Ay," Strangwayes panted, "I'm hit."

CHAPTER VI

THE END OF THE JOURNEY

For perhaps an hour the black and the bay crashed at a fierce pace across the dark countryside. Hugh had afterwards a confused remembrance of thickets where he must bend his head to escape the swishing boughs, of a ford where the water flew high as the girths, of a cluster of cottages, black and silent in the night. Cleared land and highway sped by him hazily, but always he had the mist in his face, faint hoof-notes that ever grew fainter behind him, and just before him the black horse with the piteously slouching figure in the saddle. Once and again Hugh had cried out to him: How grievously was he hurt? Could not he stay to look to it? Each time the terse reply had come: " 'Tis nothing. Ride on."

But the pursuing horses were at last no longer audible; moment after moment passed, and still no sound reached them but the echo of their own gallop. Slowly the black's pace sobered to a trot, and Hugh rode up knee to knee with his friend. " Dick, 'tis not mortal? Tell me," he entreated.

" ' Not as wide as the church door,' as saith the gentleman in the play," Strangwayes replied, but for all his gay tone Hugh caught in his voice a strained note that frightened him; " a mere pistol wound. That knave in the window gave't me. Why did you not shoot him down?"

" 'Twas my uncle," Hugh replied.

" A sweet family you belong to, then," Strangwayes muttered.

" I would it had been me he shot. If he has killed you—" Hugh gulped out.

" Nonsense!" Strangwayes answered testily. " Ride on, and trouble me with no more such talk."

For another long space they rode in silence, Strangwayes with his head sunk on his chest and his left arm motionless. Hugh pressed close to him, lest he fall from his saddle, but he did not venture to trouble him with further speech. Thus the breaking day came upon them, as they trotted through a bit of wet woodland, and Hugh at last could see his comrade's white face, that looked gray in the uncertain light, and thought to make out a dark splotch upon the back of his coat. At the farther verge of the wood, where a small brook, flowing across the road, broadened into a pool on the right, Strangwayes reined in his horse with two or three one-handed jerks at the bridle. "You'll have to try your 'prentice hand at surgery," he said, as Hugh sprang down from the bay; "adventures do often entail such postscripts."

"Do not make a jest of it," Hugh answered chokedly, and putting his arm about Strangwayes helped him to climb from the saddle and to seat himself on the brink of the pool. He still kept his arm about his friend, and now, feeling something damp against his sleeve, he looked closer

THE END OF THE JOURNEY

and found the back of Strangwayes' coat was all wet and warm. "'Tis here you're wounded?" he cried.

"Yes, in the back," the other replied, with a half-suppressed groan. "A brave place for a gentleman to take his first hurt! Draw my coat off, gently. Now take my knife and rip off my shirt. 'Twill serve for bandages."

Somehow Hugh mastered the nervous trembling in his fingers sufficiently to cut away the shirt, upon which the broad stain of red showed with sickening clearness. Beneath, Strangwayes' back was slimy with blood, and the dark drops were oozing from a jagged wound in the fleshy part of the left shoulder. Strangwayes, who was sitting with his full weight thrown upon his right arm, never uttered sound nor winced, but Hugh sank down on his knees, and for a moment felt too faint to do more than support his friend with his arm.

"'O dinna ye see the red heart's blood
  Run trickling down my knee,'"

Strangwayes half hummed, and turned his head to look at Hugh. His brows were puckered with pain, but there was the ghost of a smile on his lips as he drawled, "Why, Hughie, man, methinks I be the one to feel sick, not you."

Thereat Hugh set his teeth, and, shamed into strength by the other's courage, dipped half the cut shirt into the brook and washed the wound, tenderly as he was able, then made shift to bandage it, as Strangwayes directed. "Well, I'm still wearing a shirt," the latter said, as Hugh carefully helped him into his coat, "but 'tis not in the usual way. You must fasten my coat up to my chin, Hugh, and pray none note my lack of linen, nor the bullet-hole in the back. What a place to be wounded!"

The rim of the sun was just showing above the eastern trees when they started to horse once more. Strangwayes, leaning heavily on Hugh, managed to climb into his saddle, and then he let his hand rest a moment on the boy's shoulder, while he looked down at him. "So you are troubled for me?" he asked dryly.

"More than I would be for any man, unless 'twere my father."

"You're a brave lad, Hugh," Strangwayes said irrelevantly. "I would fain hug you, if I would not topple out of my saddle if I tried. I thank Heaven 'twas not you got hurt by my fool's trick last night." Then he put his horse slowly forward, so Hugh mounted the bay and came after.

They went at a gentler pace now, by the highway or by short cuts through the fields, for Strangwayes knew this country well, he explained, from his old experience in the king's army. He kept a little in advance, one hand on the bridle rein, the other arm limp, and his whole body stooping a trifle forward. Hugh realized with a helpless pang that his friend was suffering, he dared not think how much, nor how it might end, yet he was powerless to aid him. Once, when they rode through a village where the people were astir about their morning business, he begged Strangwayes to stop and have his wound looked to, at least have drink to strengthen him. But the other shook his head, then spoke with pauses between phrases: "They'd not succor me for love, Hugh; we are not strong enough to force them; and for the rest, I've not a shilling to soften them."

"How?"

"What I had was none too much to give that maid for the saving of our liberty, perchance our lives. At least, I rate my life thus high."

"And that I could be angry with you for such a matter as fooling with her!" Hugh broke out penitently.

"'Tis for a man's advantage to be friendly with all women," Strangwayes answered in a matter-of-fact tone. "Had I sulked in her presence, like some haughty gentlemen I know of, we'd be tramping the road to a rebel prison now, Hugh. That knave Emry! I contrived to reach him a crack on the head with the butt of my pistol as I rode out, he'll remember some days."

But after that one burst of everyday speech Strangwayes lapsed again into silence, with so slack a hold on the reins that Hugh, coming close alongside, ventured now and then to put hand to the bit and guide the black horse. Lines of pain were deepening in the wounded man's brows and about his white lips, and once, as they descended a steep pitch abruptly, he only half stifled a groan.

So when they reached the next village Hugh took matters into his own hands by pulling up both horses before a wayside tavern. "What's to do?" Strangwayes asked listlessly.

"I am going to get you drink," Hugh answered, and jumping down from his horse entered the tavern and made for the common room. There he found a surly tapster, and, trying hard to be civil and yet not abject, begged: "Can you give me a glass of aqua vitæ? I've a wounded friend here—"

To which the tapster simply responded: "Pack!"

Hugh gave back a step or two, and then, with the feeling that Strangwayes might be dying and he must do something, however desperate, pulled out his pistol. "I must have that aqua vitæ," he said quietly. "Either you give it me or I go fetch it. Make up your mind."

Instead the tapster drew away to the door, bawling for assistance till he roused up another man and a maid and the hostess herself. Hugh, with his back to the wall and the pistol in his hand, felt unjustified and ashamed, but, the thought of Strangwayes nerving him, repeated his request to the hostess. She fell to rating him shrilly for a bullying swashbuckler to frighten a poor woman so, and, as the men would not check her and Hugh could not use his pistol for argument here, she was like to keep it up some time. Happily the maid, who had peered out at the window, broke in with a glowing account of the fine horses and the poor wounded gentleman, whereat the landlady, after boxing the wench's ears for gaping out of doors, bounced over to the casement. The sight of Dick Strangwayes or of the horses must have softened her, for after an instant's gazing she began to rate the tapster and bade him fetch what the young gentleman required.

When Hugh came out triumphant with the glass of spirits he found the rest of the inn people gathered about the horses, and the hostess very pressingly urging Strangwayes to light and rest at her house. She was but too glad to help a gentleman fallen on misfortune, she explained, especially when the gentleman served the king, bless him! His Majesty and all his men had passed through there and some of them had lain in her house only the night before.

"Then we'll soon be up with your friends, Dick," Hugh urged, trying to speak cheerfully.

Strangwayes just nodded, then drank the hostess's health in the aqua vitæ, and with a flicker of energy bade Hugh get to his saddle. As they left the little knot of staring people behind them, he turned his face toward Hugh and, forcing his drawn lips into a smile, asked: "You raided those inn folk? You're learning bravely, my Spanish Puritan."

Then he became silent and suffered the gallant pace at which he had set out to slacken. The black showed a tendency to veer from one side of the road to the other, till at last, not above two miles from the tavern, Strangwayes dropped the bridle rein into Hugh's ready hand. "You must lead the horse a bit," he said wearily. "I'll rest me."

Of those last miles Hugh kept only blurred recollections, among which the dazzle of sunlight upon the firm road beneath the horses' feet, the sight of men laboring in tilled fields, and the smell of moist woods, recurred vaguely. Through all the shifting changes of the wayside Strangwayes, as he sat bowing over the pommel of his saddle with his pallid face hidden on his breast, was alone a living reality.

The long piece of woodland ended at last, and across the fields the roofs of a village came in sight. To the left horses grazing in a meadow whickered to the passing chargers, and then the riders trotted slowly in among the houses. There was a smith's shop, Hugh remembered, about which lounged men in great boots and buff jackets, and before the village inn were more in the same attire. Hugh reined up there, scarcely knowing what he purposed, but before he could dismount a young man with long light brown hair, who wore a scarlet sash across his jacket, advanced from the inn door. "King's men?" the stranger asked. "Why, what has befallen here?"

Strangwayes raised his chin a trifle, then his head sank again. "Who commands?" he asked faintly.

"Captain Dennis Butler."

"Tell him, Richard Strangwayes seeks him. He —" There the voice trailed off inaudibly.

Hugh leaned a little from his saddle and got his arm about his friend. Men were hurrying forward curiously, but of a sudden they drew aside to make way for a thick-set officer with a black beard, who came striding through their midst. "On my soul, 'tis Dicky Strangwayes!" he cried, halting at the injured man's stirrup. "Gad, but you're come in good time! We can give you a bottle of Burgundy to crack or a rebel throat to cut —"

"Ah, Captain, if you'll give me a bed, I ask nothing else of you," Strangwayes gasped out, and pitched forward, half into Butler's arms.

THE END OF THE JOURNEY

They had him off the horse and two of the troopers carried him into the house, so speedily that Hugh got only a glimpse of his friend's death-like face. He jumped down, intent on following, but the youngish officer with the light hair, paying him no heed, walked away and left him to the curious troopers. They asked him many questions touching Strangwayes and how he had been hurt, which Hugh, with eyes on the door by which his comrade had disappeared, could only answer disjointedly. Presently a man came out and, saying that Guidon Allestree had so ordered it, led the black and the bay off to be groomed and fed. Still unbidden Hugh followed into the stable yard, where, sitting down on the shaft of a cart, he stared at the inn till he knew every angle of its timbered roof. He realized vaguely that men passed him by, and one group, loafing near at hand in the shelter of a shed, he heard talking loudly together. Once, when they were complaining of the lack of liquor at this tavern, he was aware that one grumbled, "No wonder; Gwyeth's men lay here yesternight."

Even that seemed not to be personal to Hugh, and he still sat staring at the blank inn windows, while he wondered to what room they had carried Strangwayes. At last he could endure the suspense no longer, but taking his courage in his hand walked into the house, where, halfway up the stairs, he met the light-haired man. "I pray you, may I not see Master Strangwayes?" Hugh blurted out his business at once.

"The surgeon has forbidden it. They have but just cut out the bullet, and he is too weak to be worried."

"Is there — much danger?" Hugh faltered.

"Nay, very little. A mere ugly flesh wound, but he has lost much blood and is near exhausted. — Come, come, don't give way like that, boy," the young man added, as a sob of sheer relief escaped Hugh. "Your master'll be sound enough in a couple of weeks."

Hugh looked up with his face aflame; because his clothes were ragged was no reason that the young officer should take him for a horse-boy. "Will you be so good as tell Dick I am glad he is recovered?" he said slowly. "And give him back his pistol here, and tell him since he is in the hands of friends I have gone about my own affairs."

So saying he went down the stairs and, without a single glance at the light-haired officer, passed out into the courtyard. He would not hang about the place a moment longer, he vowed, but then he reproached himself for deserting Strangwayes and had half a mind to go back, when by chance he caught sight of the same group of loungers he remembered had spoken of Colonel Gwyeth. On the impulse he went to them and, questioning them, learned that not only had Colonel Alan Gwyeth been that very morning at the inn, but he was now not above eight miles distant at Shrewsbury.

At that Hugh faced about and took the highway for the great town. It was not deserting Dick Strangwayes now, he told himself, for his father would doubtless let him have a horse and ride back next day to see his friend, and in any case he must go forward, lest his father be off to some other part of the country. So during the

THE END OF THE JOURNEY

sunny last hours of the afternoon he hurried along, scarcely observing the villages through which he passed nor the men on foot or horseback whom he met or overtook, in the eager hope at each turn of the road that he would come upon Shrewsbury steeples. He hardly felt sleepy from last night's long watch, nor stiff with his rough ride, just eager and happy. When he thought of Strangwayes it was only to be thankful that his hurt had not proved mortal, and to be glad that the skirmish at the "Golden Ram" had happened. For now he could go to his father, not a raw schoolboy, but a young gentleman who had been under fire; he was just a bit sorry he had not himself been wounded.

But when at length he saw the last horizontal rays of the sun upon the clustered roofs of Shrewsbury, his happy mood seemed to end. It was all too good to be true; once before he had thought himself almost in his father's arms and he had been deceived. He hardly dared ask a countryman if the king were lodging in the town yonder, and, finding it true, could not walk forward fast enough, lest before he came up his Majesty should move away.

Walk fast as he would, twilight was deepening when he entered the town, but hordes of people — gaping country folk, sober burghers, swaggering troopers, gayly dressed gentlemen — made the dusky streets lively as by day. Among them all Hugh forced a path, jostled and pushed, and pushing in his turn. He began inquiring of those he met if Colonel Alan Gwyeth lodged in the town, and some had not heard the name, and some knew such an officer was with the king but knew not where he lay. At last he chanced upon a foot soldier who directed him for Alan Gwyeth's lodgings to the west gate of the town. Thither Hugh tramped to search the neighborhood for the house and get cursed for disturbing people, but still he persisted in his search, though there would creep in upon him a hopeless feeling that it had all been delusion from the first and he never would find his father.

In the end he got a direction that took him out a quarter-mile beyond the west gate to an old timbered house that sat close upon the road; knocking and making his usual inquiry of a curt servant, he found that Colonel Alan Gwyeth lodged there. Almost unable to believe it, Hugh repeated the words blankly after the servant, then stood staring at him without speaking till the door was nearly shut in his face. He stayed it with one hand, while he asked to see the colonel.

"He is hence with other gentlemen this evening; I know not when he will return," was the short reply before the door was closed in good earnest.

Hugh still stood on the steps, trying to comprehend that it was all true; in a few hours his father, the tall reddish-haired man, would be walking up to that very door. He would see him, at last. He went slowly down to the road, and then paused; if he walked away his father might come, for the evening was already half spent. He decided it would be better to wait there, so he went up the steps again and sat down.

THE END OF THE JOURNEY

At first he had no lack of company; horsemen went swinging by, and groups of men, some staidly, some boisterously with shouts and songs, passed in the road below him. Hugh listened with ears alert and as each dark form drew near asked himself if that might be the one. Gradually as the evening wore on passers-by became less frequent and Hugh wearied of starting at each new step. He became aware, too, that he was stiff with sitting in one position and the night was cold enough to make his clothes of small protection. He looked up at the sharp stars and counted them and picked out those he knew. Then he changed his position once more, and fell to thinking how good a hot meal would taste; he had not eaten food since the supper of the night before. And he was tired, too; he leaned his head against the railing of the stairs, and, just closing his eyes, saw the trees and fields of the night ride go by, and saw Strangwayes' white face, and saw the face of the tall man who used to carry him on his shoulder.

A great noise of talking made him rouse up, wondering dazedly if he had slept. Somebody was shouting out a drinking song, and others, with voices crisp in the chilly air, were disputing together. A torch seemed to glare in his very face, and a man, the first of several stumbling up the steps, nearly fell over him, and swore at him, then dragged him to his feet with a rough, "What are you doing here, sirrah?"

Rubbing the dazzle of the light out of his eyes, Hugh saw five or six men about him on the steps, two with torches, who seemed mere troopers, and the others finely dressed. "Is—Colonel Gwyeth here?" he faltered, with a half hope that the meeting might be deferred a bit longer.

"Here, Alan, this gentleman has commands for you," some one called, and laughed.

At that another man came briskly up from the street and, shoving the others aside, pushed under the light of the torches. A man of short forty years, and but little above middle height, Hugh perceived, in a velvet suit with a plumed hat and a cloak wrapped up to his chin. Beneath the torchlight his long hair and close-trimmed beard seemed the color of gold, and he had blue eyes that looked angry and his face was flushed. "What's to do here?" he asked curtly, and a trick of the tone set Hugh's memory struggling for something that had long been past. "What do you want of me, you knave?"

Hugh looked up at the flushed, impatient face, and, stammering to find words, wished it were all over and these men gone, and he were alone with this stranger; then he hesitated desperately, "Colonel Gwyeth, if it like you, I am your son."

Somebody laughed foolishly, and another began, "'Tis a wise child—" but Alan Gwyeth looked Hugh over and then, turning on his heel with a curt "The devil you are!" walked through the open door into the house. The others tramped noisily after him; some one gave Hugh a hasty shove that sent him pitching to the foot of the steps, and as he recovered himself he heard the house-door slammed.

CHAPTER VII

HOW THE WORLD DEALT BY A GENTLEMAN

HE could get only a broken sleep, because of a door that was always slamming; sometimes men were laughing, too, but the crash of the closing door was louder still, so loud Hugh woke at last. " It was all a bad dream," he said in his thoughts, with a lightening of the heart that made him feel like his old self. But next moment his hand touched the damp boards of the doorway in which he was crouched and found them real; across the roadway the dim houses, with the mist that comes before day hanging over them, were real; and so was the blank sky. Then all that had happened last night was true: there was a lad named Hugh Gwyeth, whose father would have none of him, who had not a friend to turn to, nor a penny to his name, nor, except for this cold doorway whither he had crawled, a place to lay his head. Hugh sat up and, as if it were another man's concern, checked it all off dispassionately.

Just then a drunken trooper came reeling down the empty street, and Hugh found himself making nice calculations as to whether the man's zigzag progress would plunge him into a muddy puddle just opposite the doorway, or bring him safely by on the far side. When the fellow staggered past unsplashed Hugh lost interest in him, and began counting the windows of the opposite houses, that were slowly lighting up with the dawn. Presently a man on a red horse came clicking down the narrow way, then two men helping a comrade home, then a little squad of foot soldiers under a brisk officer; and after that townsmen and stray troopers came in greater numbers, the doors and windows opened, and the day began.

All the long morning Hugh tramped the streets of Shrewsbury, aimlessly, for he had nowhere to go. Everscombe was not to be thought of; even if he had been at the very gates of the manor house, even if his grandfather had found it in his heart to relent, the affair at the "Golden Ram" would have made forgiveness impossible to his kinsfolk. Neither could he go back to Strangwayes, who had lent him a horse for which his father was to pay; at least the bay would compensate for that, but he had no right to ask farther kindness which he could never return. And then Strangwayes' new friends had shown him out of doors; perhaps Dick would not care to have him come back.

With such broken reflections Hugh loitered through the town, and now and again, in gazing at the swarming men and brave horses that filled the streets, tried to forget his miserable plight. About noon he stood many minutes in a gutter and listlessly watched a great body of horse march by. He heard some one say the king was going northward on an expedition, and he asked himself if Colonel Gwyeth went too, and was troubled an instant till he realized that he had now no call to follow.

Then he let all that pass, and thought only that the autumn air was chilly and he was hungry, so that though he pulled his belt a notch tighter it availed nothing. A man must eat, and out in the world food came only by work, he realized; and with that he fell to wondering if there were any labor to which he might turn his hand. A small knowledge of Latin, small skill with a sword, and the ability to back a horse, — that summed up his accomplishments. Hugh told them over with a feeling that either he had not been equipped for such a fortune as this, or he had struck out for himself long before his education was completed. But if he could ride and handle a sword he might turn trooper, so, coming in sight of a smith's shop and men, one of whom looked a petty officer, lounging about it, he ventured up shyly and, as the fellows were in good humor, questioned them tentatively, if they might not perhaps care to enroll him among them. They only laughed at him, and the petty officer bade him run home and grow. With his hopes a bit dashed Hugh walked away, but, strengthened by having a purpose, tramped the town all the afternoon in search of employment among the horse soldiery. But those he applied to either lost their tempers and swore at him, or laughed and chaffed him; and the foot soldiers, to whom he finally offered himself, were even more contemptuous. "You? 'Twould need another fellow to bear your musket," the last man he questioned answered him gruffly.

That night Hugh slept in the sheltered corner

of an alley, and two officers, tramping through at midnight with a torchbearer, stumbled over him. One kicked him, the other, glancing at him, flung him a penny before he passed on. When the coin fell beside him Hugh did not move, but after the torch had blinked out of sight he groped his hand along the damp ground, shaking with nervousness that he did not find the penny, and, as his fingers closed on it, almost sobbed with relief. He sought out a bakehouse at once, and sitting on some dingy steps opposite waited the hungry hours till morning broke, the shop opened, and bursting in headlong he could buy his bread. It went very quickly, leaving him hungrier than ever, but he got no more till next morning, when a gentleman paid him twopence for holding his horse.

He had now given over tramping the town, for he knew it was useless; he had sought employment in every troop in Shrewsbury, and everywhere he had been rebuffed. So the most of the day he sat on a doorstep and, idly watching the street and the sky, tried to forget what life had looked like four days ago. When he was ordered off the step he loitered slowly out by the western gate, and, finding him a snug corner in the lee of a shed opposite a wayside alehouse, lay down for the night. He was beginning now to get a realization of what had befallen, as a man who has been stunned recovers consciousness with a sense of pain, and he had a feeling that if he could have cried a long time it would have eased him, but the hard manhood that had been thrust upon him would not suffer that nor anything which might relieve him.

Toward morning a noise of loud singing woke him. He tried to sleep again, but the singing worried him and besides he felt cold and cramped. He rose at last to stretch himself, and stepping out into the road saw, sprawled across the door-stone of the alehouse, a big dark figure that was yelling lustily at the sky. "Have you come at last?" the fellow cried, "I said to myself,—maybe you heard me,—'Bob, if thou keepst it up time enough some mother's son will come.' Look 'ee here, lad, you're to do me a kindness. I am quite sober, mark you, sober as parson himself, but somewhat is amiss with my legs. An you'll aid me to the stable you'll do his Majesty a great service."

There might be a ha'penny at the end of it, so Hugh suffered the trooper, as he judged the man to be, to lean on him, and they set out unsteadily. What with keeping his charge erect and looking to the rough highway lest they both go down, he paid little heed to the landmarks, though once, at a half-articulate order from his companion, he swerved over to the left and, keeping a dark house on one hand, walked toward a dim light. They were just near enough for Hugh to perceive it shone from an isolated low building, when an armed man challenged them, but at a thick reply from the trooper let them go stumbling on. The familiar stamp of horses was now audible, the light shone clearer, and at last Hugh guided his shambling comrade in at the open door of a stable. On either hand the uncertain light of a brace of lanterns showed rows of dim stanchions and tethered horses, before it merged away into the dark lofts and vast roof. In the centre of the stable the lanterns flung a clear circle of yellow light, and there four fully armed carabineers, seated on kegs or sprawling on the floor, were playing at dice. The sound of footsteps made them look up, and one half swore, while another started as if to sweep up dice and boxes. "Does this man belong to you?" Hugh asked desperately, for his companion, with his florid face suddenly turned melancholy, was leaning against the doorpost and blinked at the light, but said nothing.

"Yes, he belongs to us," replied one with a beard, who seemed the leader of the party, "the more sorrow to us." He threw his dice deliberately: "Seven-tray-cinque. — Pitch him down on the hay yonder."

"Nick, how can you use a comrade so?" maundered the prodigal, as Hugh helped him across the stable and suffered him to roll over on a heap of hay.

"Be thankful you get no worse. If old Jack Ridydale had not shogged off with the troop to Chester, you'd get the devil for this; he's the man could give it you."

"Hardwyn has mind to make himself such another," said one of the younger and less assured men.

"Jeff Hardwyn is a cursed better soldier than ever thou'lt be," Nick replied concisely, and the play went on.

None took heed of Hugh, so, after a moment's hesitation, he sat down on the loose hay, where his drunken friend had fallen sound asleep. He

VII THE WORLD AND A GENTLEMAN

had no call to linger, but the hay was far softer than the ground of the streets, so he sat there and listened to the gruff talk of the men and the click of the dice. At length he stretched himself out, and, watching the dim lanterns flicker, he, too, went to sleep.

Of a sudden he was wakened by some one's pitching him roughly off the hay. There was dull morning light in the stable now, men were feeding and grooming horses, and right over him stood a shock-headed fellow, with more of the peasant than the trooper still visible in him, who demanded, "What beest thou here for?"

"'Twas no harm," Hugh answered, getting up stiffly; he had meant to walk away, but in the stable there was at least a roof over him, and he hesitated. "I can feed your horse for you," he ventured.

"Then run fetch a bucket of water," the other commanded. Hugh caught up the bucket, and, hurrying out into the chill of the morning, found between the stable and the big house a well where he drew the water, as he was bidden. After that he fetched more water, brought fodder, rubbed down a horse, — it was marvellous the amount of work that could be found for an extra pair of hands to do. But, weary and faint though he was, Hugh labored on bravely, with a special effort to satisfy Jonas Unger, the trooper who had first roused him, in which he succeeded so well that when at last the men tramped away to breakfast Unger permitted him to follow along. Crossing an open space betwixt the great house and the stables, they came out through a hedge-gap upon a byway and scattered cottages where the carabineers were quartered. Hugh slunk into the common room of one of these cottages at the heels of Unger and the man called Nick Cowper, and there, sitting at table, with white lips and heavy eyes, found the roisterer he had helped home the night before. Bob Saxon, as his mates called the fellow, was past much talk this morning, and the others were in tolerably good temper, so Hugh was suffered to take a share of their rations, which he ate on the doorstone. The food was coarse, but there was almost enough to satisfy him, so, in the hope of earning more, when the men went back to the stables he followed them.

After a time a curt officer entered the stable, and, ordering the little troop to horse, led it away to be exercised. Hugh cleaned out a stall and had some speech with other ragged hangers-on who made refuge in the stable, but, liking the company little, soon held his peace and gave heed only to his work. About noon the troop returned with the horses all sweaty, and a deal of unharnessing and rubbing down to be done. Hugh came forward to take his share and was removing the saddle from Saxon's horse, when he thought to hear mention of a name that made his hands shake at their task. Pausing to look up, he saw it was a sunburned man with a twist of mustache who was speaking: "Ay, 'twas one of the colonel's men brought the tidings. The king has surely taken in Chester."

"Good news, in truth, Corporal Hardwyn!" replied Cowper, whom the man addressed. "And we tied here to hammer wit into dunder-pated raw levies! Ay, 'twas like Colonel Gwyeth to serve us such a trick."

Hugh heard no more for the rush of blood to his temples; still he could not believe his bad fortune had served him such a cruel turn, so, when he had put Saxon's horse into its stall, he went up to Cowper and asked point-blank: "An't like you, who commands this troop?"

"What is that to you, sirrah?" asked Cowper.

"Is it — Alan Gwyeth?" Hugh persisted.

"Yes, hang you!" replied the man, and boxed his ears for asking.

Even as he reeled back with his face tingling, Hugh found room in his heart to be thankful that he had told no one his name. These knaves must never know it was their commander's son whom they had the right to knock about. Perhaps the dignity of his family required that he should leave the place at once, he reflected dolefully, as he groomed Cowper's horse; but, after all, it was better to drudge for his father's troopers than to beg in Shrewsbury streets.

So Hugh stayed on at the troop stables, where he groomed horses, and cleaned stalls, and fetched and carried with all the strength and readiness necessary to please a score of rough masters. From day's end to day's end it was hard, hateful labor with no sign of release. Once, to be sure, at the news that the king had returned from Chester, something that was half hope and half dread awoke in him, for there was a chance that at any hour Colonel Gwyeth might come to the stables. But soon he learned that his father had gone foraying to the eastward, so even that small hope vanished, and life meant only to work with all his strength, sleep on the hay, share the troopers' rations, and through all endure such abuse and brutality as they might choose to inflict upon him.

It was not long before Hugh dropped his old methods of classification and grouped men in two great divisions: those who struck at you for the fun of seeing you dodge, and those who struck to hurt you. Of the former class was Bob Saxon, who had a certain good nature about him, though his horseplay was apt to be rough. He had been to the wars in Germany, Hugh gathered from the big stories the fellow told, and for that reason Hugh felt drawn toward him; at least, Saxon knew the land where he had been born, and he knew Colonel Gwyeth. "There's a man would take a trot through hell, if he had the word," he once said admiringly of the colonel, whereat Hugh felt a feeble thrill of pride, and held his chin higher, till Cowper happened along and set him to cleaning his boots. Hugh considered there was nothing good to be said for Nick Cowper; he had an unconscious knack of setting tasks that peculiarly unbefitted a gentleman, while at all times he was brutal with the fierce roughness of a seasoned campaigner, who struck to hurt. To be sure, no malice seemed behind his brutality; it was merely his way of reducing command to terms of the senses, but that gave small remedy to Hugh's skin or to his wounded dignity, when Cowper sent him stumbling about his work with his lip cut or his nose bleeding.

But Hugh was to learn there were rougher

dealers even than Cowper, when he came into conflict with Jeff Hardwyn, the corporal. He was one who seldom lifted his hand against any man, but when he ordered the troopers obeyed; and Hugh, with a feeling that he must not get the fellow's ill-will, jumped to do his bidding and called him "sir." But, for all these poor defences, he at last fell under the corporal's displeasure, by such trivial happenings that even looking back he did not understand how it had come to pass. There had been a day of heavy rains that turned the roads to mud, in the midst of which Unger sent Hugh tramping through Shrewsbury in quest of a man he was not able to find. When the boy returned late in the afternoon, drenched and tired, he discovered the whole errand had been a mere hoax for the diversion of Unger and Saxon and the half-dozen others who were loafing in the dry stable. "Next time, pray you take a fair day to be witty," Hugh said, trying not to show temper, and was starting out to forage hungrily for dinner when Hardwyn bade him stop and tighten a buckle on his saddle girth. Pulling off his coat, Hugh turned to the job, which he found harder than he thought, so he did it hastily, then ran out to seek his dinner, and, for his late coming, got none at all.

But when he splashed wearily back to the stable he suddenly forgot all the petty misadventures of the luckless day, for over by the stalls Hardwyn was standing with his brows drawn together ominously. "Can you not tighten a buckle better than that?" he asked, and tapped the saddle at his feet with the toe of his boot.

"I did it as well as I knew, sir," Hugh replied.

"Well, I'll learn you to do it better next time," said Hardwyn without temper, and crossing the stable picked up a heavy horsewhip.

Hugh thought that the heart had gone out of his body, so weak and empty of strength did he feel. He had been whipped many times, at school and at Everscombe, but he knew this would be different, and he was half afraid, yet he did not run. Indeed, when Hardwyn took him by the neck of his shirt, he looked up and said quietly, "I am not going to run away."

"No, I'll wager you're not," Hardwyn answered, and brought the whip stinging down across his back.

Hugh heard his shirt rip in the grasp on his neck, and he felt a foolish concern over it; he saw the loose spears of hay scattered on the dingy floor at his feet; and he wondered why, since he had not meant to struggle, he had twisted up one arm and griped Hardwyn's wrist that held him. He knew that he was counting the blows, eleven so far, but he durst not open his lips lest in spite of himself he cry out. Were the cuts of the whip bringing blood, he wondered? He did not hear the strokes, but he counted them by feeling; at first each had seemed distinct and left a lingering smart, but now his whole back was wincing and quivering. He heard Hardwyn draw a deep breath and for a second hoped he might stop, but there came another slash of the whip. Then, of a sudden, it was borne in on him that Hardwyn meant to flog him till he cried. Hugh set his teeth tight on his lip and only thought, "I will not, I will not," and felt the whip-cuts, nothing more, till the floor seemed blurry and came nearer, and his shirt ripped again. Then he heard Saxon's voice: "Don't kill the lad, sir."

"Curse his stubbornness!" Hardwyn panted out, and then there were other blows of which Hugh kept no count. He only knew that at the last he found himself free to reel over against the boards of a stall, and, without glancing at the other men around them, he looked up into Hardwyn's flushed face a long minute. Then, still keeping hold on the stall, he made a step toward the door, but Hardwyn picked up the saddle and flung it down before him. "Mend that aright now," he ordered, "and, harkee, if ever you bungle another piece of work like that, I'll flay you alive."

Without a word Hugh took up the saddle and tightened the buckle. His fingers shook, he noted, and once, when he put his hand to his mouth, he felt his lip was bleeding where he had bitten it. But he had not cried or spoken, nor would he; when the saddle was put to rights he flung it over its peg, and, still keeping silence, walked out of the stable toward the highway.

So long as he was in sight of the men he walked with tolerable erectness, but he knew it could not last long and he must get away from every one, so he struck across the road into the fields. There he turned eastward on a course that would finally bring him round Shrewsbury to the main highway. For eastward lay the village where he had left Strangwayes; Dick would protect him, he knew, and yet he knew he was not going to him.

As well walk eastward as another way, though,

but he ached from head to foot and his back throbbed painfully; so at last, on a bleak hilltop, he sat down to rest, and watched the twilight close in. A little below him he could see the dim roofs of Shrewsbury and the purpling sky above. The western star came out first, and, as the night darkened, many more showed till he lost count of them and turned his eyes to the lights of the town. As he gazed thither he caught, clear and vibrant on the still air, the note of a bell. On the instant the foolish old tale of Dick Whittington came back to him: "Turn again, turn again." Then he remembered how Lois and he had spoke together the day before he set out from Everscombe; and, when he had hoped for Whittington's fortune, she had answered that his father would be glad to see him.

Of a sudden Hugh found himself lying face down in the wet grass of the hillside with his fingers digging into the turf. If he were only dead, now while he still possessed some shred of self-respect! He could not go on living, a mere horse-boy, everybody's drudge, with his highest hope to be some day a swaggering private trooper, and then to be knocked on the head in a petty skirmish. It was so piteously different from the soldierly life he had planned, but he did not ask for that now, only not to be bullied and flogged any more.

Then that mood passed, and he knew only that he was cold in his torn shirt and his back was sore so he was loath to move. But the cold at last forced him to his feet and set him pacing up and down the wet grass; he still loved life enough

VII THE WORLD AND A GENTLEMAN

to exert himself to keep it. Then he began to realize that, after all, he had acted like a child. Was this life so much less endurable than that at Everscombe? Was it worse to earn his living of a gang of brutal troopers than be dependent on grudging relatives? If he did get more blows, a man must not whimper for that, and he was now a man. Neither must a man go crying to his friends; rather the thing that best befitted a gentleman was to accept the life he had taken up and go on bravely.

So, in the early hours of the morning, Hugh Gwyeth faced westward and tramped back to the stables. Reaching there about dawn, he walked in as usual, and taking up a bucket, went to draw water. He had a curious sense of not feeling ashamed nor abashed, as he thought to feel when facing the men once more, but rather proud of himself and of more dignity than ever. He had no hope, however, of being a hero in the sight of the troopers. Some of them chaffed him over his beating and his slinking back again. "You wanted more of the same, did you?" Hardwyn asked dryly, whereat the others laughed. Saxon chaffed him too; but later, when Hugh came to the cottage for breakfast, he asked him roughly if the whip had drawn blood, and then he helped the boy to wash off his hurt back.

By next day every one had forgotten that Hardwyn had flogged him, and life went on in its old course. Only Hugh took it now as an accepted thing; there was no escape, so he would make the best of it, do as he was bidden, dodge what blows he could, and, what he could not dodge, bear without flinching. He even contrived, so long as he could busy himself about the horses, to find a sort of negative pleasure in the life. To groom and feed and water the great, friendly animals did not seem menial, but this made only a part of the day's routine, and Hugh's pride could not yet stoop willingly to cleaning boots and fetching beer. The last was the most humiliating employment of all; though he might reconcile himself to slipping into an obscure corner and cleaning the boots of a man who was older than he and a better soldier, he felt that to tramp a quarter-mile on the highway with a brace of jugs and fetch bad beer from an alehouse for a crew of peasant troopers could never befit a gentleman.

Late of an October afternoon he was trudging back to the stable from such an errand, when he met a gay company of horsemen and, to save being trampled on, halted at one side of the road till they should pass. By chance he glanced up and among the riders saw one very young gentleman with yellow curls, who wore a fine blue velvet suit and a big hat, and bestrode a dainty roan mare. Hugh caught his breath and looked again, then dodged headlong back from the road, in behind a cottage out of sight. Halting there a moment he instinctively looked himself over,— ragged shirt with the sleeves rolled up to the shoulders, ragged breeches stained with mud, half-worn boothose, and shoes that were falling to pieces. He wondered if Frank Pleydall, in his fine clothes, on his good horse, had recognized him, and he thought it unlikely. With a foolish dread of a second encounter he made his way back to the stable through the fields; the going was rough, and he now perceived much of the beer had slopped out of the jugs. "I shall be flogged for that," he told himself, and, with something that was not jealousy but hurt him keenly, he wondered if Frank Pleydall knew what a happy lad he was.

But, much as he expected it, Hugh did not get a flogging; for when he came into the stable yard he found strange horses standing there, and two or three troopers he did not know, and his own acquaintances looked energetic and on good behavior, so much perturbed they did not even rate him about the beer. "The colonel is back from the eastward," Unger explained, "and Corporal Ridydale is on our shoulders again."

"He'll send you packing," Cowper spoke cheerfully to Hugh.

Just then Saxon, riding in, called to Hugh to groom his well-bespattered horse, so the boy, eager though he was to hear more, must walk away with the beast to the open floor of the stable, where he fell to work. It darkened and lanterns were lit; one was hung from a stanchion, and just beneath Hugh saw a stranger standing, a tall, thickset man of middle age with a heavy beard, who seemed to have an eye for all the business of the stable, and at whose word men moved to obey, even more readily than they did for Hardwyn. He must be John Ridydale, Hugh decided, so he got Saxon's horse betwixt them, and, working briskly, hoped he might not be noticed. But presently Ridydale stopped giving orders, and Hugh, getting uneasy at his silence and looking sidewise at the man, found he was gazing at him with his brows drawn together. Hugh feigned to be very busy with the horse, but the currycomb moved unsteadily in his hand, while he waited, and wondered if Ridydale would kick him out of the stable at once or let him stay long enough to get his supper. Then he heard a heavy step and, looking up and finding the corporal beside him, drew back a pace warily; but the other griped him by the shoulder with a sharp, "What's your name, lad?"

"Hugh."

"What else?"

"Nothing else, sir."

Hugh had his arm half raised to shield his head, but Ridydale did not strike at him, only said with something strangely like kindliness, "Come outside here."

There were horses at the trough by the door, Hugh noted, and through the stable yard a twilight mist, in which the cottage lights looked blurry, was shutting down. They had drawn away from any stray troopers, and now, right by the hedge, Ridydale, with his grasp still on Hugh's shoulder, halted him and asked, "The rest of the name mightn't be Gwyeth, perhaps, master?"

CHAPTER VIII

THE INTERPOSITION OF JOHN RIDYDALE

It shamed Hugh afterward to remember how overwhelmingly, at that first dim prospect of relief, the realization of his friendlessness and degradation came over him, till not even sufficient spirit was left in him to make his usual evasions. "Yes, I am Hugh Gwyeth," he answered simply; "I am the colonel's son."

Then he felt the sharp sting of twigs across his face, as he pressed his head upon his folded arms against the yielding hedge, and his breath came stranglingly for a great lump that had gathered in his throat and was near choking him. Ridydale was patting him on the shoulder, he knew, and he heard him say: "Come, come, master, don't go play the woman now. 'Tis all well, I tell you."

At that Hugh lifted his head from his arms. "Did my father send you to seek me?" he asked, eagerly, as the griping feeling in his throat would let him.

Ridydale hesitated a moment. "I'll wager he'll be glad enough that I have found you, sir," he said at length. "For now, get you over to the cottage where the light shows yonder and bide till I come."

"But Saxon's horse," — Hugh's long drill in stable duty made him protest.

"Hang the horse and Bob Saxon, too!" growled Ridydale, with an expletive or so. "A pretty trade for your father's son to turn a hand to!"

Still muttering, he strode back to the stable, while Hugh obediently made his way, by the hedge-gap and the well-trodden path, to the farthest of the cluster of cottages that quartered the troop. By virtue of his coming from Corporal Ridydale he was suffered to enter the low-studded living room and sit down on a stool in the chimney corner. It was a poor smoky room, but with the fire and candle it was warmer and brighter than the stable, and there was a home-likeness about the children sprawling on the hearth, the woman cooking pottage at the fire, even about her stolid peasant husband, that made Hugh content to sit in a kind of open-eyed drowse and watch them. In these hours of negative comfort the whole burden of responsibility seemed slipped from him, and he neither thought nor vexed himself with anticipation, only waited for Ridydale.

All save the cottager's wife had packed to bed in the loft before the corporal returned. Hugh heard him outside, rating some unknown trooper with bullying volubility, and then he came in, grumbling about the mismanagement of Hardwyn, who in his absence had got the men out of all conceit of obedience. By the time they sat down to supper he had almost calmed himself, however, and was kindly spoken to the woman who attended them and brusquely civil to Hugh, who after his vagabond period felt ill at ease, even at so poor a board. Ridydale noted all that, and apparently he had made inquiries too, for when they were left alone at table he spoke out, half angrily and half sorrowfully, "So you've been drudging in the stables ever since that night, sir?"

"There was nothing else to do," Hugh answered, and took another piece of bread, with a comfortable sense that he could have all he wanted.

"'Twas hard to think at first it could be the colonel's son," Ridydale went on, "though I was on the watch for you. I heard of that blockhead Rodes, — he who bore the colonel's torch that night — how you came unto him. Rodes told it for a jest the colonel's comrades would put upon him, but I that had been with him nigh twenty years, I had a shrewd doubt there might be some truth lay at the bottom of it. So I took it on myself to make search, so soon as we returned to Shrewsbury. Lord save me, sir, when I used to see you, there where we were in Lower Saxony, such a well-favored little rascal, I never thought to come upon you currying horses for your father's men."

"You were in Germany?" Hugh asked.

"Where the colonel has been I have been, these twenty years. I went as his man when he first crossed to the Low Countries — a proper young soldier he was! Then I was back with him in Warwickshire, seventeen years agone; it seems longer."

"Then — you knew my mother?" Hugh asked, pushing aside his trencher.

"Ay, Mistress Ruth Oldesworth, and a gallant-spirited young gentlewoman she was. To leave her knave kinsfolk so, for love o' the colonel! And she was that kind spoken to all of us that followed him. Faith, a man could nigh forgive her, even for deserting the colonel so."

"But my mother was not to blame therein," Hugh broke out.

"Now, sir, what know you thereof? You were just a younker that scarce could stand then. There was blame lay with her as well as with the colonel."

Hugh rumpled the hair back from his forehead, while he strove to grasp the significance of this new information. He realized that these last weeks there had been in his heart an unphrased feeling that his father was cruel, and his mother must have suffered much, just as he was suffering. Once he had held both parents something nobler than human creatures; and latterly his mother had seemed more than ever a saint, and his father an utter wretch; but now, what was he to think?

"Did she ever lay blame on him, sir?" Ridydale spoke presently.

"No," Hugh replied, and snuffed the candle with his fingers a moment, then broke out: "Corporal Ridydale, they have told me different stories. I know not what to believe, but you were there; on your honor as a soldier, what was betwixt my father and my mother?"

Ridydale thoughtfully eyed the fire smouldering on the hearth, and tousled his beard with one hand. "I should say the blame rested with both, sir," he began at length. "They were both very young and high-tempered, and he would have his pleasure. He was stubborn, though I grudge to say it of him, and she was not over-patient. There was words betwixt them, and that same day our troop was sent foraying southward and he did not even take leave of her. But he faced the troop about ere the sennight were over and brought us home at a gallop. And when he came to quarters she had taken you and gone for England. He never said word of it, even to me, save, 'She might ha' left me the lad; he was as much mine as hers.'"

"Then — he did have some care for me once?" Hugh asked; he was keeping his face turned toward the fire, away from his companion.

"You were his only son, sir, and you were a marvellous pretty little rogue."

Hugh smiled at the fire, rather tremulously; it was dawning upon him that Ridydale, for all his formal respect and kindness, was disappointed that he did not bear out the promises of his babyhood, and he had a doleful feeling that in the same way Colonel Gwyeth, too, would always be disappointed in him.

"After that we went into Pomerania," Ridydale began again, "and joined ourselves unto King Gustavus. For the colonel would not make a start to follow his lady; perhaps 'twas stubbornness, but he had no word of her since she quitted Germany, and he was too proud to go a-begging to her, so we just stayed on in the Swedish army. Once — 'twas the year we fought at Wolfenbüttel — there came a gentleman volunteer from England with tidings out of Warwickshire, and so we learned that she was dead."

Hugh blinked at the fire and made no answer.
"Ay, she was a good lady and of a fine spirit," Ridydale mused aloud. "And as much blame lay with the colonel as with her. But she might have been more patient."

Then, as Hugh still kept silent, Ridydale suggested they get to bed, and led the way up the steep ladder to the loft. There were two pallets in Ridydale's rough chamber, and Hugh wondered impersonally, as he lay down on one, what trooper the corporal had violently dispossessed of his quarters to make room for him. At the foot of the pallet, in the sloping roof, was a small window, through which Hugh found, after the candle was out, he could see five bright stars and a patch of purple-black sky. He lay staring at the stars and saw no meaning in them, for thinking busily to himself and trying to comprehend that his parents had been neither all good nor utterly depraved, but just frail everyday human creatures, whom he must love and bear with for their humanness.

Next morning he awoke of his own accord, without being kicked, and, finding the room empty and a sunbeam coming through the little window, rose up and went briskly below stairs. Late though he was, the woman gave him all the breakfast he wanted, and then force of habit took him over to the stable. "What have you done to set Jack Ridydale in such a sweet temper?" Saxon greeted him, and the other men merely pestered him with questions but gave him no blows.

With a feeling that it was not yet time to proclaim his identity to all, Hugh answered evasively, and then, because it was irksome to be idle, he watered one of the horses, and, as Unger had bidden him the day before, began patching up a headstall. He was sitting on a keg, fumbling with a refractory buckle, when Ridydale bore down upon him with a fierce, "What are you about? Put that down and get back to the cottage."

Arguing that if he were still a stable-boy Ridydale had the right to command him, and if he were a gentleman Ridydale's friendliness had given him the right to make requests, Hugh laid aside the headstall and went meekly back to the cottage, where till dinner time he lounged ingloriously on the doorstone. After the noon meal Ridydale, very sullen and wrathful, beckoned him outside and rated him, respectfully but severely. "'Tis not becoming a gentleman like you to fetch and carry for those dogs of troopers," he explained. "Truth, you seem to have small regard for the dignity of your family, sir."

It was so ludicrously like the view of what befitted a gentleman which up to a fortnight ago he himself had held that Hugh could not help smiling. "Methinks 'tis not what a gentleman does but how he does it makes the disgrace," he said.

Ridydale shook his head and looked dubious, then, coming apparently to a better temper, changed the subject by offering to lend Hugh money with which to buy fresh clothes. "The colonel will be here to-night," he concluded, "and I've a plan to wait a good-natured moment and tell him of you. I'm thinking he'll ask to see you, and you should not come before him in such rags as these."

But Hugh had had enough of borrowing on the chance of Colonel Gwyeth's making repay-

ment, and he refused the loan; if the colonel
chose to provide for him, he reasoned to himself,
he need wear his rags but few hours longer; and
if the colonel rebuffed him again he would liefer
have rags than whole clothes and a debt to so
short-pursed a man as a corporal of carabineers.
Ridydale fairly let slip his self-control at the boy's
obstinate refusal. "If 'twere not for your red
hair and your trick of setting your lips together,
I'd doubt if you were a Gwyeth," he broke out at
last, and marched away to the stables in some
temper.

Whereat Hugh felt angry, then grew thoughtful, and, reflecting that the man, for all his
arbitrary ways, had treated him with real kindness, wondered if he might not have somewhat
tempered his refusal. So, when he next saw
Ridydale, at supper, he tried to talk him into
good humor by questioning him of his father,
which much mollified the corporal, and then of
the troop, and finally of the progress of the war.
It seemed Colonel Gwyeth's force had shared
with Sir William Pleydall's troop some brisk
skirmishing about Worcester; Hugh wondered if
Frank had had the good fortune to be present,
and sought to get news of the Pleydalls from
Ridydale, who, when he learned Hugh had acquaintance with such gentlemen, looked a trifle
more favorably upon him. The boy was sorely
tempted to tell him the story of Dick Strangwayes
and the skirmish at the "Golden Ram," but,
after all, that was a kind of self-glorification that
would become Bob Saxon better than Hugh
Gwyeth. So he held his peace, and was thankful

that he had got Ridydale into a mood where, if he still esteemed him rather a weak-spirited fellow, he did not utterly despise him.

But early as next morning it was Hugh's ill luck to destroy whatever good impression he had made. Having risen late, he had fetched a bucket of water up to the chamber, and, stripped to the waist, was bathing himself with much splashing, when Ridydale unexpectedly came in. "The colonel has granted to speak with me ere noon," the corporal announced his business at once, "so you shall speedily — " There he paused, looking sharply at Hugh, who stood sidewise toward him, then strode over to the boy. "How got you those fresh scars on your back?" he demanded.

"No matter," answered Hugh, facing hastily toward the speaker.

Ridydale took him unceremoniously by the shoulders, and turned him round. "'Twas done with a whip!" he burst out. "What means this? Have you been flogged?"

"Yes," Hugh replied. "Now have the goodness to take your hands off me."

"Was it done here at the stables?" Ridydale persisted. "Answer me, master."

"Do you look for me to turn tale-bearer?" Hugh retorted.

"I look to cut some combs for this," Ridydale stormed. "Though you lack in spirit you bear your father's name, and for that they that misuse you shall answer — "

"I pray you, let it all go," Hugh interrupted. "I have suffered no harm — "

Ridydale stamped his foot down on the floor. "Harm, quotha! Why, you might be a brat out of the kennel for all the shame you take from it. Tell me, what can befall a man of gentle birth that's worse harm than to be banged by a pack of knaves?"

Hugh busied himself in pulling on his shirt, and made no reply.

"Well, 'tis time the colonel took you in hand," Ridydale blustered. "You need to be taught what befits a gentleman."

Then he went noisily out of the room, and Hugh heard him clatter down the ladder from the loft. Looking out at the little window he saw Ridydale head for the stables, and he hoped the man might not make inquiries there or bring any one into disgrace for what had befallen. Then, as he turned back to finish dressing, a new alarm seized Hugh: what if the corporal, in his irritation, should refrain from speaking for him to Colonel Gwyeth? But next moment he had quite accepted the thought; indeed, he seemed all along to have half suspected some miscarriage would destroy his faint hope of the last few hours. It would only be of a piece with all that happened to him since he set out from Everscombe.

So, on the whole, he was surprised when about an hour later the cottager's wife knocked at his door with the news that a trooper was below, come to take him before the colonel. No, he was not excited, Hugh told himself, for he cared not what the issue might be; he had twice gone so eagerly to meet his father, and each time been so bitterly disappointed, that now, whatever good fortune might be before him, it could awake in him no fresh anticipation. Yet, for all that, he came down the ladder rather briskly, and, when he found himself actually setting forth to Colonel Gwyeth's quarters, felt a thrill of something like apprehension.

The bit of walk up the byway and along the main road to the great house, the back of which Hugh knew so well from his stable days, ended all too soon. Still repeating to himself that he did not care, he was not frightened, Hugh followed the trooper through the doorway; and then the door had closed, he was left alone in a dim back room, and suddenly he realized that in sober truth he was near to trembling with nervous dread. He was afraid of that flushed, red-haired man who had publicly rejected him; he was afraid of his roughness and more afraid of his tenderness, and if it had not been for shame at running away so ignominiously he would have bolted out of the house. Since that was not to be thought of he sat down on the window-seat and studied the dead leaves and withered flower-stalks of a strip of garden outside. Then he looked about the room and counted the oak panels in the walls and the diamond panes in the windows, but after all his eyes strayed to the door opposite, by which his guide had left him, and he found himself listening to the subdued hum of men's voices that sounded within. Once a single voice rose choked and impatient, and immediately after feet scurried down the passage outside the entrance door. Getting up, Hugh tried hard to stare out at the window, but soon found himself facing the door and listening. All within was quiet now; indeed, there was not a sound nor a warning when at length the door was flung open and Ridydale himself beckoned him to come in. "Don't be afeard, sir," he said under his breath as Hugh passed him, and even in the midst of his own agitation Hugh noted that the corporal's face was anxious and his manner subdued.

"No prompting, Corporal Ridydale," interrupted a stern voice that Hugh remembered. "Come hither, sirrah."

Hugh halted where he was, a few paces from the door, and looked toward the fireplace. Before the hearth Colonel Gwyeth was standing with his hands behind him; the set of his lips could not be judged because of his thick beard, but his brows were contracted so his eyes looked black beneath them. "So this is my son," he began more quietly.

Hugh bowed his head without speaking; for the moment he dared not trust his voice.

"Come, come, hold up your head, man," the colonel broke out impatiently; and then, with a visible effort to maintain his quieter tone, "Why have you not come to me ere this?"

"I did not court a second rejection, sir," Hugh answered, with a steady voice, though his hands were crushing his cap into a little wad.

"There was no need of a first rejection, as you call it. You could have spared us both all this shame had you chosen a proper time and place to seek me."

"I had come some miles and I was eager to see you," Hugh answered slowly.

"Had they used you ill at Everscombe that you ran away?" the colonel broke in.

"N-no, sir," Hugh must admit in simple justice. "My grandfather always used me rather kindly."

"Gilbert Oldesworth?" Colonel Gwyeth turned impatiently from the fireplace. "'Twas of him, I doubt not, you had your good Roundhead doctrine."

"I — do not understand, sir."

"The doctrine of giving your cheek unto the smiter. That cut on your face, now, was that, too, given you by one of my grooms?"

Hugh felt the blood sting in his cheeks; he looked at his father but made no answer.

"Perchance, sir —" Ridydale ventured in a subdued voice.

"Be quiet, John. — I have heard the whole history of your last fortnight, Hugh Gwyeth, your honorable associates, your gentle bearing, all you have done to uphold the credit of your house."

"On my soul, sir, you do the lad wrong," Ridydale struck in rashly. "Though his way be not your way, he is but young and —"

"Hold your tongue, John Ridydale!" the colonel cried, banging his fist down on the table beside him. "And for you, sirrah Hugh, if you have aught to say for yourself, say it out now."

"I know not why I should defend myself, sir." Now they would hark to him at last, Hugh was amazed to find how hot and thick his words came. "I know not what I have done shameful, unless it becomes a gentleman better to starve than to work for his bread."

"You have only done this much, that you have

bitterly disappointed me," Colonel Gwyeth answered sharply. "For my gallant young gentleman I had thought on, those crop-eared kinsmen of mine have sent me a snivelling young Roundhead—"

"For my hair, that is not my fault," Hugh blurted out, "and for snivelling, you have no right to put that word to me. You may ask any one—"

Colonel Gwyeth swept back one arm with an impatient movement that sent some loose papers from the table crackling to the floor. "Can you not understand now what you have done?" he cried. "When you ran away from your school you looked for me to make a soldier of you, did you not? Tell me now, how can I set over my troopers a fellow their whips have lashed?"

For the moment Hugh found no words; the full significance of his father's speech, the totally new view of his weeks of discipline, dismayed him beyond reply. With it all came a feeling that he was bitterly sorry that the matter had gone amiss; in time he might have come to like the red-haired man, who was disappointed in him, and the red-haired man might have come to like him. Even yet it was possible he might win the colonel's favor, if he could show his mettle, if he were only given a chance! Then he heard Ridydale venture, "An't like you, sir—"

"Enough, Jack," the colonel replied, with a poor assumption of a casual tone. "I want you now to take Master Hugh here and get him fitting clothes and a steady horse. By to-morrow night I shall have procured a pass—"

"What mean you to do with me?" Hugh cried out, making a step toward his father.

"I am going to despatch you back to your kinsfolk at Everscombe."

There was an instant of silence; then, "You hold me so mean-spirited a fellow that you will not keep me with you?" Hugh asked slowly.

"Your ways suit your Puritan kindred better than they suit me," Gwyeth answered, fumbling among the papers on the table. "'Tis too late now for me to mend what they have marred. So I shall furnish you with a horse and clothes—"

"I did not come out of Warwickshire to beg a new coat and a nag of you." As he spoke, Hugh half turned away to the door and he perceived now that Ridydale was violently signing to him to be quiet and stay where he was. He did not heed, but, stepping to the door, laid his hand on the latch. "And I shall not go back to Everscombe, sir," he finished his speech deliberately.

"Tut, tut! You are too old for such childishness," answered the colonel, with exasperating contempt.

"I will not go to Everscombe," Hugh repeated.

"Do you turn saucy, you young crop-head?" replied Colonel Gwyeth, letting slip his assumption of calmness. "You will do as I bid you."

"You have no right to say 'do this' unto me," Hugh flung back. "And I want nothing of you,— nothing that you have offered me. I had rather get my head broke in a troop stable twenty times over. But I'll leave your stable. And I'll never trouble you more, sir, with coming unto you, unless you choose to send for me again." All this he said fast, but without raising his voice, and throughout he kept his eyes fixed on the colonel, who stood with his clinched hand resting on the table, and a black look on his face. But Hugh gave him no time to answer, just said, "Good morrow, sir," with much dignity, set his cap on his head, and walked out of the room. He took great pains to close the door carefully behind him.

Once outside upon the highway, he became aware that his face was burning hot and every fibre of his body seemed braced as for actual battle. Heading blindly toward Shrewsbury he tramped along fiercely, while he went over and over the incidents of the last half-hour. If any man but his own father had dared speak so contemptuously and so untruly of him! No, if it had been another than his father, it would not have mattered. But that Colonel Gwyeth, of all men, should hold him such a miserable fellow, and give him no chance to prove himself better!

Just then he heard behind him Ridydale's voice: "Master Hugh! Stay a moment, sir." The corporal had plainly run from the house, but, so soon as Hugh halted, he sobered his pace and came up at a more dignified gait. "On my soul, sir, I meant not to put all awry," he broke out at once.

"Did you bear the tale of that flogging unto him?" Hugh asked hotly.

"Ay. But not as you think, sir, on my honor." Ridydale strode at Hugh's side while he poured out the story: "I had taken me to the stables and dragged the truth from the knaves there.

Well, I'll settle that score with Jeff Hardwyn. I was hot with it all when I came to the colonel, and he bespeaks me very careless and cool, if 'twas his son indeed, belike in time, and so on. I might ha' known 'twas but the way of him and he would yet make it right, but I blurted out he'd best move quickly for his son's sake, not leave him to be buffeted by every cullion in his stables. Well, he got the whole story of me then, sir, and off he goes into one of his fine Gwyeth rages, and packs off Rodes after you, and rates every one in the house on whom he can put hands until you come. And I left him in such another rage. Why in Heaven's name did you go about to defy him so, sir?"

"Because he drove me to it," Hugh retorted, and pressed on with his face set to the front.

"Well, no one is driving you now that you keep such a pace. Whither are you going, an't like you?"

"Shrewsbury. To seek in all the troop stables till I find those who will employ me."

"Nay, nay, lad, come back with me, if you have it in heart to forgive me. On my soul, I meant not so to dash your fortunes. By the Lord, I've a liking for you, sir, in spite of your meek bearing. And I doubt not your father would see there was some good in you, in time. Only come back, and mayhap he —"

"Before I'd beg of Colonel Gwyeth now, I'd go carry a musket for a common foot soldier," Hugh answered.

"Well, you've not your father's spirit," Ridydale jerked out impatiently.

K

Hugh turned on him: "I trust I've not. I trust I'll never live to cast off a son of my own."

At that Ridydale stared blankly, then stopped short and burst out laughing. "By the Lord, you are the colonel over again, sir, whether it like you or not! My faith, and he does not realize it even now, no more than I did. Why, there's mettle in you, sir, after all. Now come back."

But Hugh very plainly showed his whole intent was turned to Shrewsbury, so at length Ridydale abruptly yielded. "I'll come along with you," he offered. "Very like I can find employment for you there, sir. If you care to trust unto me—"

"Ay, and I thank you too," Hugh answered, touched for the moment, till he remembered that Ridydale cared for him only as he would have cared for a dog, had it borne the name of Gwyeth.

After that they trudged on in silence, past the huddled, outlying houses, through the west gate of Shrewsbury, and so into the crowd and confusion of the garrison streets. It was somewhat past noon, Hugh judged by the position of the sun, and then the sun was shut out, as they turned into a narrow byway where the mud was deep in the shadow of the tall houses. "This has not much the look of a troop stable," Hugh suggested, as Ridydale halted and knocked at the dark rear door of what seemed a considerable mansion.

But Ridydale was speaking a word aside to the serving man who opened, and paid no heed. Presently he stepped in, bidding Hugh follow, and then, leaving him alone in a dingy anteroom, he walked away with the servant. Seating himself on a bench by the wall Hugh tried to run over the morning's events, and then to put them by and think only of what was before him: stable-boy, trooper one day, perhaps. Only it was not a good thing to hope forward to, so he drummed his finger-tips on the bench and wondered why Ridydale delayed.

Just then there came a quick, light step outside the inner door. "Where is he?" a shrill voice cried. The door was kicked open, and there plunged in headlong a slim figure in blue. "Hugh, you scoundrel! Where have you been? Why did you not seek me out at first? Hang me if I be not glad to see you, old lad."

"Frankie Pleydall!" was all Hugh could get out for the arms about his neck that were near to strangling him.

CHAPTER IX

THE WAY TO WAR

"That was friendly conduct of you!" Frank Pleydall, having ended his last hot tirade, suffered himself to fall back once more with his shoulders against one arm of his big chair and his legs hanging over the other. "I take it, had not that tall corporal of yours come hither and opened up the matter to us, you'd have gone sweat in a stable, eh? On your honor, Hugh, did you enjoy the life?"

"Would you?" Hugh retorted, and then, as he looked at Frank's curls and fair skin, the impossibility of his going through such experience came home to him. He shrugged his shoulders and, turning to the mirror, went on dragging the comb through his rebellious hair, rather slowly, for to be cleanly and freshly clad was an unwonted sensation, to enjoy which he was willing to dally a trifle in dressing. From time to time he paused to glance at Frank, who lounged and chatted, just as he had done in the old days at school, or to look about the dark room, with great bed and heavy furniture, that recalled to him his grandfather's chamber at Everscombe. After all, he still felt at home in well-ordered life; "outcast" was not stamped upon him for all time. In

Frank's stockings and shirt, which was rather scant for him, and a certain Cornet Griffith's gray breeches, and another officer's half-worn shoes, swept up in the general levy Frank had made on the nearest wardrobes, he thought himself for a moment the same young gentleman who had left Everscombe a month before. Then, chancing to meet the blue eyes that looked back at him out of the mirror, he realized this was not the face he used to know; this face was thin, so the jaws seemed squarer, and there was a firmer set to the lips, and a new depth to the eyes. A slight cut on one cheek and a bruise above one eye he noted, too, without great resentment against those who had given them; such marks would pass quickly, he knew, but the endurance and obedience he had acquired with them would remain.

"I should think it would pleasure you to study that well-favored face," Frank chuckled lazily. "When you're done, sir, get on your coat, and I'll take you to my father."

Hugh pulled on Cornet Griffith's gray jacket, which was somewhat too large for him, and stood turning back the long sleeves. "What a tall fellow you seem!" his comrade broke out, bringing his feet down to the floor and sitting forward in his chair. "On my conscience, I could swear you were more than six months elder than I."

"So could I," Hugh answered thoughtfully.

"Well, for all that you are not to treat me like a boy as the other men do; you're nothing but a lad yourself."

Hugh laughed, and put his hand down on

Frank's shoulder. "We'll be good comrades as we ever have been," he said. "I shall never forget how kindly you have used me this day."

"Oh, hang all that!" Frank put in hastily. "You'd do the like for me. And 'tis pleasure for me to have you with me. You can share my chamber, — there's space enough for one to be lonesome, — and we'll go to the wars together, eh?"

The realization of part of the boyish plan he had brought with him from Everscombe pleased Hugh gravely, but he had been too often disappointed to clutch eagerly at any hope, so he only said, "I'd like it right well, — if your father wish me to stay."

"If I wish it, he will," Frank answered confidently, and so they went arm in arm down the stairs.

Large as the house was, Sir William and the officers of his troop contrived to fill it only too full, Hugh concluded, after Frank had haled him, to his great embarrassment, into several rooms, and presented him formally to all the men on whom he could lay hands. Of the number he best remembered a dry-spoken Captain Turner, who told him, with an implication that made Hugh's face redden, that he ought in justice to notify the rebels that he had joined the king. He remembered, too, a long-legged Cornet Griffith, whose boyish face at sight of him took on such a rueful look that Hugh suspected the loan of the gray clothes had been a forced one. He ventured a private expostulation to Frank, who merely laughed: "Oh, Ned Griffith is a cousin of mine, so he ought to be glad to lend me his goods. — And here I have found my father out at last."

With that he dragged Hugh by the sleeve into a retired parlor, where Sir William Pleydall, a stout florid man of near sixty, was sitting at a table dictating to a secretary. "Here is Hugh Gwyeth, sir, of whom Colonel Gwyeth's corporal told you," Frank announced. "You'll entertain him as a gentleman volunteer, will you not, sir?"

"Will you be silent, Francis, till I have done with this piece of work?" Sir William burst out.

Frank knelt down on a chair with his elbows on the table and his chin in his hands, so the candlelight fell across his girlishly fair face. "I am right sorry, sir," he began winningly, "I did not mark you were busied. I had thought — you would gladly aid a friend of mine. Have I offended you greatly, sir?"

"No, Frank," Sir William answered hastily, and, putting by the papers he held, motioned Hugh to come over to him. "I remember you very well, sir," he began. "You were home with Frank one Michaelmas time. So you ran away from that school? 'Twas very well done of you. That man Masham is a cozening, foul-mouthed knave of a crop-headed Puritan." Sir William's face flushed and Frank made haste to change the subject. "You promised me Hugh should stay with me, sir, you'll recollect."

"If he care to," Sir William made answer. "You look sober enough, Master Gwyeth, to keep my lad in proper behavior."

"I would gladly serve you, Sir William, in any

way I could," Hugh said earnestly. "I think I could fight—"

Sir William began laughing. "Call yourself a gentleman volunteer, if 'tis any satisfaction to you," he said, and seemed about to end the conversation; but, after a second glance at Hugh, asked abruptly in a lower tone, "Between ourselves, sir, what vice was there in you wherefore your father would not entertain you?"

"I did not chance to please him," Hugh answered.

"But you are his only son, are you not?" asked Sir William, looking, not at Hugh, but at Frank, who was still kneeling by the table.

"Yes, Sir William," Hugh replied, with his eyes suddenly lowered.

The baronet was silent a moment, then, "Stay with us as long as you please, my lad," he said in a kinder tone than he had yet used, and with that, abruptly taking up his papers, turned again to his secretary.

Hugh came out in silence from the little parlor, and for a time, while he enjoyed the realization that he had not lost a boy's capacity for feeling happy and hopeful, could make no reply to Frank's brisk chatter. But, before the evening was over, he made amends to Master Pleydall, for, snugly settled in a window-seat with his friend, he recounted to him not only the distinctions he hoped to win in the war, but all that had befallen him in the last six months. Frank, hugging his knees in his excitement, wished audibly he had been with Hugh to run away; two days without food seemed so slight a thing when told.

But Strangwayes' share in events surprised him enough to make him leave clasping his knees and sit up straight: "Met my Cousin Dick? What good fortune for you! He used to be a gay kindly fellow, the best liked of all my father's nephews. What manner of man is he grown now?"

Hugh's eager account made Frank look dubious. "Very like when he comes again you'll not wish to be my comrade any more," he suggested jealously.

"You're somewhat of a fool, Frank," Hugh answered candidly. "Tell me now, have you had news of Dick of late?"

"Ay, he's still with Butler's troop; we only learned that on coming out of Worcestershire two days back. He is but just recovered from his wound and fever —"

"Do you think, Frank," Hugh interrupted, "to-morrow we might walk over to the village and see him?"

"I take it you'll not," Frank retorted. "Where have you kept yourself from the news? To-morrow we march southward to flay the skin off that old fox, the rebel Earl of Essex. We'll make short work of him, and then —" he trailed off into an exact exposition of the way the war would go, which ended only at bedtime.

Next day, as Frank had promised, in a keen, clear weather that made the throngs of troop-horses prance and gave a vividness to every bright coat and sword-hilt, the southward march began. Hugh, riding forth bravely with Frank, Captain Turner, and others of Sir William's officers, felt he could have shouted for mere pleasure in the sight of the plunging horses, the troops of men, and the throngs of friendly townsfolk that lined the streets of Shrewsbury. In every fibre of him was a bracing sensation, not only from the crisp air and the sunlight, but from the mere feeling of the horse moving beneath him and the ordered motion all about him of men and beasts. Now first it came over him that, even if he might not serve with his father, he was glad that he was one of his Majesty's great marching army, bound to fight for the king.

At the east gate, by which all must pass, horses and men were wedged thickly, so presently Hugh found himself forced to one side of the gateway, where his progress was checked. An ammunition wagon had broken down and blocked the way ahead, the word ran through the crowd, whereat some men swore, and others, laughing, took the delay merrily. While they were waiting thus, an officer with one trooper attending rode headlong into the thick of them and there stuck fast. "You'll need slacken pace, sir, you'll find," Turner called to him.

"I've no wish to show my steed's quality," replied the other. "But I'd fain be with a troop of mine that's somewhere ahead on the road 'twixt here and Staffordshire." He impatiently thrust back the flapping brim of his felt hat, and Hugh was made sure of what he had guessed by the voice, that it was Colonel Gwyeth himself.

At first he felt a kind of trembling, which was foolish, he told himself; for he no longer feared the man. So he did not even try to urge his horse forward, but suffered the beast to keep his stand, while he gazed fixedly at the colonel. All through the press ran a swaying motion, which soon forced Colonel Gwyeth, still in loud speech with Turner, knee to knee with Hugh, and at the touch he faced toward him. Hugh felt a thrill go through him, but he looked his father squarely in the eyes and, lifting his hat a trifle, said, "Good morrow, sir."

"In the name of the fiend!" Gwyeth broke out; he had to turn in his saddle to say it, for the movement in the throng had now brought him level with the nose of Hugh's horse. "Well, sir, you seem fully able to fend for yourself."

So he was swept away, and next instant Ridydale following him was up alongside. "'Tis all well, Master Hugh?" he asked in a low tone as he brushed by.

"Ay, thanks to you," Hugh replied, and then Ridydale was forced away, so he lost him in the ruck of horsemen. After that he gave heed only to edging his own beast forward till they were out upon the highway, where they found the road so nearly choked with the riders of their troop, which they presently overtook, that a swift pace was still out of the question. This was somewhat of a relief to Hugh, for the borrowed sorrel which he bestrode was of no great speed, and made him think sadly of the bay horse he had ridden on the headlong dash from the "Golden Ram." Frank, however, who was capitally mounted on his roan mare, The Jade, so named for her wretched temper, lamented all the morning that he had not space sufficient to show his steed's fine paces.

About noon, as they passed through the village

where Hugh had met with Butler's troop, he coaxed Frank out of the ranks and, with an eager hope of seeing Dick Strangwayes again, headed for the inn. But the place was filled with thirsty troopers, so the tapsters were too busy to pay much heed to the boys till Frank tried bribery. Then they learned that the day before Butler's dragoons had started southward to capture some arms at a Puritan country-seat; and, though he looked scarce fit to ride, the gentleman who had lain ill at the house had gone with them. "Well, Cousin Dick must be a hardy fellow," said Frank, as the two boys got to horse again. "Though, to be sure, all the gentlemen of our family are." He flung out his chest as full as possible while he spoke, and presently got his hat tilted over one ear at a swaggering angle.

Thus the march went on, by south and east, over ground Hugh had already once ridden at a time that now seemed immeasurable years behind him. He had let his life at Shrewsbury and his father's rejection of him slip backward in his memory, till now he found himself living heartily in the present. Existence meant not to worry at what was past, but to sleep in an inn bed or on a cottage floor, whatever quarters fell to the troop, to eat what fare Sir William's officers could procure, and through all, wet or dry, to ride on whither the king led.

Very early in the march they entered the hamlet of the "Golden Ram," where Hugh, as he held it to be his duty, sought out Sir William and laid before him the story of Emry's treachery. The baronet, after some moments of explosive swearing, sent men to apprehend the fellow, and bade Hugh go to guide them. But when they came to the inn they found that at their approach Constant-In-Business Emry had discreetly removed, and there was left only the red-cheeked maid with the black eyes, who joked and flirted with the troopers while she drew them ale. At first she did not recognize Hugh, and, when she did, seemed to take little interest in him; but, as the men tramped out, she ran after him, and catching his arm asked him in a whisper how the dark gentleman fared, and if he had been hurt in the scuffle. The news of Dick's illness made her half sniffle, which touched Hugh so that, having no money to give her, he tried his friend's tactics and kissed her. Whereat the wench, after a feint at boxing his ears, darted back to the door of the common room, where she paused, laughing shrilly. "Ride away, my lad," she called after him. "It takes more than jack-boots and spurs to make a man."

Hugh went back to his horse in some mortification; it might be well enough for Dick Strangwayes to be on good terms with all women, but he had no will to meddle farther in such matters.

Yet, scarcely a week later, he found himself seated at a table in a stuffy chamber, trying by the flicker of a guttering candle to blot out a letter to a girl. For the army was now among the Warwickshire fields, and the sight of home country brought back to Hugh's thoughts Everscombe and the good friend he had left there. So, while Frank jeered from the bed about his sweetheart, and urged him to put out the candle and lie down, Hugh, sitting in his shirt-sleeves, painfully scrawled some ill-spelt lines to Lois Campion. Much had happened that would only make her miserable to know, so he spoke little of his father, only told her he was well and happy, and, as Colonel Gwyeth could offer him no place in his troop, was serving with Sir William Pleydall. He sent his duty to his grandfather, too, and his obedient faithful services to her.

Just there Frank sat up in bed, and, throwing a boot at the candle, contrived to overturn the ink-bottle. Shutting his lips, Hugh mopped up the stuff, then, still without speaking, began to undress. "Now you've lost your temper, Master Roundhead," Frank teased; but Hugh held his tongue till he had blown out the candle and stretched himself in the bed, then said only, "Good night."

He was almost asleep when Frank began shaking him. "Hugh, prithee, good Hugh," he coaxed, "are you truly angry? Pray you, forgive me, Hugh."

"Don't I always?" Hugh answered, half waked. "Go to sleep, Frank."

So they began next morning on as good terms as ever, and before night had barely avoided two of those quarrels which Frank made a daily incident to friendship. But by the following sunrise even Frank was too busied with other matters for such diversion. "The rumor's abroad that we're to bang old Essex soon," he broke out, as he and Hugh rode a little before Sir William's troop along the stony Warwickshire road.

"We've been going to ever since we left Shrewsbury," Hugh replied. "I hope— Perhaps if I did somewhat in battle some one would bestow a commission on me; I'd like not to tax your hospitality longer." Then he repented of the last as an ungracious speech.

But Frank, without heeding, ran on: " I hope I shall get a share in this work, and I will, if I lose my head for it. You'll understand, Hugh, my father let me have no share in the fighting in Worcestershire; they left me at home when they went out to Powick Bridge. On my honor, Hugh, I wish sometimes one or two of my sisters had been boys. 'Tis a fine thing, no doubt, to be sole heir to a great property, but a man would like a little liberty now and again, not to be ever kept close and out of harm like a girl. Now I'll lay you any amount of money my father will strive to keep me from this battle."

Hugh did not look properly sympathetic, so Frank added pettishly: " And he'll rate you no higher than me, so if you are to have a hand in the fighting and get you a commission, you must look to yourself."

None the less Hugh cherished a suspicion that if a battle took place under his very nose he would be aware of it, and in that hope he went trustingly to sleep next night. Sir William's troop was quartered about a small manor house, some three miles to the west of Edgcott, where the king lay. Hugh noted the place merely as one that gave comfortable harborage, for he and Frank were assigned a chamber to themselves, where they went promptly and wearily to bed. But barely asleep, as it seemed, a troublesome dream disturbed Hugh; he thought himself back in the Shrewsbury stables, where the horses had all turned restless and stamped unceasingly in their stalls. Then of a sudden he sat up in bed, broad awake, just in time to see the door kicked open, and Griffith, with his coat in one hand and a candle in the other, stumble in. " Up with you, youngsters! " he cried. " Essex is coming."

" Essex? " Frank whimpered sleepily. " We'll kill him."

" Leave us the candle, Cornet Griffith," Hugh cried, springing up and beginning to fling on his clothes. " How near are the enemy? " His teeth were chattering with the cold of the room and a nervous something that made his fingers shake.

" The Lord knows!" Griffith replied, struggling into his coat. " The word to get under arms has but just come."

" Where is my other stocking? " Frank put in piteously from his side of the bed. " Hugh, have you seen it? "

" Stockings! " the cornet ejaculated. " There's a fellow would wait for lace cuffs ere he went to fight."

Thus warned, Hugh put his bare feet into his riding-boots, and, fastening his jacket without the formality of donning a shirt, ran for the door at Griffith's heels. Frank, after an unheeded entreaty to wait for him, tumbled into his shirt and breeches, and came headlong after out into the corridor.

Below in the great hall, under the dim light of candles, men were jostling and shouting and pulling on coats and buckling sword-belts, as they passed hurriedly out by the black open door. Running blindly after the crowd, Hugh collided by the entrance with Captain Turner, who came in jauntily, albeit he was in his shirt-sleeves. "How near are the enemy, Captain?" Hugh cried, catching him by the arm.

Turner looked down at him with a dry smile. "Not so near, Gwyeth, but you'll have time to wash your face ere they come up."

Even the mocking tone could not recall Hugh to his self-composure, but he ran on out of the house, where he was jostled by troopers and nearly trampled on by horses that were being led up. Getting out of harm's way at last in an angle of the front of the house, he became aware that the stars were few in the sky and on the horizon a light streak showed; it must be nearing dawn. Just then he heard the deadened sound of a horse's being rapidly ridden over turf, and then a strange officer came galloping up to the very door. Running thither, Hugh saw him disappear into an inner room, whence a little later Sir William Pleydall, a bit excited but carefully accoutred, came forth with the announcement that the enemy were near by at Kineton, and the troop was to hold itself in readiness to march to meet them.

There was sufficient time to follow Captain Turner's advice, so Hugh and Frank went back to their chamber and, while their candle paled in the daybreak, dressed methodically. Hugh turned up his boot-tops and fastened his buff coat up to his chin, telling himself he should be too grateful to Sir William for such a stout jacket to envy Frank his cuirass, then, while his companion was tugging a comb through his curly hair, sat down on the window-seat to wait. The manor house looked out across a valley toward the east, where a light rift in the dun clouds showed till presently the sun broke through, and turned the mist in the lowlands to silver. "It will be a fair day," Hugh said, half aloud; "'tis a Sunday, too, is it not?"

"Yes," sneered Frank. "How can so godly a man as Essex fight of a Sabbath?" Then he broke off speech for the serious business of strapping on his sword, which was long enough to threaten to trip him up. Hugh looked on rather enviously, for no one had yet offered him a sword, and, as he felt he should not ask for one, he had to content himself with sticking in his belt a spare pistol Captain Turner had lent him.

When the two young soldiers came downstairs they found the candles were long since out and gray daylight was glimmering through the hall. There tables were spread, about which the officers of the troop, all equipped, sat or stood while they ate; and, as they had good appetites, Hugh, though he was not over-hungry, felt obliged to take bread and meat and try to make a hearty meal. All about him was talk of nothing but the battle, the numbers the Earl of Essex had in his army, the numbers the king could put against him, and the surety of a mighty victory. "Do not you be all so certain," croaked Turner, who had seated himself to make a comfortable meal. The others hooted him down, so he changed the subject by chaffing Frank on his prodigiously long sword. The boy retorted saucily enough to make those about him laugh; indeed, for the most part, all were gay now daylight had come and the work before them was clear to see. There were wagers laid on the length of the battle, promises of high revelry on the spoils of the enemy, and above all calls for wine. When the glasses were filled, Sir William, rising at the head of the table, gave the king's health. Hugh remembered afterward the instant's tense hush that came in the talk and loud laughter, then the sudden uproar of fists smiting on the table, boot-heels stamping on the floor, and through and above all cheers and cheers that made the high-roofed hall reëcho. Then, as the tumult died down, the major, Bludsworth, cried: "Now, then, lads: To the devil with the Parliament and Essex!"

After that was shouting that made the lungs ache, and glasses shattered on the floor, then, as the storm of curses and calls abated, one of the officers struck up a song against the Parliament, and some joined in, some laughed, and others still cried, "Down with the Parliament!"

Just then a messenger, pushing in, spoke a word to Sir William, who gave orders for the troop to prepare itself to march, for the main guard would soon be under way.

"Mayhap we can get sight of something from the hill here," Frank cried. "Come out, Hugh, and see."

Running out into the cold of the nipping morning air they set their faces to the steep pitch of hillside behind the manor house. The turf was stiff with frost, so climbing was easy, and in a short space they were at the summit. Instinctively they turned their first glance to the west where the enemy lay. "But 'tis useless gazing," Frank said, next moment, "for 'twixt here and Kineton rises a piece of high land; they call it Edgehill. Face back to the east, Hugh. Look, look, 'tis the vanguard!"

Winding down the opposite slope they could now distinguish a long line of moving figures, horsemen upon horsemen, with the sunlight glittering ever the stronger on their cuirasses and helmets. Moment after moment the boys delayed there, till the foremost of the riders toiled up a lower ridge of the hill, not an eighth of a mile distant from them. The hum of the moving files reached them; almost they thought to distinguish the devices of the fluttering banners. "But the king's standard will come only with the Life Guards and the foot," Frank explained. "This evening 'twill be waving over all England. God and our right! God and King Charles!"

"Yonder below marches a black cornet," Hugh broke in. "See you, Frank? My father's troop goes under such a banner."

"Say we draw down nearer to them," the other cried, and started to descend the hill.

"Stay, Frank," Hugh called, "it must be midmorning. I think we were best get back to our troop."

"Name of Heaven! I had near forgot," Frank replied, and, facing about, started back to the manor house at full speed.

Hugh followed after, slipping upon the steep hillside, and so they came down behind the stables, where after the tumult of the earlier morning was a surprising quiet. "Some must have set out already," Frank panted, as he headed for the house.

"I'll fetch our horses," Hugh shouted after him, and ran to the stable. Within he saw The Jade and the sorrel had already been led forth, and in their places, all a-lather and with drooping heads, stood the black and bay captured from the Oldesworths. "When were they put here?" Hugh cried to the hostler, and, without waiting for an answer, ran for the house; if the horses were there, Dick Strangwayes must be close at hand.

But when he came to the house he found neither horse nor man, only off to the right the last of Sir William's troop were pacing round a spur of the hill, and on the doorstone stood Frank with his hands tight clinched. "Hugh, they've taken our horses!" he cried shrilly.

"Have you seen anything of Dick?" Hugh asked in his turn.

"And Bludsworth,—the fiend come and fetch him!—he answered me: 'The men that can strike the stoutest blows for the king must have the horses to-day.'" Frank plunged a step or two across the trampled turf, as if he had a mind to run after the troop. "He'd not a dared use me so, if he knew not my father would approve. I told you they'd cheat us of the battle. Never mind, I would not fight for them if I could."

As Frank's voice trailed off into inarticulate mutterings Hugh found opportunity to question: "Has Dick been here? Tell me."

"Ay, 'twas he and another from Butler's troop.

Had spurred night and day. Their horses were spent. And Dick Strangwayes has taken my Jade. Plague on him! He's too heavy for her; he'll break her legs. My Jade—"

"He has gone into the battle and I did not see him," Hugh broke out. "He may be hurt again."

"I care not if he be," Frank cried, "so he bring her back safe. She was the prettiest bit of horseflesh! And I was going to ride her in the battle.—Did I not tell you they'd not let us come? And no doubt they'll beat the rebels and 'tis the last encounter and I shall not be there. And she was my horse, and she loved me; she almost never kicked at me." Frank's shrill voice broke suddenly. "Oh, hang it all!" he cried, and, dropping down on the doorstone with his head on the threshold, began sobbing piteously and choking out more oaths till his voice was lost for weeping.

Hugh forgot his own bitter disappointment at not seeing Dick and having no chance to earn a commission in the battle, in his first alarm for Frank. Then alarm gave place to something akin to disgust at the boy's childishness, and he half started to walk away, but he turned back. After all, Frank was younger than he, and he ought to be patient with the lad, just as Dick Strangwayes had been patient with him. So he stood over Frank and tried to joke him into being quiet.

"But 'twas my horse," the boy sobbed, "and there'll never be another battle, and I had no part in the last."

"Well, it does not befit your cuirass to cry like that," Hugh answered; and then, " Look you here, Frank, 'tis not above six miles to Kineton and we've good legs to carry us. Why should we not have a hand in the fighting even now?"

CHAPTER X

IN THE TRAIL OF THE BATTLE

It was long past the noon hour, as the westward bent of the sun showed, when the two boys panted up the northern pitch of the rough Edgehill. From the manor house to the field they had come at their best pace, running at first even up the hillsides, till sheer lack of breath made them somewhat moderate their speed. A couple of miles out from the house, as they headed aimlessly, with only a vague notion that somewhere to the west the battle would be joined, they came up with a body of foot alongside which they marched clear to the southern verge of the hill. Coming thither, they at last heard the rumor that, while the foot would be massed in the centre for the fight, the Prince with the mounted men, among whom served Sir William's troop, would hold the right wing. Thereupon they forsook the foot soldiers and, heading to the northward, plunged down a steep pitch and across an open bit of ground, where they got entangled in a body of pikemen and were nearly ridden down by some straggling dragoons, and so came breathless up the last hillside. There upon the high ridge, whence for miles they could see the low country spreading away toward Kineton and

CH. X   IN THE TRAIL OF THE BATTLE   153

right beneath them the mustering squadrons, they made a moment's halt.

"Below here to the right our men are," Frank gasped, without breath enough to shout. "If I only had The Jade."

"'Twill be the enemy far over yonder in the plain, where I can just make out black things to move," said Hugh. "There look to be a many of them."

"There'll be fewer ere night," Frank replied.

"Sure, we'll scarce give battle so late in the day?"

"There's time enough 'twixt now and sundown to trounce them roundly," Frank answered cheerfully. "Come, let us go down and seek our people."

They had gone barely a rod along the brow of the hill, when right behind them, deadened till now by the yielding turf, sounded the galloping of a horse. Glancing over his shoulder, Hugh got sight of a rider spurring in their steps with no evident intention of swerving, so he caught Frank by the arm and jerked him to one side, none too soon, for the horse's nose almost grazed the boy's shoulder. "Look how you ride!" Hugh shouted angrily. The horseman never deigned to look at him, but, with his dark face set to the front and the ends of his scarlet sash fluttering, shot by and disappeared down the hillside.

"Curse him!" Frank sputtered, "'twas a coward's trick; 'twas like him."

"Like who?"

"'Tis Philip Bellasis, a son of my Lord Bellasis. I pray his comb be cut some fine morning."

"The Lord Bellasis who is of the king's council?" Hugh asked, as they tramped along the hilltop, with ears alert now for more reckless riders behind them.

"Ay, a scurvy civilian," Frank said, with extra swagger; "we of the army have no love for them nor they for us. Why, his influence came near losing my father his independent command. He would have lumped us in with my Lord Carnavon's horse. Well, we'll show to-day who'll save the kingdom, meddling lawyers like Bellasis or soldiers like ourselves."

Then conversation ceased, for reaching a gully in the hillside they gave all their thoughts to descending it, and slipped and scuffled in the dry bed till Frank had wrenched his ankle and Hugh had a torn coat-sleeve to his credit. The gully ending in a small stream, they followed it down through a copse of bare bushes that snapped against the face, and so came out upon the open plain. Not an eighth of a mile distant, sitting ready with their backpieces gleaming and their carabines slung across their shoulders, they could see the ranks of horsemen. In the open betwixt the boys and the ordered troops messengers were spurring to and fro, and now and again, in small groups or man by man, stray horsemen straggled by. One such they came upon by the brook, as he was patching a broken girth, and Hugh, pausing to lend his aid, asked him what news there was in the field. "Why does not the battle begin at once?" Frank urged, and, when the man answered the troops were but waiting the word to fall on, he caught Hugh's arm and bade him come forward quickly to seek their regiment.

At that the trooper struck in: "Best keep out o' the press, sir. You'll be trampled to pieces there with small good to the king or to yourself. Better bear off to the northward out of harm's way."

"But I am here solely to get in harm's way," Frank protested; and, when Hugh, taking the advice, made for a log bridge to cross the stream, followed grumblingly.

Once over, with the intention of taking their final stand at the extreme right of the line of waiting horsemen, they pressed northward across the uneven plain. They were sliding down the bank to a shallow hollow, when the thud, thud of hoofs warned them to look to the westward and there, over a slight rise in the ground, a belated troop came at a smart trot. Pressing back against the bank Hugh watched the crowded column's approach, the bespattered breasts of the horses, their tossing heads, and above the waving manes the white faces of the riders. As the head of the column came close upon him his eyes rested on its leader, and he saw he was a man of middle height with reddish hair, who rode in his shirt with neither cuirass nor helmet. Then the troop was sweeping past, black, red, and gray horses straining at a trot, and men with steady faces and silent lips, among whom, looking closer, Hugh recognized some he knew.

But he only gazed without speaking till the last horse had swung down the hollow, and Frank, who had been cheering mightily, settled his hat on his head again, with an excited, "A brave troop, was it not, Hugh?"

"It was my troop," Hugh answered. "Did you not note? 'Twas my father led them."

"Oh, ay, to be sure," replied Frank, making for the opposite side of the hollow. "I scarce remembered him, and, to my thinking, he has used you so knavishly that he does not merit to dwell in any gentleman's remembrance, and — Hark, there!"

Both halted a moment as from far off on the left came the dull boom, boom of cannon. From far to the front an answering crash sounded. "They're falling to it," Frank cried. "Briskly, Hugh!"

One last spurt that sent the blood beating to the temples and turned the breath hot in the throat, and they were stumbling up the little hillock for which they had headed. Still, before and on the left, the cannon were pounding, and there came, too, in long, undistinguishable shouts, the noise of men cheering. The withered grass of the hillside wavered before Hugh's eyes with the very weariness of running, yet he found strength in him to pull off his hat and breath to pant out: "For a king!"

Then, coming over the brow of the hill, he had sight of the rough plain stretching off to the gray west, and across it saw the long ranks of horsemen sweeping forward. A gleam of cuirasses and helmets, a glimpse of plunging horses and waving swords, a flutter of banners; they had charged onward, and only the echo of their shouts still lingered and was lost in the throb of cannon. Now first Hugh realized his throat was near cracked with cheering and his arm ached with waving his hat; so he paused breathless, with his eyes still fastened on the brown dust-cloud toward the west. There came a touch on his arm, and putting out his hand he grasped Frank's wrist. Young Pleydall was gasping for breath with a choke like a half sob. "If we had only been with them!" he broke out.

"My father is there," Hugh said, half aloud. He did not tell Frank what he was thinking: that, after all, he would rather have a father who, even if he did despise and reject his son, was striking good blows over yonder, than an indulgent parent like Master Nathaniel Oldesworth, who could bear to sit idle at home.

"What if your father is there?" Frank panted in retort. "It does not better matters for us. They're hard at it. Listen to the muskets yonder. Come, let us go thither."

Hugh gave one glance to the west, where even the dust-cloud had faded in the distance, and to the south, where a slight swelling of the plain hid the sight of conflict; it was from there the tantalizing noise of firing came. "'Tis not in human endurance to stay here and not know how the day is going," he burst out, and led the way down into the plain. They struck toward the brook they had crossed, and followed its course northwestward, almost in the track the Royalist horse had taken.

"They've all passed out of sight," Frank said as he pressed forward, half on the run. "They must have driven the rebels clean into Kineton."

"Hark to the southward!" Hugh answered.

"They will only be shooting down stragglers," Frank replied confidently. "The day's ours. No living thing could stand up against such a charge. Was it not brave? I tell you, Hugh, war is the grandest—"

There the words died away on Frank's lips, as a few paces before them near the brookside he caught sight of a dark, motionless thing. "'Tis not—" he faltered, and made a movement as if he had half a mind to fetch a circuit about the place.

"Come along," Hugh said firmly, though he felt the heart contract within him. "If he be alive, we must help him." Walking forward deliberately, he halted a step from the object,—a common trooper, he now saw, and by his colors one of the king's men. He lay on his back with his hands clinched above his head, and the blood bubbling out through a bullet wound in his throat, but he still breathed in short, rattling gasps. Perceiving that, Hugh ran to the margin of the brook, and, dipping his hat full of water, splashed it over the man's face; he remembered afterward what a dull, dogged face it was under the pain that was distorting the brows and lips. He raised the man's head up against his arm. "Fetch more water, Frank," he bade; then, as the boy turned, it seemed something caught and clicked in the trooper's throat, and his head slipped down from Hugh's arm. Hugh suffered him to sink to the ground, and was kneeling beside him, half dazed with the awesomeness of what had happened, when

Frank came stumbling back. "What!" the younger lad cried; "is he—"

"He is gone," Hugh answered simply. He got up, and walking to the brook lay down on the brink and drank; the chill of the soggy turf beneath him and the cold water he gulped down seemed to wash away something of the horror he had just seen. He rose fairly steadied. "Shall we go forward, Frank?" he asked. "There'll be more such to see."

"Yes, let us," Frank said, rather subdued, and so, passing the body of the trooper, they went on down the brook.

The farther they advanced, the more ill sights there were to see: horses that lay dead or sprawled with disabling wounds yet struggled to rise, men with gashed bodies or blackened faces, who were beyond aid, and others, bleeding with wounds, who had crawled to their feet and were heading for the rear. One horse, a roan, Frank persuaded Hugh, for The Jade's sake, to shoot with his pistol; but after that Hugh, sparing his scant supply of ammunition, refused to carry on such work. But they tried to aid the wounded men, who came ever more frequently, and with them one or two of another sort, unhurt but riding too hastily to pause to speak. "The cowardly knaves!" Frank cried. "If I find one of our troop turning tail so, hang me if I do not recommend him for a flogging."

But just then there came a white-faced horseman, who, reining up at their call, gladly gave them what tidings he could, which were vague enough, only the king's men had swept the rebel

horse from off the earth, and chased the rest of
the army away, and there had been great fighting,
and a scurvy Roundhead bullet had broke his
leg. Would one of the young gentlemen reach
him a drink of water? He could not dismount.
Hugh filled the man's steel cap at the brook, and
then he rode slowly away.

Farther on, where the conflict had been hotter,
they passed more bodies, and just the other side
of the brook, which they leaped at a narrow turn,
came upon one lying face down whose long hair
gave him to be a gentleman. Hugh had bent to
see if by any chance he still lived, when Frank
thrust by him. "Do you not know that head-
piece with a nick in it?" he cried. "'Tis Ned
Griffith."

At that they had him over on his back and
found he was breathing, in spite of a great gash
in his shoulder that had sheered through the
cuirass. Tearing off his armor, they splashed
water over him till the young fellow revived
enough to blink his eyes open, groan, and shut
them again. "Live?" said Frank, pouring another
capful of water over him. "Do you think a man
will die who can fetch a groan like that?"

Griffith's eyes slowly opened again. "You
youngsters?" he asked feebly. "Was it the
whole troop rode over me?"

Hugh laid open his coat, and, with a certain
grim thankfulness that what he had unwillingly
seen now enabled him without physical shrinking
to help a friend, bandaged his hurt. "We must
carry him to the rear," he finally ordered Frank.
"You take his legs, and I'll manage his head."

They lifted up Ned Griffith, who hung limp and heavy in their hands, and set their faces toward the dark hill whence the king's army had charged forth. The walk out into the field had gone briskly enough, but there seemed no end to the return journey. Again and again they had to lay the injured man down while they recovered breath; but though wounded stragglers passed them, they saw none who could aid them, so of necessity they lifted up their burden once more and struggled on. Sometimes Frank panted out a grumbling complaint, but Hugh made no reply, for his eyes were on the wounded man's white face and parted lips, and he found himself wondering how his father was faring in the battle, and what might have befallen Dick Strangwayes.

Of a sudden Frank, letting Griffith's boots come to the ground abruptly, began shouting with all his strength to a brace of loiterers. "Men of our troop," he explained to Hugh, "and not much wounded, Heaven be thanked for't! They can convey Ned to a surgeon, if such a one is in the field, and we'll back to see more."

Relinquishing their charge on such terms, they set their faces again to the field of battle. It was now drawing toward sundown, and the fire to the south had slackened. "Mark my words, the war is ended," Frank lamented; "and we have had no part in it, only to tramp about and look on those others have killed."

Hugh must acknowledge to himself it had been a grim afternoon's work, so with some hope of brisker adventures he followed willingly, as his companion headed southerly toward the clearer line of a road. "Maybe we'll find our troop if we walk toward Kineton," Frank suggested. "And we could ride back with them."

"Yes, they should have taken some horses from the rebels by this," Hugh replied, with a nod toward a corpse with an orange sash that lay on the edge of the roadway. He stubbornly told himself it was only another monument to the Royalist fighting quality, and tried to believe he had nearly deadened sympathy in him and calloused his senses to the horror of what he must endure if he would follow this life he had chosen.

They faced westward and tramped along the road, but what with ruts and mire it proved heavier walking than the fields. "Faith, I'm weary of this," Frank grumbled. "How much farther to Kineton?"

"Let's bear off on the other side," suggested Hugh, peering through the gathering twilight. "Yonder's a bit of a hollow and it may be easier going."

They crossed a piece of open level, and, holding this the quickest way, jumped down the slight pitch at its farther edge. As they recovered footing, they perceived close before them in the lee of the bank two bodies lying motionless, one of which seemed that of an officer by its better clothes and of a rebel by its orange sash. It was the first officer of Essex's army they had yet noted among the dead, and, with a sudden fear that it might be one of his own kindred, Hugh bent over the corpse. Finding, to his relief, that the face was strange to him, he was turning away, when his eyes chanced to rest upon the other body, that of a hulking common foot soldier. As he gazed he thought to see a slight tremor pass over it, so, stepping to the man as he lay on his face, he shook him by the shoulder.

At the touch the fellow suddenly scrambled to his knees. "Don't kill me, master," he whined. "Give me quarter."

Hugh had started back a step or two and pulled out his pistol; the man was not even scratched, he perceived, but had feigned dead. Then he noted a basket-hilted sword with a leathern baldric that had been concealed beneath him as he lay, and he noted, too, that not only did the dead officer wear no sword, but his pockets had been turned inside out. "So that's your trade, is it?" Hugh cried. "Robbing the dead of your own party, eh?"

"I'll never do so no more," whimpered the fellow. "Don't 'ee shoot."

The craven tone of the creature harked back to something in Hugh's memory; he leaned a little forward and studied the man's bearded, low-browed face, then drew back with his pistol cocked. "I remember you," he said. "Are you ready to pay back the two shillings and sixpence you took from me on the Nottinghamshire crossroad?"

"Is this the padder?" Frank struck in. "Put a bullet through him, Hugh."

"Don't 'ee shoot me, master," the other begged. "I did not kill 'ee then, and I might ha'."

"I am not going to shoot you," Hugh replied, "but you can give me over that sword to pay for what you owe me. And remember, this pistol I hold now is in good order," he added, for he half suspected the fellow was plucking up courage as he discovered it was only two lads, not a whole troop, had come upon him. So he stood back warily out of the plunderer's reach, while Frank, who was viewing the whole proceeding happily like a holiday sport, took up the booty and passed it over to him. Hugh gathered the baldric about the sword in his left hand, a little hurriedly, for it was beginning to dawn on him that he and Frank had strayed pretty far, and where one live rebel was there might be others. Just then, over in the plain, he got sight of a straggling horseman or two, so he turned upon Frank with a quick order: "Clamber up the slope there and make for the road briskly."

He heard behind him the boy's quick retreating step, but his eyes were still fixed on the scowling rebel, whom he thought well to cover with his pistol. "Sit where you are," he commanded the man, "and offer to play me no slippery tricks if you value your skin." Thus speaking, he backed toward the bank, which he ascended slantingly, so as to keep an eye on the fellow. But, chancing to look beyond him, he saw one of the horsemen was already heading in his direction, so he turned and fair ran for the roadway, where Frank was halting for him. "Run," he called to the boy; "'tis a hornets' nest here."

Without staying for farther questions, Frank took to his heels down the road toward Kineton, and Hugh, after one glance to the right where he saw no stragglers of his own party, ran after him.

At each stride he gained on him, for Frank's boots and cuirass encumbered the youngster; capture was possible, it flashed through Hugh's head, and with it came the reflection that it would be discreditable to be taken in the act of plundering a private of foot, for others might not see the justice of the case as clearly as he had seen it. Then he found wit to think only of the hoof-beats that were now sounding on the roadway behind him, louder and louder, and, looking at Frank stumbling on before him, he thought what an ill return it would be for all Sir William's kindness to let harm come to the boy. So he halted short and faced back; close behind him was one trooper with a yellow sash and somewhat in his rear came three others. How long the horse's head looked, Hugh reflected dazedly, and would the man slash down at him with his sword and make such a gash as he had seen upon Ned Griffith? Then there was no space for reflection or remembrance, only the horse's head grazed by him, he saw the man lean forward in his saddle, and, thrusting up his pistol with the muzzle aimed under the man's upraised arm, he fired. The sword grazed down weakly across his shoulder, the edge slipping harmlessly over the stout buff; then the sword fell to the roadway, the horse clattered forward a pace or two, and the rider reeled headlong from the saddle. The horse went galloping away down the road with the stirrups beating against his flanks.

A shout from behind brought Hugh to his senses. He ran forward, got a fleeting sight of the rebel trooper, who lay outstretched on his back in the roadway with a grayish shade gathering on his face, then came up with Frank and caught him by the arm. "Off the road, quick!" he panted. "They'll ride us down."

They went headlong over the low embankment and struggled blindly forward into the field. Hugh had jammed his pistol into his belt, wondering how many seconds it would take him to draw his sword clear for a final stand, when Frank reeled up against him, crying: "My ankle! I've wrenched it again." With that he pitched down at Hugh's feet, and Hugh, clapping his hand to the hilt of the sword, stood over him and faced about. Then he saw the rebel horsemen had drawn rein in the roadway and were watching them but not following, behind him he heard horses coming, and Frank, suddenly scrambling to his feet, began shouting, "King's men! Hurrah!"

Hugh turned about in time to see a little squad of eight or ten horsemen with scarlet scarfs come riding out of the twilight and pull up alongside them. There was something familiar in the broad shoulders of the leader and the gruff voice in which he began: "'Tis happy for you, gentlemen, that we—"

"Corporal Ridydale, have you forgot me?" Hugh interrupted breathlessly, going up to the man's stirrup.

"Forgot you, sir?" Ridydale made answer, "Lord, no, sir. Jump up behind me. 'Tis not a healthy place hereabouts for men of our color. — Here, Rodes, take t'other young gentleman up behind you."

After delaying long enough to slip his new

baldric over his shoulder, Hugh scrambled up behind Ridydale, and the little squad headed across the field toward Edgehill. How had the battle gone, Hugh asked, as soon as he had recovered breath; and Ridydale told him the Prince and Colonel Gwyeth had hunted the rebels clear beyond Kineton. "The knaves banged our troop some deal, but we had brave plundering in the town," the corporal ended. "'How has the day gone in the rest of the field?' I know not; we have done our part."

"Colonel Gwyeth had no hurt?" Hugh broke in.

"No thanks to him that he hasn't, the madman!" Ridydale answered. "He would fight in his shirt, for he swore these fellows were too paltry for a gentleman to guard against. So he laid off his armor ere he rode into the fight. Now that, sir, is the temper the gentlemen of your house have ever been of, and 'tis the only fitting temper."

It looked like the beginning of their usual disagreement, so Hugh kept silent, the more willingly since he found himself tired so that even talking required exertion. He leaned rather heavily against Ridydale, and watched the field, that looked gray in the deepening twilight, slip by them, and, when he shut his eyes, still saw the field with the trampled bodies of men and writhing chargers. Then, of a sudden, their horse pulled up. "I take it we'll rendezvous here," he heard the corporal say. "Perchance you'll bide with us till the colonel comes, sir?"

"No," Hugh said hurriedly, slipping down from the horse. "Thank you, Ridydale. We'd have been in a bad way but for you."

Then he stumbled away with Frank across the hummocky plain, which darkness made all the more treacherous, and, scrambling up the hill to the broad summit, toiled about among the scattered troops that were straggling back. "I am clean spent,' his companion said sorrowfully. "I would not be a foot soldier for all the gold in the kingdom. Where think you my father is, Hugh?"

"We'll try to find him," Hugh answered, with what cheerfulness he could summon, and turned aside to ask a friendly-looking soldier if he knew where Sir William Pleydall's troop was stationed. The man did not know, and, indeed, in the confusion and darkness no one seemed to know anything; so the two boys could only tramp up and down, Frank expostulating crossly and Hugh too utterly weary to respond, till at last they got sight of a figure that looked familiar in the dusk. Running thither they found it was Major Bludsworth, whereupon Frank nearly hugged him. "I never was so glad to see you before, sir," he cried. "Where is my father, and when are we going to have anything to eat?"

Bludsworth took Frank by the arm, and half carried him a rod or so to a small fire beneath a bank about which Sir William and a little knot of his officers were standing. "Here's a runaway in quest of you, Sir William," he announced brusquely.

"Francis, you here?" Sir William asked, with some displeasure.

"Prithee, do not be angry, sir," Frank protested, "I've had a gallant day of it. And I have not had the least hurt. And Hugh here killed a man, sir. And has Dick Strangwayes brought back my Jade?"

"The beast is unscathed," answered Sir William, drawing Frank to him with a hand on his shoulder. "And another time you may as well ride in on her back at the start and done with."

"Master Strangwayes has come out safe, then?" Hugh's eagerness made him strike in.

"No hurt at all, his usual fortune," Sir William replied, before he turned away to one of those beside him.

Hugh had to check his questions on his tongue's end, and wait and look about in the hope each instant that Dick might come tramping to the fire. But the minutes ran on, Frank had settled himself by the blaze, and Sir William had no time to heed a boy's concerns, so Hugh must finally take courage and, going to Bludsworth, ask of Dick's whereabouts. "Young Strangwayes?" replied the major. "Why, he has gone back to the house we quartered at; some one had to convey Cornet Griffith thither."

"Well, he's left the road behind him," Hugh answered stoutly, and, turning from the fire, faced into the black of the night.

At first, what with the foot and horse soldiers and camp followers to be met, the gleam of the bivouac fires on either hand, and the tumult of the army all about him, it was brisk enough journeying. But, as he passed out from the circle of the encampment and the bustle around him subsided, he found his riding-boots felt heavy and the going was far slower than it had been that morning. It was dark overhead, so he stumbled, and once his new sword tripped him. He put his hand to the hilt so as to strike up the blade, and then as he trudged he fell to wondering what manner of man the sword had belonged to, and he thought on the trooper with the wound in his throat, and the many faces of dead men. When a branch snapped in a copse to his left he halted short with his heart thumping, then told himself he was a fool and tried to whistle as he walked. But there came on him a desire to look back over his shoulder, and the echo of his whistle made his blood thrill unpleasantly. There was a thicket he must pass through, he remembered, before he reached the manor house; he dreaded it long, and, when he came to it, clinched his hands tight and walked slowly, while the gray face of the trooper he had himself slain dazzled up and down before his eyes. Half through the thicket he broke into a run, and, with not even will enough left in his tired body to restrain himself, plunged heavily across the open to the door of the hall, where there was light. He stumbled against the door, which resisted, and, in a panic he could not comprehend, he shook it.

"Gently, gently," came a voice that calmed him. The door swung open, and in the candlelight that shone within he saw Dick Strangwayes, with his cuirass and helmet off, his coat hanging unfastened, and the same old half-laughing look in his eyes, while his lips kept sober.

Hugh pitched in headlong and blindly griped his friend in his arms. "Dick, Dick," he burst out, "I have found you. And, Dick, I — I killed a man to-day."

"Is that all?" Strangwayes drawled with one arm about him. "Why, I killed three."

CHAPTER XI

COMRADES IN ARMS

THERE were no dreams for Hugh after he had stretched himself out on a bench in the hall as Strangwayes bade him. He was too exhausted in body and spirit to question or speak; he only knew he was glad he had found his friend once more, and the cushion beneath his head felt soft, so he went dead asleep, and lost at last the remembrance of the sights of the day's carnage. He had no dreams and he was loath even to have a waking; some one shook him again and yet again, but he only murmured drowsily, with a voice that seemed far off to him, till he was pulled up sitting. He screwed his knuckles into his eyes, turning his face from the candle-light, and he heard Strangwayes laugh: " Look you here, Captain Turner. This gentleman must have a clear conscience by the way he sleeps."

The thought that Turner's sharp eyes were on him made Hugh face about and sit blinking at the candles. The hall where they had that morning eaten was quite bare now and dark, except for the two flickering candles and the uncertain firelight. In front of the chimney-piece Turner, all equipped to ride forth, was making a lunch of a biscuit and a glass of wine he held in his hands, and the only other occupant of the apartment was Dick Strangwayes, who, wrapped to the chin in his cloak, stood by the bench. "Awake, eh?" he smiled down at Hugh. "Good morrow, then."

"What's the time?" Hugh asked, peering across the hall at the windows, which were squares of blackness.

"Past two and nipping cold. Are you fit to ride back to the field with us?"

For answer Hugh staggered to his feet, marvelling at the stiffness in his legs, and tried to hold himself erect. "Here, on with this," said Strangwayes, throwing a cloak about him. "I judged 'twas yours, and if 'tis not, the man who left his goods so careless deserves to lose them. And slip this sash over your sword-belt. It was Ned Griffith's, but he'll not need — "

"He's not dead?" Hugh broke out.

"No, no; but he'll be of little more use than a dead man for the next four months. Slash in the breast and his leg broke by some of our horse as he lay. You'll need to look you out a new cornet, Captain Turner."

"They dropped my lieutenant, too, down by Kineton," said Turner, putting by his glass. "Gwyeth's troop and mine, there on the flank, we suffered for it. Do you judge those knaves will have the horses saddled ere daybreak?"

"Is there more fighting to come?" Hugh questioned sleepily, as he tried to tie the scarlet sash across his chest.

"Enough to flesh that maiden sword of yours," Turner paused at the door to reply. "By the bye, Master Strangwayes, is it true that Captain

Peyton was slain in the charge? He owes me five sovereign on my wager that neither side could call the day theirs, and if he has got himself killed!" Turner shrugged his shoulders and passed out.

"What has brought him hither?" Hugh yawned.

"Poor old lad! Eat a bit and try to wake up," urged Strangwayes. "What has brought Michael Turner? Why, his love for that poor little troop he let get so wofully peppered in the fight. He has been ravaging the country for a horse-load of bread with which to fill their stomachs, ere the battle he is sure will come this day. And now, question for question, what brings you here, so far from Colonel Gwyeth?"

Hugh put down on the table the piece of bread he had been eating, and looked across at Strangwayes, then blurted out plainly the whole story. He was glad to find he could tell it almost without passion now, with not a censuring word for Colonel Gwyeth, and even with an effort to make a jest of some of the happenings. He heard Strangwayes mutter something like an oath when he described his first meeting with the colonel, but there was not another sound till he told of the affair with Hardwyn; then Strangwayes drew in his breath between his teeth and turned toward the fire. Hugh concluded hurriedly and half frightened, and waited for an answer; then broke out, "Dick, sure you're not going to despise me for it as he does?"

Strangwayes came to him and put both hands on his shoulders. "No, Hugh," he said, "I need all the scorn that's at my command for that precious father of yours."

The jar of the opening door made them stand apart and face to the end of the hall, as Turner looked in to say, "Do you ride with me, gentlemen?"

Outside, a chilly wind that stung the face was abroad, and the sky was black with clouds. Hugh paused on the threshold to blink the candlelight out of his eyes, then, peering into the dark, made out the dim figures of Turner, already in the saddle, and of two of his mounted troopers who held led horses, and, last of all, let his gaze rest on a half-wakened groom who came up with two fully equipped chargers. At sight of them Hugh jumped down from the doorstone, and, after one closer glance, cried, "Why, Dick, will you suffer me ride the bay?"

"The bay?" Strangwayes answered from the black horse's back. "Your bay, you young fool! Why in the name of reason did you not keep the beast with you, since you captured him?"

Hugh settled himself in the saddle and turned the horse's head in his companion's tracks, too full of joy to heed anything, save that the bay that had known him in the Everscombe stables, that Peregrine Oldesworth would not suffer him even to stroke, was now his, all his. He put out one hand to stroke the warm neck, and whistled softly to see the slender ears erected.

"Hold up, man! You're riding me down," came Strangwayes' voice beside him, and he found he had pushed forward till they were crowding knee to knee.

"Do you honestly mean me to keep this fellow?" Hugh asked.

"If you can," Strangwayes replied; "I'm thinking you'll keep him on three legs if you do not spare talk and look to him over this rough ground."

Hugh laughed happily, then drew the reins tauter in his hands, and strained his eyes into the dark ahead lest some pitfall open to swallow up the bay horse from under him. The road was so short, as he traversed it now, that he was sorry when the fires on Edgehill twinkled in the distance, and, picking their way cautiously, they came to the rendezvous of Turner's troop. "I am keeping by the captain, do you see?" Strangwayes whispered Hugh as they dismounted. "He has lost his lieutenant, and Sir William has promised to set me in the first vacancy."

Of the rest of the night Hugh only remembered that his knees were very warm with the fire by which he sat, and his back was cold in spite of his cloak. The flames crackled bravely, and Strangwayes talked nonsense, to which Captain Turner listened in deep and sober approbation. But Hugh, crowded close up to Strangwayes, said nothing, just gazed at the fire and closed his eyes once in a while, till at last he went ignominiously asleep with his head on his friend's shoulder.

Waking with neck stiff and arm cramped, he found to his delight the east all pale in the dawn, so, slipping the bridle of the bay horse over his arm, he went strolling across the encampment till he could find out Frank and show him his new mount. But Frank, now confident in the possession of The Jade, discovered many flaws in the bay, which he set forth in horseman-like phrases till Hugh went sauntering back again to Strangwayes. At Turner's fire he found a newcomer, a brown-haired young officer, who had once taken him for a horse-boy, whom Strangwayes now made known to him under the name of George Allestree, guidon in Captain Butler's dragoons, and serving as a volunteer at Edgehill. Discreetly ignoring their former meeting, Allestree was effusively grateful to Hugh for the use of the bay, which Strangwayes had lent him to ride thither, and altogether proved so pleasant spoken a fellow that Hugh ended by putting out of mind the memory of his previous conduct.

With Allestree and Strangwayes Hugh passed the long day, now talking a bit by the ashes of last night's fire, then rising to stretch his legs and look to his horse, then back to the fire again, where he ate such rations as were dealt to him and felt rather hungry afterward. It was a day of uncertainty and idleness beneath which lay a tense expectancy; any moment a blow might be struck for the king, yet the moments passed and nothing was done. About noon Turner stalked off to confer with Sir William, but he came back whistling and non-committal; indeed, there was nothing but the old story to tell: his Majesty's army rested on Edgehill and my Lord Essex's army was drawn up in the plain below, and each looked at the other, but neither moved to strike.

They were not up in action till mid-afternoon of the next day, when there came word the rebels were retreating, and, right on the heels of that, a

definite order for the horse to form in the plain.
Once more Hugh scrambled down the slope of
Edgehill, but this time his feet were braced in the
stirrups, his sword smote against his horse's flank,
and all about him, in loud talk of the victory they
were soon to gain, other mounted men were descending. Once more he had sight of ranks of
horsemen marshalling for a charge, but now he was
himself in the thick of it, and, when the word was
passed along, waved his sword with the rest, then
galloped forward amidst his comrades. Before him
the plain swept into the western sky, where the
clouds were shiny with the sun they hid, the wind
came sharp in his face, and around him men shouted
and horses plunged till his own beast, too, catching the joy of movement, reared up. This was
war, Hugh thought, and only for a second recalled
it was the same bloody field over which he had
tramped not eight and forty hours ago. Then
across the plain he saw a cluster of roofs, and,
as they spurred faster, made out the windows of
the cottages, and men moving in the street. At
that the shouting in the ranks about him became
a yell of onset, and he, too, rising up in his stirrups,
screamed, " For a king, a king!"

Of what followed nothing was quite clear.
There were houses, a woman that ran shrieking
in front of his horse, and a Roundhead soldier he
saw bleeding upon a doorstone. He heard shots
to the front, saw some of his side press past him
in flight, and after that he was mixed in a confusion of horses and men of both parties. He
struck wildly in with his sword, whereat a Royalist
dragoon, swinging round in his saddle, cursed him

volubly in German and in English as not old enough to be trusted with cutting tools, and crowding past the man he left him still cursing. Then he was wedged into a lane, where was a baggage-wagon with a teamster on it who tried to lash forward his four horses. One Cavalier trooper slashed up at the fellow where he sat, while another was cutting the traces. Up at the far end of the lane was a shouting, "The rebels are coming!" Hugh urged the bay forward to the heads of the leaders, and, bending from the saddle, cut the traces with his sword. Then a ruck of the Royalist troops was about him, and, as men caught at the freed horses, he judged it proper to seize one of them by the bit and hold to him, while the crowd forced him back down the lane, past the wagon and the teamster dead beneath its wheels. From the rear came shots, but there was no facing about in such a throng, so with the rest Hugh swept back at a gallop through Kineton out into the open country.

The pace slackening now, he slipped his sword back into the sheath, and, taking time to look about him, saw some of those who rode near had been cut, but he himself and his two horses were without a scratch. Turning in the saddle to gaze back, he saw other bands of horse come straggling behind them. "Is the fight all over?" he asked a trooper who trotted beside him.

"Over?" swore the fellow. "What more d'ye want?" Then he looked pretty sharply at Hugh, and ended by offering to lead the wagon-horse for him, an offer the boy refused. Next the trooper, assuring Hugh he might have no end of difficulties in maintaining his right in the capture, proposed to give him ten shillings for the beast. What more he would say Hugh never found out, for, as they rode at a slackened pace a little on the flank, a horseman from the rear came charging into them, stared, and cried Hugh's name. It was Bob Saxon of Gwyeth's troop, who, scenting a matter of horse-dealing, voluntarily came in, and, falling upon the other man, bepraised the captured horse till he clean talked the fellow out of the field.

"Ten shillings?" Saxon repeated contemptuously to Hugh, "Lord forgive the knave! The beast is worth fifty. Come along with me, sir, and I'll find you a market."

They made a great circuit off to the north of the field and about dusk fetched up in a hamlet to the rear of the army, whither Royalist troops were now marching from Edgehill to seek quarters. Saxon gathered some half score of dragoons and a petty officer or two in the street before the village inn, where, with loud swearing and shouting, he showed off to them the captured horse. There followed much chaffering and wrangling, with Saxon's voice loudest, which ended in the paying of the money and the delivering over of the beast. "Fifty shillings, as I promised you, sir," Saxon announced, as he told them into Hugh's hand, with a suggestive look that made Hugh pass him back five for himself.

"You're a good piece of a gentleman, sir," the trooper said candidly, as they rode out from the hamlet. "Be you never going to serve under Colonel Gwyeth?"

Hugh winced and answered "No," then, bidding Saxon good-bye, headed for the manor house, which he was not able to discover till mid-evening. It was a relief to find himself safe among his comrades, for he was so conscious of the forty-five shillings in his pocket that he felt sure every prowler and hanger-on of the camp must have marked them for plunder.

From the field of Edgehill the royal army marched to Banbury, which yielded to them unresistingly. To Hugh this was far pleasanter marching than the passage through Warwickshire, for not only did he now wear a sword and a red sash that marked him of the king's men, but he had his own horse, Bayard, as he had named him for his bay color. The animal contented him very well, though Frank and The Jade distanced him whenever they raced a piece. "Bayard is no ambler; he was built for serious work in the field," Hugh replied loftily to Frank's jeers, and betook himself to Dick Strangwayes, whose mere presence was comforting. He trailed along at Dick's side, ate with him, and shared his bed, and, in return, would gladly have cleaned Dick's boots and groomed his horse, the horse that had once belonged to Captain Oldesworth. He knew better, however, than to offer such service, so he satisfied himself with taking their two horses to stable, and standing over the groom who cared for them to see the task was done without shirking.

On the night they lay at Banbury he came in from such labor and in their chamber found Strangwayes unbuckling his cuirass, and singing, which was with him a sign of either very good or very bad fortune. "What's to do, Dick?" Hugh asked, lighting a candle at the fireplace.

"What do you say to a lieutenancy to the front of my name again, and over seasoned fighting men this time, not Jacks such as I misgoverned in the Scots war?"

"Sir William has given you the lieutenancy under Turner?"

"Ay, and on the heel of that comes better: Turner's troop rides for service into Northamptonshire to-morrow."

"That's well," Hugh answered rather sorrowfully, as he put the candle on the table. "Luck go with you."

"Come along and bring it to us. Ay, you're to go. I told my uncle we could use you as a volunteer. You see, the troop is short one officer since Griffith left."

"Yes?" Hugh urged, with curiosity.

"I'm promising you nothing, remember," Strangwayes continued soberly. "But there's that vacant cornetcy, and you're a lad of a steady courage,— I pray you, spare blushing,— and of a discreeter head than most of your years. Now, first, you're to ride with us and do all you can to satisfy Captain Turner."

"Dick, I cannot satisfy him," Hugh gasped, almost bewildered by the coolness and breadth of Strangwayes' plan. "Captain Turner never does aught but mock me; I'm near as unhappy with him as with my father." He could have bit his tongue for the ease with which it let slip such a piece of the truth, but Strangwayes only gave him one involuntary look, then changed the subject hastily to the matter of the raid into Northamptonshire.

Next day, when his Majesty and his men rode south for Oxford, Captain Turner, Lieutenant Strangwayes, and Volunteer Gwyeth, with some forty troopers, got to saddle and went cantering eastward, to their own pleasure and the discomfort of more than one Puritan of Northamptonshire. It was partisan warfare, but Turner waged it honorably; and Hugh, after he once got used to riding with his hand on his hilt through villages of hostile, scowling people, had no quarrel with the life.

They made their first dash for a country-house where arms and powder were stored; there was slight resistance, a shot or two without damage, a door battered in, and then Hugh was detailed with five men to ransack a wing of the house where were the kitchen and offices. As they found nothing they only wearied themselves with the thorough search Hugh insisted on, and got laughed at for their pains by a fat kitchen wench. But Strangwayes and his squad captured six muskets and a keg of powder, though he came away grumbling. "No more work of that sort for me," he confided to Hugh. "You, you rogue, were safe in the buttery, while I was rummaging the parlor, and the gentlewomen stood off with their skirts gathered round them and glowered on me as if I were a cutpurse. I'm thinking the time will never come that women understand the laws of war."

Afterward they struck into a small town where

more powder was said to be hid. Across the narrow part of the main street the people had built a barricade of carts and household stuff, so Turner, after reconnoitring, determined on a charge. "You had best bear the colors, Gwyeth," he said, as the troop fell into order outside the village. "Strangwayes must ride at the rear, and, in any case, his two arms are of more profit to us than yours."

Hugh forgave the sneer as the cornet of the troop was put into his hands. Like all Sir William's cornets, it was a red flag with a golden ball upon it, the prettiest colors in the world, Hugh considered, except the black flag with the cross of gold that Colonel Gwyeth's troop marched under. Settling the staff firmly against his thigh, he glanced up to see the folds of the flag droop in the still air, then took his place by Turner at the front of the troop, and, a moment later, charged in behind him. The stones clicked beneath the horses' feet, the cottages sped by, the barricade, whence came the hateful spitting of muskets, was right before them. Hugh swerved for the left end, where the structure was lowest, and Bayard, gathering himself up, cleared it at a leap. Behind the barricade were men of all coats, some loading and steadily firing, but more already scrambling down to flee. One, crying out at sight of Hugh, broke away the faster; another levelled a pistol at him, but before he could fire Bayard's hoofs had struck him into the kennel. Then the whole barricade seemed to go down as the Cavaliers, some still in the saddle, others dismounted to scramble the better, came pouring over.

Thus the king's men possessed themselves of the town and took the powder, which for some days to come supplied them. But there was a price to pay, for in the encounter they had two men wounded, one of whom died that night, and on the morrow before they marched was buried in an orchard. Hugh never forgot the look of the leafless trees, the frosty ground, and the silent men, who stood drawn up, with their breastpieces strapped in place, all ready to mount. Each tenth man sat his horse with the bridles of his comrades' steeds in his hand, and there, at a little distance from the horses, some of the townspeople, loitering with curious, unsympathetic faces, peered and pointed at those about the grave. They buried the dead trooper without his armor, but with his cloak wrapped round him, and Strangwayes, standing with his helmet under one arm, read the burial service. For the life of him Hugh could not help thinking of that sermon Dick had once preached to Emry and his friends, and there came on him an unbecoming desire to laugh, which mixed with a choke in his throat so his lips moved till he was well assured Captain Turner must think him no better than a child.

The morning sunlight was strong when they rode away from the orchard, and half a mile out the troopers were swearing good-humoredly at each other, and Strangwayes was jesting at the bravery of the town watch, a single countryman whom he had hauled out, roaring for mercy, from beneath an empty cart. Hugh laughed at the tale, and laid it to heart that in war no man can hold regrets long, for his turn may come next, and what little life may be left him is not given to be needlessly saddened.

So he designedly carried a light heart under his buff jacket, and seized what enjoyment he could from the small matters of everyday work. He was happy when they had broiled bacon or a chicken for supper, which was not often, and thankful for any makeshift of a bed; he took pleasure in cantering Bayard at the head of the troop, and watching the red and gold cornet flutter and flap above him; and he liked the fierce, hard knocks of the skirmishes they had, in little villages and at lonely country-houses, here and there through the shire. But when food failed and there was no bed but the ground, when he was weary and sore with much riding, even on that one wretched day when a troop of Roundhead dragoons fell on them and sent them scampering with three saddles empty, he got his best content from Strangwayes' friendship, which made him surer of himself and readier to face the world, yet humbler in his efforts to keep the affection of the older man.

The thought that the winning of a commission in that troop meant more such days of service with Strangwayes caused Hugh to redouble his efforts to please Turner, and he succeeded so far that after the first skirmish the captain suffered him to carry the cornet. For the rest, Turner met all his honest efforts and prompt obedience with sarcasms on his youth and simplicity, which made Hugh wince and go on laboring bravely. Only one word of approbation did he get of Turner; that was on a pouring wet night when

Hugh came in from a watch with the pickets, soaked to the skin, and, finding no food, lay down without a word on the floor of the cottage where the officers were quartered, and went sound asleep. Through his waking he could have sworn he heard Turner say, "After all, Lieutenant, there's the right mettle in this crop-headed whelp."

Though when Hugh opened his eyes and saw Turner standing over him with a candle in his hand, the latter only said, "My faith, sir, do you ever do aught but sleep?"

Thus with work and enjoyment of work the month of November passed, and meantime his Majesty with the bulk of his army had marched to London, and then marched back again. Afterward men said a kingdom might have been gained upon that journey and had been cast away, but at that time Turner's troop had only rumors of marches and countermarches, till in the early December a definite order reached them to repair to the king's headquarters at Oxford and join themselves to their regiment.

It was in the mid-afternoon that they at last rode into the city, where the High Street was gay with bravely dressed men and sleek horses, and the old gray buildings seemed alive with people. So many fine troops were passing and re-passing that none gave special heed to the little muddy band out of Northamptonshire. They passed unnoticed out by the North Gate toward the parish of St. Giles, where quarters had been assigned Sir William's regiment, and there, in the dingy stable, the officers parted. Hugh of necessity surrendered the cornet into Turner's hands with a last regretful look at its idle folds. "You made shift not to lose it, did you not, sir?" the captain said with some kindness. "Why, you're no more of an encumbrance to a troop of fighting men than most youngsters are."

Then Turner and Strangwayes walked away to report themselves to Sir William, while Hugh remained to see that Bayard and Dick's Black Boy were well groomed. To tell the truth, he was glad to linger in the stable with the men among whom he had spent the last month; he wondered if he was to have the chance to serve with them always, and the thought made him nearly tremble with expectancy.

He was loitering by the stable door, when he caught sight of a familiar blue jacket, and Frank Pleydall, in company with two lads of his own age, came swaggering up. "So you're back again, are you, Hugh?" he cried, with a boisterous embrace. "And more freckled than ever, I swear! Is that heavy-heeled horse of yours still unfoundered? Nay, don't scowl, I mean nothing. But tell me, is Michael Turner's troop here or in the stable across the way? I want to have a look at its fighting force."

"Wherefore?" Hugh blurted out suspiciously.

"Why, I'm to hold Griffith's cornetcy in it. Such labor as I had to win it, Hugh. Talk to my father night and day, swear I had the strength and discretion of twenty, vow to run away if he gave it not to me, so in the end I secured it of him. Cornet Pleydall; how like you the sound? I told you I'd coax a commission of him."

"You will find Captain Turner a gallant man

to serve under," Hugh said, after a moment. "Good-bye, Frank, I'm weary now. I'll speak with you to-morrow."

With that he passed out into the street and headed aimlessly, he cared not whither. He had not known till now how sure he had felt of that cornetcy. And that a mere boy like Frank should be preferred over him, because his kinsfolk gave him their countenance! For one instant he almost had it in his heart to wish himself back at Everscombe, still believing in his father, and still confident the world stood ready to receive a man kindly for his own endeavors.

Too wretched to think or lay a plan for the future, he plodded up and down the crowded streets till it grew dusk and pitchy dark, when sheer weariness turned him to his quarters; at least Strangwayes was his friend. The thought put more life into his step and made him hurry a little with impatience till he had sought out the baker's shop, in an upper chamber of which they were to lodge. To his disappointment Dick had not yet come in, so Hugh, without spirit enough to light a candle, sat down on a stool by the fire with his chin in his hands and waited.

When he heard Strangwayes' step outside, he endeavored to force a gay tone and shouted him a greeting, but now he tried to use it his voice broke helplessly. "There, I've heard it all, Hugh," Strangwayes said, and made no movement to get a light; "and I'm thinking Turner takes it as ill as we do. He kept an assenting face to Sir William, of course, but he blurted out to me that the deuce was in it that a little popinjay like Frank must be thrust into our troop."

Hugh forced a desperate laugh that ended in a choke.

"And I've another piece of news for you," Strangwayes went on, sitting down beside him. "Now you can take it as good or bad, which you please. I'm not resolved yet myself. You'll recollect Peyton was shot at Edgehill, and we lost many men from the regiment. Well, they've taken another troop that suffered much and used it to fill up the place. And a new captain has been put over it under Sir William."

"Is it you, Dick?" Hugh asked.

"Nay," Strangwayes answered, with a chuckle; "'tis a one time independent colonel, Alan Gwyeth."

CHAPTER XII

FOR THE HONOR OF THE GWYETHS

"You're free to take it as you choose, good or ill," Strangwayes went on; "but I can tell you Colonel Gwyeth is in no two minds about it."

"I am sorry for him," Hugh answered, after an instant. "I know it does wring a man to lose a commission out of his very hands."

"Since I must steer to the windward of hypocrisy, I am *not* sorry for him," Strangwayes returned. "And do not you worry yourself over his broken spirit, Hugh; so far he has borne up stoutly. At the last report he was ranging about with his sword at ready, bent on scoring out all his wrongs upon Master Philip Bellasis."

"Philip Bellasis?" queried Hugh, struggling to recall what that name stood for. "What has he to do in this matter?"

"The simplicity of untutored youth!" Strangwayes' voice came pityingly. "Why, 'tis clear as most logic: my Lord Bellasis of the king's council disapproves of these small independent troops, and has given his voice loudest, 'tis said, for merging Gwyeth's horse into Sir William's regiment; *ergo*, Colonel Gwyeth has taken my Lord Bellasis into his hatred. My Lord Bellasis is blessed with the gout; *ergo*, Colonel Gwyeth, not to waste so precious a commodity as hatred upon a disabled man, transfers all his intentions to my lord's swashbuckling son Philip. For, granting the colonel's temper, he must fight something now, and he would vastly prefer something of the name of Bellasis."

Hugh still kept his old place without offering comment, so Strangwayes, after a moment or two, rose and lit a candle at the hearth. He did not pause even to slip off his accoutrements, but, holding the light, began roaming about the chamber on inspection, and communicating the results of his researches to his companion: "We might be worse placed. Two flights of stairs upward from the ground, so the air should be delicate and wholesome. Also the room is so small the fireplace ought to heat it well. And for the lack of furnishings, the emptiness near cheats a man into believing he has space enough to stretch himself. A contented spirit, mark you, is an admirable necessity in a soldier."

In the end he brought up at the nearer of the two windows, which he opened, and, after a long look out into the night, drew in his head again with a soberer face. "If I risked myself a handbreadth further from the casement, I think I could make out the roofs of St. John's," he said, sitting down quietly, with the one small table betwixt himself and Hugh. "'Tis the good old college of which I was so unworthy a son. I am glad we lie near it."

"Where is the rest of the regiment?" Hugh asked.

"Sir William and most of his officers lodge just over the way at a merchant's house; Turner and Chadwell and Seymour are here under the roof with us. We'll all meet together at Sir William's table."

Hugh started back on his stool so he nearly overset himself. "Dick," he burst out, "that means that thrice a day I shall be forced face to face with Colonel Gwyeth."

Strangwayes nodded, and then, the sheer absurdity of the whole position coming over them, they both went into a fit of laughter.

Hugh recovered himself with a saner feeling of self-possession. "After all, it's very simple," he said aloud; "he'll take no note of me, I know, and I'll bear me as I would to Captain Turner, or any of the older men."

But, in spite of his stout words, when he woke in the dark of next morning Hugh could not sleep again for thinking of Colonel Gwyeth, and wondering if he would see him at breakfast and if the colonel would speak to him.

When he first entered the long upper chamber of the house across the way that served the officers for dining hall, he looked about him, half eager and half in dread, and despising himself for both emotions. But he saw no sign of Alan Gwyeth, Colonel Gwyeth, as he named him to himself, for all he was now a mere captain. Two of the officers of the old independent troop, a German, Von Holzberg, and a certain Foster, who had come over into the regiment with the colonel, Frank pointed out to him; but Hugh only glanced at the men and went on eating. He wondered if it had been either of them that shoved him off the steps that night at Shrewsbury, and he had no desire to come in contact with them.

After breakfast Frank Pleydall haled him off to view the city. "You might spare me one hour away from your Dick Strangwayes," the younger lad complained. "But I knew after you got sight of him you'd not have a word for me."

Hugh felt conscience-stricken, so he forced himself to be very pleasant to Frank, in spite of the boy's persisting in talking of Turner's troop and his new cornetcy. Before they reached the High Street of the city, however, they were joined by several other youngsters, one a lad from Magdalen, the others, boys whose fathers were serving the king, with all of whom Frank seemed to have a ripe acquaintance. Hugh concluded Master Pleydall was not suffering for companionship, and presently he concluded, too, it was a companionship into which he could not hope to enter. He had an unhappy feeling of aloofness from the amusements of these boys; he knew next to nothing of bowls or dice of which they spoke, and when one lad began to jeer another about a girl, he did not understand. So presently he took his leave of Frank, who was too busied with his comrades to take much heed of his going, and started back by himself to his quarters.

He was walking rather slowly, to study the landmarks he had noted and find his way without inquiry, when some one took him a boisterous clap on the shoulder. Facing about with a deal of indignation in his movement, he found it was George Allestree, who merely stood back and laughed at him. "You need but two wings to make a paragon of a turkey cock, Hugh Gwyeth," he said amusedly. "Are you looking for diversion? Come along with me. I am sick for some one to talk with."

Perhaps it was not a complimentary invitation, but Allestree followed it up by being so cordial and jolly that Hugh went with him out to the walks of Magdalen, and back into the city to dine at an ordinary. They had only just come out into the street again, when Hugh perceived a sudden surging of the foot passengers about him to the edge of the kennel, and such horsemen as were passing drew to the side to leave the way clear. Then some one raised a cry, "The king!" and others began cheering. Allestree caught Hugh's sleeve and drew him up a flight of steps, whence, looking over the heads of the people, they could see a little band of mounted gentlemen come slowly pacing down the High Street.

"Look you there, 'tis Prince Rupert," Allestree cried loudly, to be heard through the cheering, and Hugh took a long look at a tall young man in a scarlet coat, whose whole attention was fixed upon his restless horse. Then he heard the cheers redouble, and Allestree had now joined his voice to the uproar. Right before the spot where he stood Hugh got sight in the midst of the horsemen of one with a pointed beard and slender face, who bowed his head never so slightly to those who cheered around him.

Then the horsemen had passed by, men turned to go their way once more, and Allestree replaced his hat on his head. "Had you lost your voice, Hugh, that you could not cheer?" he asked curiously.

"No," Hugh answered, as he followed down from the steps, "I was thinking."

"'Tis a bad practice. What was it of?"

"I was thinking his Majesty looks much as other men."

"Indeed? And what else?"

"I was wondering," Hugh said half to himself, "which had the right of it, you that do ever so extol him, or my grandfather who laid the blame of all this on him."

"Because your hair is clipped you've no need to wear 'Roundhead' in your heart," Allestree answered sharply. "None but a boy or a fool would speak so." Then, as Hugh looked abashed, the other moderated his tone, and, talking carelessly of this and that, they came at length to Allestree's quarters, close outside the North Gate.

There Allestree would have Hugh out to the troop stables, to show him Captain Butler's gamecocks; and, in the midst of it, Butler himself walked into the stable. Hugh remembered his dark, low-browed face very well from their first encounter, but he was surprised and a little flattered also to find the captain knew him at the mention of his name. "The brave lad that saved me my old friend Strangwayes," Butler said, with a bit of an Irish accent, and shook hands kindly, then lingered to set forth the graces of the gamecocks. "Gloucestershire birds, those," he explained. "They were hatched of rebel eggs, but I held it sin to leave them to tempt a good

Puritan brother into seeing a cockfight. So I just made bold to muster them into the king's service."

"We must put them to't soon, Captain," said Allestree, and, when Hugh left them, a good hour later, they were still discussing the cocks.

It was near dark when Hugh came at last to Sir William's quarters. The loud talk of the men above stairs brought him at once up to the dining room, where he found several officers loitering. "Trust that red devil Gwyeth," Lieutenant Chadwell was saying; "he ran Bellasis down, be sure."

"Fight, did they?" asked another.

"They set out together this afternoon. Yes, they've crossed blades ere this."

"Do you know who had the better of it?" Hugh cried, thrusting himself into the circle.

Chadwell looked up at him impatiently, then answered, "No"; and Hugh, staying for no more, ran out of the room.

Clattering down the stairway to the outer door, he dodged by Turner, who, facing about on the stair, called, "Whither are you summoned in such haste?"

"To the city. To get news of the duel," Hugh replied, over his shoulder.

"There's no need to go that far," Turner answered moderately; and then, as Hugh came stumbling back to him up the stairs, went on: "Bellasis was worsted, a thrust through the shoulder. Captain Gwyeth came off unscathed."

"I was afraid—" Hugh said, clinching his hand about the balustrade as he stood.

"Of what?" Turner questioned dryly. "Has the gentleman been such a good friend—" He broke off there, and looked at Hugh. "I crave your pardon for that last, Master Gwyeth," he said, without sarcasm, and walked away up the stairs.

That night at supper it seemed marvellous to Hugh that men could speak or think of anything but the duel. However, there was more speech of fortifying the city and of the storming of Marlborough than of Captain Gwyeth's affairs, so he was glad to get away to his room, where at least there were none to interrupt his own thoughts.

Late in the evening Strangwayes joined him. "Yes, yes, you can spare words; I've heard all about that duel," he greeted Hugh; "and the town'll hear more to-morrow. Captain Gwyeth has just sent a message to Sir William; he passed it on to me, and I'll do the like by you. Hang me if the provost did not pounce down on the captain almost ere he quit the field, and haled him off to the Castle. They want no duelling among the king's men."

"Will they punish him?" Hugh asked breathlessly.

"Much!" Strangwayes answered, with vast contempt. "He did but nick Bellasis, and if report be true that fellow's injury is no loss to the kingdom. If he had killed him it might be otherwise, for Bellasis has great kindred, civilians, too, who would not scruple to bring the law on his slayer, but as 'tis— Why, they'll but hold him at the Castle a few days to encourage those of us who are of like inclination, and then he'll come abroad again." Then something of the warmth of his tone abated, and he laughed to himself. "'Tis an ill wind that blows no one good, eh, Hugh? You can eat your daily bread in peace now; for the present Captain Gwyeth cannot vex you."

Indeed, now the constant expectation of meeting with Alan Gwyeth was removed, Hugh found it far easier to fit himself to the routine of his new life. At first, to be sure, it cut him every time he saw Strangwayes buckle on his sword and clank away to the exercise of his troop, and he winced at every boasting word Frank let fall of the great things he meant to do now he was a full-fledged cornet. But he soon found that even a gentleman volunteer who had failed of a commission could be of use, where the fortifications on the north and southeast were digging; so for some days he spent hours in the varied assembly of college men and townsfolk, who labored with pick and shovel at the trenches. It was inglorious work for a soldier, and it was hard work that sent him to quarters with blistered hands and aching back. Frank joked him a little on turning ditcher, some of the other men chaffed, and even Strangwayes raised his eyebrows with the dry question, "Is it necessary?"

"If the king cannot use me in one way, I must serve him in another, since I am eating his bread," Hugh replied doggedly.

Whereat Strangwayes' eyes laughed, and he prayed Hugh, if he thought 'twould make no difference to the king, to quit the trenches for that afternoon and come ride with him. "Your aim is to be a soldier, is it not?" he asked, as they paced along the western road beyond the High Bridge.

"Yes, if I can get me a commission; 'tis all there is for me."

"Good. I began to doubt if you had not determined to turn pioneer. Dig in the trenches somewhat, by all means, and learn what you can of how men build fortifications and how the engineers devise them. But you must not for that neglect your horse and your sword. That brings it to my mind, Hugh; you should know something of rapier play as well as the broadsword. There's a Frenchman in the city shall teach it you."

Hugh stammered something, with his eyes on the pommel of his saddle.

"'Twill be a favor to me if you will take these lessons of him," Strangwayes put in hastily. "I knew the man in my college days; he owes me somewhat from them and would gladly return it thus."

So, early as next morning, Strangwayes marched Hugh over to a dingy lane that led from the Corn market, and up a narrow stair to a bare room, where he presented him to Monsieur de Sévérac, a fierce small man with mustaches. De Sévérac stood Hugh up with a rebated sword in his hand, and thrust at him, talking rapidly in a mixture of French and English, while Hugh vainly tried to parry the point that invariably got home upon his body. He came away bewildered and sore, to find the dull labor of the trenches, where at least he knew what was expected of him, a downright comfort. But little by little, as the lessons went on, he began to find a method beneath it all, and to get real pleasure from wielding the long, light rapier, so different from the broadsword to which he had been used. De Sévérac even admitted one day that he had a steady hand, and with practice might make a creditable swordsman.

With a great desire to whistle, Hugh walked back to dinner, and, two steps at a time, ran up the stairs at Sir William's house, a bit before the hour, he judged, for he found the dining room to all appearances empty. Then, as he stepped across the threshold, he caught sight of Von Holzberg, standing in one of the deep window recesses, and beside him a man with red hair, who at his step turned and looked at him. It was Alan Gwyeth. For a moment he stared steadily at Hugh, and by his face the boy could not tell whether his humor were good or ill; then he bowed to him curtly, as any one of the captains might have done, and continued his speech with Von Holzberg. They spoke in German, Hugh observed, in the instant that he halted mechanically before he turned on his heel and went out of the room. He had no desire to whistle now; he only knew that he was heavy with a great disappointment, that was none the less overwhelming for being utterly vague.

But, in the end, he found that matters went the more smoothly, now the dreaded meeting was over. It grew in time a mere daily and expected occurrence to see Captain Gwyeth among the officers, and to receive from him, in the course of ordinary civility, sometimes a short bow, once or twice a curt good morrow. But, though Hugh repeated to himself it was all he had looked to receive of the man, there slowly grew in him an unrealized sense of resentment that hitherto had had no place in him. He ceased to look wistfully toward Captain Gwyeth, but made it a point to talk busily with Frank or Dick or others that he knew when he came in his father's sight, and to return the other's scant bows with equal curtness.

Meantime other occupations and interests than the affairs of the mess room were busying him. The ground was now too hard for digging, but the fencing lessons still went on, as Hugh's bruised face and aching body often testified. He had also come once more, at a hint of an invitation from Turner, to take his place in the ranks and go through whatever exercises the troop was put to. Try as he would, though, a little bitterness still came into his heart at sight of Frank, carrying the red and gold cornet, so he was happier when, formal drill over, he could ride away whither he listed on Bayard.

When rapier and horse both failed of interest, Hugh had recourse to John Ridydale, whose quarters in a by-street he had speedily discovered. With small coaxing he persuaded the corporal to drill him in handling pistol and carabine, an exercise which involved the shooting off of an amazing quantity of his Majesty's powder and ball at practice marks in the fields of the west suburbs. Hugh, after peppering away bravely, came home in great enthusiasm to Strangwayes, who laughed a little, and finally remarked one day, "And do but think, too, how that honest corporal will go singing your perfections to Captain Gwyeth." Whereat Hugh grew thoughtful, and somewhat curtailed his shooting trips.

After that, especially as fouler weather closed in, he exercised much in Turner's troop stable, where Frank kept a wooden horse for vaulting, which he took great profit in seeing Hugh use. "'Tis such a pleasure to look on animation of a cold morning," young Pleydall remarked one day, as he stood shivering in his cloak. "But do you get enjoyment of it?"

Hugh, who sat in his shirt-sleeves swinging his legs on the back of the horse, merely laughed and drew his left hand up and down his spare, sinewy right arm. He had grown a little that winter, and he was beginning also to learn the power that was latent in each muscle. Just now he was thinking to himself that if it ever came again to rough and tumble hand-grips with Peregrine Oldesworth, such as they had had in the days at Everscombe, his cousin would not be quite so sure of the mastery.

Aside from the fact that he was still an uncommissioned volunteer, Hugh's only quarrel with his busy life that winter was that he saw little of Dick Strangwayes. His friend's chamber and purse were at his disposal, but his time Strangwayes himself was not master of; not only did his duties in the troop require him, but he had in the city and in the colleges many friends to whom he gave much of himself. Hugh valued the more the moments he had with his comrade at their chamber, and, for the rest, sought himself companionship where he could. Frank, too, had associates of his own, for whom Hugh had no great affection, so as a last choice he resorted to George Allestree, who showed his friendship by introducing him to all the taverns and ordinaries in the city. It was Allestree, too, who, when he found Hugh took in great seriousness his intention of becoming a soldier, unearthed a fat book, "The Soldier's Grammar and Accidence," by one Gervase Markham, and told the boy he would get from that all the theory of war he wanted.

"I'll read it speedily and return it to you, George," Hugh said gratefully.

"Prithee, don't hurry yourself," Allestree answered quickly. "Ten years hence is quite soon enough for my needs."

Indeed, Hugh did not find Gervase Markham exciting reading, but, to the silent enjoyment of Strangwayes, he dutifully labored through his pages. He was hard at work on Markham one morning, with his chin on one fist and his elbow on the table. Only his eyes were not on the book, but ranging out at the casement, for it was in early February and the sky was blue, and Hugh was thinking how the buds would be bursting soon on the beeches in the park at Everscombe.

"Did you note the Worcestershire parson who sat at our table last night?" suddenly spoke Strangwayes, who was shaving at the little mirror between the windows.

"Frank said he was an old tutor whom Sir William held in much respect," Hugh answered, bringing his gaze back to the room.

"Well, he was set next Captain Gwyeth, and I was the other side, so I enjoyed their discourse. It seems the parson was much attracted by you." Strangwayes tipped his head on one side while he scraped the razor along his cheek, and spoke disjointedly. "Something, either the way you thrust up that square chin of yours, or your pretty habit of not speaking to your elders unless they address you,— except in my case, for you constantly fail in respect to me,— well, you much pleased the gentleman, so he asked the captain your name. And the captain told him. 'Your son, sir?' says he, and falls to congratulating the captain on your fine bearing and — nay, I'll spare you. But I'm thinking Captain Gwyeth did not relish his supper." There was an instant's pause while Strangwayes, with his head thrown back, shaved warily beneath his chin; then he laid down the razor and faced about. "Will you believe it, Hugh?" he said, in something between jest and seriousness, "I'm thinking if you should go very humbly, hat in hand, to the captain and say, 'Sir, I bore myself very frowardly and peevishly toward you, but now I am ready to submit me,' I'm thinking he would rate you soundly and — henceforth maintain you himself."

"Doubtless he will,— when I go unto him so," Hugh said shortly.

Strangwayes laughed a little, then fell to talking of indifferent matters, while he put on his coat and fastened his belt. "I saw Phil Bellasis in the city yesterday," he ended. "Perhaps to even matters he's looking for Captain Gwyeth now."

"I should think one lesson would suffice for him," Hugh replied; and then, as Dick tramped away, turned his attention again to Gervase Markham.

But reading or any serious pursuit was out of

the question on those blue spring days in the midst of winter. There was near a week of such weather, in which poor Gervase was left to gather dust on the chimney-piece, and Monsieur de Sévérac expostulated at Hugh's inattention. The boy's heart was idling out in the open air, and his body must needs follow. He galloped Bayard round about the city till he knew the roads to weariness, and then, descending upon George Allestree, he dragged him out to tramp in the slushy remnants of the last snow.

"We'll even up scores now," Allestree said one afternoon. "You've haled me through the mire, which I loathe, and now I'll make you sup in the city with me, which I know you abhor."

So it was that in the evening Hugh found himself blinking sleepily in a brightly lighted room above a city ordinary, and roused up only at the click of the dice. At one of the small tables Allestree and Lieutenant Seymour, who had joined them, were deep in play, so Hugh got up and stood watching them. In spite of all urgings he did not play himself; the forty-five shillings he brought from Edgehill had lasted him well for spending money, but he had none to squander on the dice.

He looked up to the door as several new-comers entered, — civilians, from their lack of any regimental badge. "Why, is't not Bellasis yonder?" Seymour asked, dicebox in hand.

"Hm," grunted Allestree. "Throw."

Hugh glanced curiously at the men, who had placed themselves at the next table. One that sat on the farther side — a sallow, long-legged fellow of thirty — he held to be Bellasis; meeting the man's eyes, his thoughts went back to the day of Edgehill, when Bellasis had nearly ridden down Frank, and he felt sure of the identification. Then he turned to watch Allestree's play; how many throws had passed he did not know, when, hearing some one speak near by, he listened carelessly.

"Oh, you do not know him, then?" a curt, incisive voice reached him. "Well, 'tis no wonder. The puppy was whelped in a gutter."

Hugh felt a hot prickling clear to the back of his neck; but, although his whole attention was now riveted to those behind him, he did not turn.

"Yes, groom to a gang of common foot soldiers. A fellow of the name of Strangwayes took him thence in charity and employed him as body servant."

"I stake you ten shillings," said Allestree, reaching well across the table.

"I take it," answered Seymour.

Hugh leaned a little forward with his clinched hands resting on the table, and listened, not to them, but to Philip Bellasis.

"Pshaw! how would you have it?" the scornful voice went on. "'Tis bad blood there. Now Alan Gwyeth —"

Hugh swung round on his heel; the candles dazzled up and down before him, but he could make out Bellasis, resting his chin on one hand as he sat, and speaking straight at him: "Alan Gwyeth, you'll remember, was but a broken German cutthroat, who lost his commission here for cowardice —"

"Sit down, Hugh!" Allestree cried.

Hugh could feel Allestree's grasp tighten on his arm, but, shaking him off, he walked across to the table where Bellasis sat. The room was very still, and in the silence his voice sounded husky and low. "You spoke of Alan Gwyeth," he began slowly. "When you call him a coward, I tell you you lie in your throat!"

Then he leaned across the table and smote Bellasis on the mouth.

CHAPTER XIII

IN THE FIELDS TOWARD OSNEY ABBEY

It was dark in the passage outside the door, and Hugh fumbled stupidly to find the latch. Inside two patches of moonlight, checkered like the diamond panes of the windows, lay on the floor. Hugh stood staring at them dully a moment before he spoke, "Dick."

"Well?" came from the black corner where the bed stood; it was Strangwayes' assertion that he always slept with one eye and one ear alert.

Hugh stepped over to the bedside. "I have met with Philip Bellasis," he began quickly, as if he had a lesson he knew must be repeated. "He slandered my father. I gave him the lie. We are to fight with rapiers to-morrow at twilight in the fields toward Osney Abbey."

Strangwayes was sitting upright in bed now. "You are to fight Bellasis?" he repeated.

Hugh nodded. "Have you the time to come out to the field with me, Dick? George offered, but I'd rather—"

"Did George Allestree suffer you enter on such a quarrel?" There was a sharp, ringing quality in Strangwayes' voice Hugh had seldom heard.

"Nay, 'tis no fault of George," he answered quickly, and detailed all that had befallen at the ordinary.

Strangwayes dropped back on his elbow. "Hugh, you fool, you babe!" he broke out, still with that odd quality in his voice. "That scoundrel trapped you deliberately; he durst not meet your father again; he tried to trap you, and you suffered him!"

"I could do nothing else," Hugh answered.

"Well, get to bed now," Strangwayes said in his kindest tone. "You must have all the rest you can before you go to spit our friend Philip."

Lying down obediently, Hugh stared at the moonlight creeping along the floor, and listened to the watch that paced the street below. Strangwayes at his side breathed uneasily and once or twice turned somewhat; but Hugh lay quiet till his opened eyes ached and were heavy, and he slept a sleep full of dreams.

When he came broad awake again there was chilly daylight in the room, and Strangwayes was up and half dressed. "What sort of day is it?" Hugh asked.

"A gray day," Dick answered cheerily. "'Tis good for your work. There'll be no sun to dazzle either of you."

Hugh got up, and in the midst of drawing on his clothes glanced at Dick's watch, where he saw it was past their rising hour. "Is this the way you pamper a fighter, as if I were one of Butler's gamecocks?" he asked.

"You were sleeping well," Strangwayes answered; "'twere pity to wake you. I'll fetch some breakfast and we'll eat together here."

"You can get food from the shop below; you've no need of your hat and cloak. Where are you going, Dick?"

Strangwayes hesitated an instant while he drew his cloak about him, then replied, "I am going to your father."

"You shall not!" Hugh cried, and, crossing to the door, set his back against it.

"Assuredly I shall," Strangwayes answered. "The matter has gone beyond jest."

"He will call me a snivelling coward," Hugh pleaded; "he will say I made a mash of it and then came whimpering to him."

"Let him," Strangwayes interrupted, "'tis his quarrel and he should manage it himself. Why did you ever thrust in?"

"I know not," Hugh answered. "Only he is my father. And he is no coward. They lied about him in that. And he was not there to reply. I had to come in."

"Well, he can come in now," Strangwayes retorted, and strode over to the door.

Hugh thrust up one arm against his friend's chest. "You will not tell him?" he begged. "I know you can put me aside, Dick; you're the stronger. But prithee, do not use me thus. He despises me so already. I'd liefer Bellasis killed me twice over. You won't speak a word to him, Dick?"

"No, I won't speak to him, Hugh," Strangwayes answered soothingly. "Come, come, you're foolish as a girl. Go get on your coat, and be ready to eat a full breakfast." He put Hugh aside with one arm about his shoulders, and went out of the room.

When Hugh had finished dressing he opened the casement and leaned out a little into the raw morning air; the chilly wind seemed to brush away something of the heaviness of his unrefreshing sleep. Down in the street below he saw men passing by, and a townswoman in a scarlet hood that showed bright against the muddy road and dark houses. Across the way he saw Major Bludsworth come leisurely down the steps from Sir William's quarters, and presently he saw a trooper, lumbering briskly up the stairs, disappear inside the house.

Just then a kick upon the door made him turn in time to see Strangwayes, keeping the door braced open with one foot, come sidewise through the narrow aperture. In one hand he held two mugs of ale and in the other a pasty, which Hugh had the wit to catch before it fell to the floor. "Ay, treat it reverently," Dick said, "'tis mutton, and age has ever commanded reverence. Part of the ale has gone up my sleeve, but the rest is warranted of a good headiness."

After he had thrown off his cloak the two set them down at the table with the pasty and the ale between them, and drew out their knives. Strangwayes scored a line across the middle of the mutton pie. "Now each man falls to," he ordered, "and he who works the greatest havoc on his side gets the mug that is full, while the other must content him with the scant measure. Now, then, charge for England and St. George!"

They were well at work, Hugh eating dutifully and Dick both eating and setting forth an interminable tale of a fat citizen's wife he had accosted in the bakeshop, when there sounded a quick stamping on the stairs. " I'll wager 'tis the popinjay," said Strangwayes, pausing with his knife suspended.

Right on the word Frank Pleydall burst into the room. " Is it true you're to fight ? " he cried.

" A guess near the truth," answered Strangwayes. " Draw up and share with us."

" I've eaten breakfast. They were talking of the duel there at the table. So you're to fight Bellasis, Hugh? Aren't you afraid ? "

The full mug of ale suddenly went crashing and slopping to the floor. " If I were the Creator and had men to make," said Strangwayes, down on his knees among the fragments, " I'd make men without elbows, at least without such elbows as mine. Come aid me, you lazy fellow."

Hugh obediently began mopping up the spilt ale, but Strangwayes did not stay to help him. He was speaking with Frank over by the window, and Hugh just caught something like, " If you don't hold your foolish tongue, I'll cuff your head off."

In any case, when Hugh rose to his feet he found Frank very subdued. " 'Twas my father sent me hither," he began, with a little trace of sullenness. " He said if you really had it in mind to fight, you were best slip out of the town early. The matter has got abroad, and the provost may send to apprehend you just for accepting the challenge."

XIII IN THE FIELDS TOWARD OSNEY ABBEY

"Then we'll disappoint the provost," said Strangwayes. "I've sent to the stable already to have our horses brought round. Clap into your boots, Hugh, but bring your shoes along. You can't fight with a ton of leather about your heels."

"Is there aught I can lend you, Hugh?" asked Frank, studying his friend with interested eyes.

"I'm well enough," Hugh answered cheerfully. "Dick is going to let me use his rapier."

"Can't I come out to the field with you?" Frank begged. "Oh, I'll not speak a word, Dick, and I'll do whatever you may tell me."

"If a second man came it would have to be Allestree," answered Strangwayes. "Better go back to quarters now, Frank. Tell Sir William we thank him for his warning, and I have taken a day's leave of absence."

But as Strangwayes was edging him toward the door Frank dodged by him and ran back to Hugh. "Good luck to you," he said, putting his arms round Hugh and kissing him. "And—and God keep you."

Then he clattered out and down the stairs, and Hugh, for a moment, neither looked at Dick nor spoke.

He was drawing on his cloak, still with his back toward Strangwayes, who stood by the window, when his friend struck in gayly: "In good time, here are the horses. Come along, now." Thus Hugh was hurried out at the door, with time only for a single backward glance at the little crowded chamber, and barely an instant in which to ask himself, would he ever look upon that room again?

At the foot of the first flight of stairs they met Turner, recognizable by his slim figure, though the corridor was too dark for them to distinguish his face. "Going out to the field, eh, Gwyeth?" he asked, thrusting out his hand. "Well, success to you, lad, good success." He shook hands a second time with a strong pressure that lingered on Hugh's fingers till after they were mounted and off.

Under foot the mud and slush were heavy, but the horses kept up a tolerable pace, which Hugh, unknown to himself, was setting for them. A feverish desire to be moving quickly was upon him, and with it a dread of being silent. He laughed and chatted indifferently of whatever caught his eye upon the western road till he soon had Strangwayes talking back glibly. "We'll dine at an alehouse called the 'Sceptre,'" Dick rattled on. "I know it well of old. I used to have a score as long as my arm chalked on the door. There's a very pretty bowling green behind the house. Which explains my long score. When the spring comes I must have you out thither and teach you to bowl. 'Tis good for the muscles of the arm, let alone the exhilaration of the spirits."

It was mid-morning when they drew rein before the much belauded alehouse, a low gray building, in a field somewhat apart from the surrounding cottages, with tall poplars in a row on either side that made it seem the more remote. The short-breathed host and his staid, gray-headed drawer had had acquaintance with Strangwayes as late as that winter, to judge by the warmth of their greeting. They had the horses to the stable at once, and the gentlemen to the big front chamber of the upper story, where a good fire was started, a cloth laid, and all made comfortable. "We'll not dine till one o'clock," Strangwayes ordered. "If you hear scuffling before then be not dismayed; we may try some sword practice. You understand, eh, Martin?"

The sober drawer showed sparks of interest. "Be you to fight, Master Strangwayes?" he asked.

"This gentleman is, this afternoon. Now keep a quiet tongue, Martin, as you always do." He slipped a piece of money into the drawer's hand, and the man departed slowly, with his gaze on Hugh.

"Now make yourself at ease," Strangwayes bade. "Or will you try a little rapier practice to limber your muscles?"

Hugh was ready enough, so Strangwayes procured from the host a pair of blunted rapiers with which they fell to fencing. Hugh watched Dick's sword-hand and did his best, but again and again the point slipped past his blade; there seemed no suppleness in his wrist nor spring in his body, and when he tried desperately to retort faster he laid himself open to his adversary. In the end, as he attempted a vigorous thrust in quarte, his foot slipped so he only saved himself by catching at the table. As he recovered himself he looked at Dick, and saw his face was of an appalling soberness. "You've a steady enough hand, Hugh," he began hastily. "Only you must quicken your thrusts somewhat. No, don't try any more; you'll only spend yourself needlessly."

Hugh handed back his weapon, and made a great work of putting on his coat again. But presently it would out. "My father is considerable of a swordsman, is he not?" he began.

"He has that reputation," Strangwayes answered dryly.

"Yet he did not contrive more than to wound Bellasis."

"I doubt if he put his whole skill into the business," Strangwayes said quickly. "Come, Hugh, try a hand at primero with me,—unless you fear I worst you there."

He drew the cards from his pocket, and they sat down to the table by the fire. How many games they played Hugh did not heed; he dealt recklessly and talked and laughed his loudest; sometimes he won of Strangwayes, sometimes he lost, but it all mattered nothing. He was in the thick of a boisterous exposition of the merits of the hand he held, when some one knocked at the door. "Come!" Strangwayes cried eagerly, and sprang to his feet.

The door was pushed open, and Ridydale, spattered to the thighs, walked in. "A letter for you, sir, from Colonel Gwyeth," he said, crossing to Hugh. "The colonel lay from his quarters yesternight, and came not back till late this morning."

This last was spoken more to Strangwayes than to Hugh, but the boy did not heed. He was tearing open the letter with fingers that shook with impatience. It was very brief, he saw at first glance; then he read:—

WORTHY SIR:
    For something like forty years I have contrived unaided to keep my honor and my reputation clear. By the grace of Heaven I hope to do so for forty years longer, still without a boy's assistance. Quit at once this absurd quarrel you have entered on. Take yourself back to your quarters. I shall myself deal with Master Bellasis.
                Your obedient servant,
                            ALAN GWYETH.

Hugh read the paper over once more, slowly, then passed it to Dick. "That is what he writes me," he said without passion, and getting up went to fetch a standish and paper from an open cupboard in one corner of the room.

He placed them on the table as Strangwayes looked up from finishing the letter. He, too, said nothing, but his mouth was set in a hard line under his mustache. "I'll write an answer," Hugh said quietly, as he seated himself.

"Will you not ride back to the city with me, sir?" Ridydale put in eagerly.

Hugh was silent a moment while he adjusted his paper and pen, then replied: "I am not coming to the city with you. Moreover, Corporal Ridydale, if you ever again mention unto me one word of Captain Gwyeth, I'll have no more dealings with you."

Then he turned resolutely to his task and wrote his answer, slowly, for he was an unhandy penman, and he wished the letter to be quite dignified in neatness.

WORTHY SIR:
    When we parted at Shrewsbury perhaps you may remember I said to you that you had no right to lay a command upon me. Since that time you have done naught to get you the

right; by your will I am no son of yours. Yet so long as I bear the name of Gwyeth it is my part to defend that name from any slander. Therefore I did enter on a quarrel with the one who defamed my family. The quarrel is now mine and I shall pursue it to the end. Though I have been flogged by your troopers, I have some notion of what becomes a gentleman of honor. Such a gentleman as my mother would wish me to be does not suffer another to undertake his defence.

Your obedient servant,
HUGH GWYETH.

He chose his words deliberately; it was amazing how ready they were to his hand, now that he had come to the realization that Alan Gwyeth had used him with brutal unjustness.

He folded the paper carefully. "Here, take it, Ridydale," he ordered. "But remember, I've no quarrel with you, Corporal. You have been a good friend to me, and I'd still keep you so. Only never another mention of Captain Gwyeth."

Ridydale hesitated a moment with the letter in his hand before he broke out: "Tell you what, Master Hugh, I'll send this by another messenger. I'm going to rest here till the fight's over. You may want me."

"That's well," Strangwayes said promptly.

After Ridydale had left them, Dick ordered up dinner, and they tried to talk over it as before. Strangwayes made out fairly, but a numb silence was on Hugh; in the bracing anger of a few moments before his resolution seemed all to have vanished and left him spiritless. He could not help looking to the window to see what time of day it was, and involuntarily he interrupted Strangwayes with a question as to how soon they should start for the field. "Not for a couple of hours," the other replied. "'Tis a bit of a walk; we'll take supper here afterward—"

With a sudden gesture Hugh pushed by his plate and swung about with his head hidden against the back of his chair. For of a sudden there came sweeping upon him overpoweringly the realization he had been battling off all the morning: this was the last meal he might ever eat.

He got to his feet unsteadily and walked to the door; the scrape of a chair told him Strangwayes had risen. "Don't!" Hugh cried. "I want to be alone."

Somehow he felt his way down a flight of backstairs, and pushing open a side door stumbled out into the air. There was a level stretch of pashy bowling green down which he splashed his way. But press forward as he would, he knew he could not run from what he had bound himself to, so, where the green ended at the hedge, he flung himself down on a wet bench and sat with his head in his hands. In one of the bare poplars a snow bird was chirruping; over toward the stable he could hear a man calling and a horse stamp. He dropped his head on his knees and stared dumbly at the trodden mud between his feet. For he knew now there was nothing to help him, even Dick's friendship and affection were of no avail; there was only himself to rely on. Once he thought of God, but the God the Oldesworths had taught him was distant and very stern; He would never take pity on a duellist, even if he cried to Him. So Hugh, with his head bowed down, wrestled through the struggle alone, and little by little forced himself to accept with a soldier's resignation the fate that should take from him the joy of battle, and of friendship, and of life that summed up all joys.

When he rose his face was quite steady, though he made no pretence to the cheerfulness he had kept up that morning. Walking briskly back to the house, he made his way to their chamber, where he found Strangwayes pacing up and down. Hugh went to him and put a hand on his shoulder. "Let's not try to pretend about it any more, Dick," he said simply. "Bellasis has handled a rapier for years where I've used it but weeks. There is no hope for me. Frankly, is there? On your honor, Dick."

"There is this hope," Strangwayes answered, after an instant. "It may be he will content himself with disabling you, and then — he will force you to crave his pardon."

"The other way suits me better," Hugh said quietly.

"You can only do your best," Strangwayes replied. "He may be careless. Be ready to use every opportunity."

"I will," Hugh nodded, and then, sitting down by the fire, he beckoned his friend to sit beside him. "I take it, time's short," he began, "so I want to tell you, Dick, you're to take Bayard and keep him, and be very kind to him, only I know you'll be that."

Strangwayes reached out his arm; the two griped hands, and sat so.

"Give my sword to Frank," Hugh went on, "and give Ned Griffith back his red sash. Ridydale can have my spurs. Then there's six shillings I've here; I want a trooper named Robert Saxon in Gwyeth's company to have them; he'll be sorry and drunk at once. Give my duty to Captain Turner and Sir William, and commend me to George Allestree." He paused a moment, then resumed: "There's a girl at Everscombe Manor, Lois Campion; we were playfellows then. She has not writ me since, but I'd like her to know that I held her in remembrance. I'd fain send my duty to my Grandfather Oldesworth, too, but I doubt if he'd accept of it."

"I'll do all as you bid," Strangwayes answered. "God! if I could but fight that coward for you."

After that outburst they sat side by side without speaking, while the quick moments slipped by, till at last Strangwayes rose unwillingly to his feet. "We must start now," he said, so Hugh put on his cloak, and arm in arm they went out from the house.

At the door Ridydale saluted them, then fell into step behind them, and in such order they splashed down the bowling green. Through a gap in the hedge they entered a field where some patches of snow still lingered in the hollows. Beyond they passed through a copse of naked trees, and so across a dry ditch entered a level piece of open ground. At the farther end two men stood waiting. "Faith, I had judged you meant to shirk your hour," cried the taller of the two in a sharp, high voice.

"Close of twilight is a rather loose appointment, Master Bellasis," Strangwayes answered curtly.

"And you fetched a third man, did you? Two to one—"

"Maybe you would wish the city guard to come upon you with blades in your hands?" Strangwayes interrupted. "I have brought a sure man to watch the road. But if you object—"

"Oh, by no means," laughed Bellasis. "And 'tis well you brought him. 'Twill need two of you to convey your gentleman from the field."

"In any case I shall have legs left to walk back to the field and find you," Strangwayes retorted, with his nostrils drawn thin. "Strip off your coat, Hugh. Take your place beyond the bushes there, Ridydale."

Hugh was glad that Dick unfastened his coat for him; for a sick instant the control he had acquired of himself seemed slipping away. But it was only an instant, and then, grasping his rapier firmly, he had stood up stiffly in the place they bade him stand. In the distance, against the darkening twilight, he could see the bare trees and the towers of Osney Abbey; then his eyes descended to Bellasis' keen sallow face, and then they dropped to the man's bony sword-hand, and he saw nothing else.

Some one said, "Now!" and the rapiers crossed, how, he scarcely knew. He heard the quick click of the blades, and with it came a sudden flash of pain in his right thigh; he thrust desperately at Bellasis' shoulder, but his point went wide.

"That shall quit the blow you struck me," his adversary spoke softly, as the blades clicked again.

Hugh shifted his body, stiffly, for his right leg felt strangely numb, yet with his utmost skill he contrived to put by two thrusts; all his attention was riveted to the blades, but some inner consciousness was telling him that Bellasis was only feinting carelessly, and had not yet shown his strength. His very despair drove him forward in a useless thrust, and at that the other's rapier seemed in his eyes, and he felt something warm on his left cheek.

"And there's for your father's blow," said Bellasis, in a low voice. "Get your breath now for the last bout."

There was thrust and parry for what seemed endless hours; click of blade, desperate effort that set Hugh, mad with his helplessness, panting to the point of sobbing. Then, of a sudden, as he made an instinctive swerve to the right, there came a rasping sound of tearing cloth, a deathly agony swept through his body. But he saw Bellasis leaning toward him with body all exposed, and, springing forward, with all the strength in him he thrust home the rapier.

The hilt of the rapier slipped from his hand. Bellasis' shirt and face showed white on the muddy ground at his feet. All the rest was blackness and pain. A second thrill pierced through his side. Some one's arm was about him, and Dick's voice cried, "Hugh, Hugh!" with an agony in it he marvelled at. He could feel Strangwayes' fingers tearing open his shirt, a cloth pressing in upon his side. "Ha' done!" he gasped out, clutching Dick round the neck.

Right upon that, somewhere very far distant, he heard Ridydale's voice: "Off with you! The guard's upon us!"

CHAPTER XIV

UNDER THE KING'S DISPLEASURE

A RACKING agony of being borne joltingly along Hugh remembered dimly, but now there came a moment of fuller consciousness. He knew it was black all about where he lay, the ground beneath him felt wet, and his face was jammed into something so cold it made his cheek ache. With a helpless catching of the breath he tried to shift his position. "Hush, hush!" Strangwayes' voice sounded right at his ear, and Strangwayes' arm pressed him close.

Smothering the cry of pain, Hugh listened breathlessly; somewhere far above him people must be moving, for he heard the snap of boughs and men's voices calling, "Have you found a trace?"

"Nay, they bore to the roadway, I'll wager."

"Have ye searched the ditch?"

On that, nearer and louder than before, came more trampling and crashing. Hugh could not hear Strangwayes breathe, but he felt Strangwayes' arm draw more tensely about him, and, when he turned his head painfully, knew it was Strangwayes' hand pressed down on his mouth. Now as he lay he could see a shred of dark sky with the outline of branches thick woven against it.

Then the sight of the sky went blurring out from before his eyes, and the crackling of the bushes grew fainter till that and all other sound ceased for him.

A sense that he had been long in a region of blankness, then once more he heard voices, but now they were beside him and he knew who spoke. "Durst you venture forth, sir?"

"I dare not risk it, Corporal. Yet if we stay in this slough— You're holding him as clear of the wet as you can?"

"What else should I be doing, sir?" Ridydale's voice came snappishly.

"You are here, Dick?" Hugh tried to say, but it took an instant to force out even a weak whisper.

A quick movement and Strangwayes bent over him; Hugh concluded vaguely that he was resting across the knees of his two friends with his head upon Dick's arm. "How is it with you now, lad?" Strangwayes asked eagerly.

"Well enough. Only my face aches," Hugh admitted in a whisper that pained him.

"I could have forgiven him, had he killed the lad clean and quick," Strangwayes broke out; "but to hack him into pieces thus!"

"Hell gnaw him for it!" Ridydale growled back.

With neither wit nor strength to reason out of what or whom they spoke, Hugh lay quiet and unresisting in the arms of his companions. He wondered if their coats were wrapped about him, he felt so warm. Then, after a space where even wonder was blotted out, he felt his shirt thrust open again and the air cold on his breast. "Give me those other napkins," Strangwayes' voice sounded hard and colorless; "he is bleeding again."

Something like a groan burst from Ridydale. "May we not venture it now, sir?" he begged.

"In God's name, yes!" Strangwayes cried.

Hugh felt himself lifted up, and with the movement came a throbbing pain through all his body, and then a deathly faintness, that left him no strength to cry out. Through it all he caught a glimpse of a blackness above him that must be the night sky, and then it was all a blackness, where he could not even feel Dick's touch.

For one instant of agony the light returned to him. It seemed they must have torn open all his wounds, and they would not spare him, even when at last he cried for mercy. Strangwayes' face came out of the blur of light, and Strangwayes griped hold of his hand, but gave him no other comfort. Then the light went out, and for a space Hugh had only ugly dreams.

It was of a morning that he opened his eyes again upon a sane and remembered world. Somewhere near crackled a fire, the light of which dazzled him so he blinked and closed his eyes once more. Gradually he became aware that he was warm, and lay on something soft. He felt no pain at all now, and he could not understand why they had so fettered his body with bandages. Presently he summoned energy to open his eyes a second time, and, with long intervals of dozing, lay staring about him: a small, bare room he did not recollect to have seen before; one high, narrow window, with a naked branch that seemed to cleave it from corner to corner; a dancing fire that for a long time fascinated him. After that he studied the blue coverlet that was flung over him, and then, dragging out one arm, rested it upon the coverlet, and marvelled that his wrist was grown so slender.

Then from somewhere Strangwayes came and stood over him, just the same as he had ever been, only now the lower part of his face was black with a half-grown beard. "Do you know me, Hugh?" he asked, and for once there was no laughter in his eyes.

"Why, of course I know you," Hugh replied, vexed at the folly of such a question.

Drawing up a stool, Strangwayes sat down beside him, but Hugh hardly noted him for still gazing at that limp arm that did not seem to belong to him. But presently he found that he could move it, if he took his time, so with infinite pains he dragged his hand up to his face, and felt a great welt of plaster upon one cheek. "What's to do?" he asked faintly.

"A beauty mark you may keep with you," Strangwayes said, with an effort at his old gay tone, though his eyes were blinking fast.

Hugh rested a time, then, with much patience, lifted his hand to his head, and gave a gasp of consternation as he drew his uncertain fingers across a stiff, prickly surface. "What have you done to me now?" he cried.

"Clipped you close. Do you think a fellow that gets him a fever can be let play Cavalier?"

"You cut my hair?" Hugh repeated. "And it

was growing bravely. He'd a had no need to call me Roundhead any more. I would not have used you so." He slipped his hand down over his eyes, and burst into a pitiful sort of whimpering, he knew not why.

"Be silent now!" Strangwayes cried, with a sharpness that made Hugh quiet with pure amazement that his friend could use such a tone to him. But after that Strangwayes put his pillow into shape, and, covering him up, bade him sleep, with all his old kindness.

After sleeping long and comfortably Hugh awoke to see a candle flickering on the table, and the small window carefully hidden over with a curtain. "Are you here, Dick?" he asked, and Strangwayes, rising from before the fire, came to the side of his pallet. "Awake again, Hugh? Come, don't you think you could eat a bit?"

"I know not," Hugh spoke with long pauses. "Why, perhaps I am hungry. I thought something was amiss."

Strangwayes laughed, for no visible reason, and, presently fetching him broth, fed him with slow spoonfuls. The food put enough life into Hugh for him to ask at length, "Where are we?"

"In a back chamber of the alehouse of the 'Sceptre.' There, question no farther. Your duty now is but to eat and sleep."

For many hours Hugh obeyed that command unquestioningly, and pained himself only to take the merest outer observation of what went on about him. A small pompous man in black, who dressed his wounds and left ill-tasting drugs, came twice to the room; the drawer, Martin, came often with food; and Strangwayes was there always, right at his bedside, whenever he chose to call upon him. For the rest, there was the crackling fire to watch, and the window. Once when he looked to it of a morning he saw it thick with white frost, and Strangwayes, coming to the pallet, flung a cloak over him as he lay. Hugh watched him an instant, then broke out irrelevantly, "Dick, have I been very ill?"

"Just a bit," Strangwayes replied, in his dryest tone.

"From the duel, was it not?" Hugh pursued; then suddenly: "Tell me, how did it fare with Bellasis? Has he recovered before me?"

"He is recovered," Strangwayes answered, and hastened away to mend the fire.

But four and twenty hours later Hugh attacked his friend with a new query: "Why does not Frank or George come to visit me now? I think I be strong enough."

"Wait a time longer," Strangwayes urged; so Hugh waited and pondered much. For his head did not ache now whenever he tried to think, so he went over all he remembered of the last days, and concluded on this and that till he was ready to ask farther questions.

The late cold that made the window white had somewhat abated, when for the first time Strangwayes propped Hugh up in bed with two cushions behind him and a cloak about his shoulders. "I want to ask you something," Hugh began then, soberly, "I am quite strong, you see. Now tell me, Dick, did I not hurt Bellasis?"

"Yes," Strangwayes answered, setting his face grimly to the front.

"Sorely?" Hugh urged. "Tell me, Dick."

"You must lie down again," Strangwayes ordered; but as he was stretched on his back Hugh caught his friend's sleeve. "You must tell me," he repeated. "Dick, I did not — kill him?"

In spite of all he could do Strangwayes' face made reply, and Hugh, after one look, turned himself to the wall.

Presently Strangwayes' arm was slipped under his neck. "You must not grieve for that man," he spoke anxiously.

At that Hugh turned and put his arm round Dick as he knelt by the pallet. "I was not grieving," he said simply, "only I was sorry that after all I could not be sorry for him." Then, after a moment: "Tell me all about it. Yes, now, I pray you, Dick."

Strangwayes looked at him, then settled himself a little more comfortably on the floor by the pallet. "You remember the fight?"

Hugh nodded. "But I cannot understand how I had the better of it."

"He gave it you," Strangwayes answered. "He scorned you so he destroyed himself. He fenced as if 'twere mere play, and his last thrust was not clean. It took you beneath the small ribs, not a mortal thrust, and there his rapier stayed hampered. And while his body was undefended, as he strove to wrench his blade free, you ran him through the bowels. They carried him off the field, I hear, but he was bleeding inside, and they could do nothing for him. So 'twas well we came out from the hands of the guard, for Lord Bellasis was mad with anger, and he has great friends and influence with the king, so by next day the ways were laid and they were seeking us to answer for his death."

"And you saved me from them," Hugh said under his breath, while he tried to hug Dick with one arm.

"Faith, 'twas saving myself at the same time, and I near killed you in the effort. Jack Ridydale and I caught you up on the alarm and plunged into the ditch at the edge of the field—"

"I remember," Hugh interrupted.

"So do I," Strangwayes said, and tried to force a laugh. "Sure, 'twas wet there. By the favor of fortune the watch passed over us, and we fetched you to the 'Sceptre' and had in a close-mouthed physician. And I was bravely frightened, Hugh, for there was no moving you hence, and here we lay in the jaws of the enemy. No, no, you're in no danger now. For so soon as we were safe in the alehouse good old Ridydale made for the stable, and the watch had not yet searched here, so the horses were untouched. He got him on his own steed, took your Bayard and my Black Boy by the bridles, and rode for the west as fast as spur could drive. Toward dawn he faced about and trotted home again, the horses all belathered and crestfallen, and, jogging along the road in such trim, he was seized upon by the zealous patrol and haled into the city to answer as to our whereabouts."

"They did not harm him?" Hugh asked anxiously.

"Harm him? Nay, the old scoundrel was more than their match. He swore we had posted all night, made a change of horses, and headed into the enemy's country to take ship out of the realm. They coaxed him and they bullied him for three days, but the rascal lied with such liberality and discretion that in the end they must release him. So the matter stands, for some do truly believe we have got beyond seas, and my Lord Bellasis has still a hope that we be somewhere in the country round about here. And the most of the people, Hugh, have clean forgot about us by this."

"None know where we are? That is why none of the others have come hither?"

"No; 'tis that I wanted few to come drawing suspicions to us. Sir William knows, and he was pleased to approve your conduct, Hugh, and sent us supply of money by the trusty old drawer here. Ridydale durst venture to us only once, for fear of being tracked. 'Twas when he was new released and he had had no word how it was faring with you. So he came and he brought news of Captain Gwyeth."

Hugh made no reply.

"If you have the strength to hear it, I'd fain ease me of it," Strangwayes went on. "This is what he had done, Hugh: When he got my word that man had forced a fight upon you because you were your father's son, and when I prayed him to meet the hacking cutthroat — Heaven forgive me! Bellasis is dead now. Well, you know the answer Captain Gwyeth sent you. Having shown his proud temper in that, he set out, not to join us and intercept the man upon the field, but to seek him in the city. Now Bellasis, like a wise man, had withdrawn himself on a suspicion of that, so Alan Gwyeth did but meet Bellasis' cousin, Herbert, who drew him into a scuffle under the very shadow of the Castle. They were promptly put under arrest therefor. Then the captain found the hour of the duel coming on, and he laid by the heels for his folly, and then—" Strangwayes paused, and tried to laugh himself into a less earnest tone. "Well, Hugh, he prayed to see the officer of the watch, and conveyed unto him full information of the place and time of the duel."

"Then 'tis he that is to thank for bringing the watch upon us?"

"Yes, and for making us hale you into the ditch and near rack your poor body to pieces. I swear the rough handling we had to give you had as much share in bringing on the fever as your wounds. And as you lay in the very heat of the fever came this fine proud message from him that his will was to come unto you. And I wrote back unto him so he has not come. But if you wish him, Hugh, I'll — well, doubtless I can crave his pardon, and then he will come to you."

"I do not wish to see him," Hugh answered coldly. "What did you write him, Dick?"

"'Twas not just a temperate letter, I'm fearing. For your fever had run four days, and there seemed no change save the worst change. Oh, well," Strangwayes laughed, "I wrote him that his cursed ugly pride had never brought anything to you but disgrace and pain, and now he had killed you he should leave you to me. I told him his blundering stupidity in sending the watch would have wrecked your honor, had they come ten minutes earlier, and now it had wrecked your life. And I told him he had been no father to you while you lived, and he should not play that part in your death. I said if he came hither I would bar the door in his face. Truth, I must have been near mad to write so uncivilly, but—I had been watching with you three nights, and I was worried for you, lad. So he did not come. And you do not wish him to?"

"No, never," Hugh said, then lay silent so long that Strangwayes, slipping his arm from beneath his head, had risen, when Hugh broke out, "Dick, you must have sent him a message the day of the duel."

"Hm," said Strangwayes, heading for the fireplace.

"You promised me—"

"Only not to speak to him," the other put in hastily. "I did not. I wrote him a letter there in the bakeshop, and sent it by a stray trooper. Dear lad, I was trained for a lawyer. How could I resist a quibble? You're going to forgive me, Hugh."

"'Tis a very little fault in you, Dick," Hugh answered. "Though if another had done it—"

"Well, I'll never attempt to incline Captain Gwyeth to his duty again, rest assured," Strangwayes ended their talk earnestly.

So, while he still had barely strength to lift

his head from off the pillow, Hugh came to full knowledge of how his affairs stood. He was glad to be told the worst, not be played with like a child, yet the realization of the desperate state to which the word and the blow at the Oxford ordinary had reduced, not only his own fortunes, but those of his friend, made his slow convalescence doubly hard to bear. Day followed day, all alike, save that on some the fire was heaped high for warmth, while on others, more frequently as time passed, the narrow window was flung wide open, and a breath of spring-like air sweeping in made confinement all the less endurable. Then Hugh fretted miserably, till he looked at Dick, and thought what it must mean to a man to be pent up in a sick room while he had all his limbs and strength at his command. For Strangwayes never left him, save for a half-hour or so at night, when he used to slip out by the back way and tramp about the bowling green, to bring in with him so fine a breeziness that Hugh used to lie awake for his coming. At first Strangwayes did not quit the chamber even for his rest, but, wrapping his cloak about him, stretched himself across the hearth, till Hugh, with gaining strength, assured him he could fare well enough without constant watching, and begged him to get a room and a bed. After that Hugh passed long, sleepless hours of the night in loneliness, while through the little window he watched the varying shades of the sky and the stars that had so many times looked back at him.

During the day the chief diversions were to eat, and to note how many minutes more he con-

trived to sit up than on the preceding day. In
the intervals he and Dick played cards, till the
pack was wofully thumbed, or chess, which Hugh
found easier, for he need only lie on his back and
look sidewise at the board. Later Dick unearthed
the whole library of the "Sceptre," a fat " Palmerin
of England," whose "gallant history" he patiently
read aloud to Hugh, who did not find the story
enlivening, but got to appreciate Dick's sarcastic
comments. Still better he liked to hear his friend
talk, half nonsense, half truth, of the things he
had seen and done when he served in the Low
Countries and made his stay in Paris. "How
should you like to go thither yourself?" Strangwayes asked abruptly one March morning, when
for the second time Hugh was sitting up in a chair.

"With you?" the boy asked quickly.

"No, not with me now," Strangwayes answered;
"I cannot quit the kingdom, Hugh, while there's
a blow to be struck. Even though I be a volunteer—"

"Dick!" Hugh cried, "you've lost your commission through me?"

"No, no, no," Strangwayes said hastily. "Only
'twould be awkward to come to the front and
claim it while this duel is still remembered. Sir
William will always keep me a place in his regiment. And when you are cured, 'tis my purpose
to go into the North to fight. I'll not be easily
recognized now my beard is grown, and I'll put
another name to me. There in the North I may
chance to do something that will bring us a pardon for what we had a share in."

All of which Hugh only half heeded as he sat

with his head in his hands. For it was worse than the realization that he had killed a man to know that he had wrought Dick's fortunes such a terrible shock.

Strangwayes said what he could that was generous, and ended with the old proposition to send Hugh, so soon as he was recovered, into the Low Countries, where he would be safe from all pursuit. But Hugh shook his head. "I cannot, Dick; I'd rather be hanged here on English ground, or whatever else they would do to me. Why, I could not speak their queer language yonder. And you've pampered me so, I durst not venture out among strangers again. I'll do as you do, change my name, and volunteer somewhere else."

It was at this time he made a resolution, which he had a chance to carry out perhaps a week later, when Ridydale paid him a cautious visit. Sir William's regiment marched northward in two days, the corporal explained, bound to garrison Tamworth, and he had thought it well to come see Master Hugh ere he went, and bring him his accoutrements from his quarters at Oxford. Hugh watched his chance till Dick had left them alone, then prayed Ridydale get Bayard from Turner's stable and sell him. "I have been a heavy charge unto my friends, and am like to be heavier," he explained painfully. "And in any case I cannot keep the horse, for he is known as mine, and might draw suspicion to me. He's a good beast and should fetch a fair price. Only try your best, Corporal, to sell him unto some one will use him kindly."

Ridydale demurred, then yielded; and before he left Oxford, brought Hugh five sovereigns, the purchase money. Then there was an explanation with Strangwayes, who was downright angry, but finally laughed at himself. "Only a fool would quarrel with such a remnant of a fellow as you look now," he concluded.

Hugh felt the term was justified the first time he dragged on his clothes, which seemed cut for a lad of vastly greater brawn, and, contriving to hobble into the adjoining chamber, got sight of himself in the glass. Eyes, mouth, and a raw scar sheer across his left cheek, seemed all that was left of his face, and his close-cut hair added to the unfamiliarity of his look. "Scars are good adornments for a soldier," he said bravely, but he tried in vain to find a complimentary phrase for the painful stiffness that lingered in his thigh.

By dint of stumbling about his chamber, however, the lameness wore off, till he could walk with some surety of not falling against the furniture; and then there came a night he never forgot, when Strangwayes helped him carefully down the stairs, and, pacing slowly across the bowling green, they sat down on a bench that Hugh remembered. It was a clear spring evening, with the stars numerous and bright, and an earthy smell in the soft air. Hugh felt the ground beneath his feet once more, and stared at the poplars that still looked bare in the nighttime, while his heart grew full at the thought that he was alive to enjoy the spring and all the deeds that were yet to do. He spoke it all out, as he leaned against Strangwayes, by saying: "I am well again now, Dick. When shall we be off to the North?"

"North? Not for you at present, lad," Strangwayes replied. "You're no figure for a camp yet. So I am going to carry you to a farm called Ashcroft, somewhat toward Warwickshire, where dwells a distant kinswoman of Sir William Pleydall and of my mother. 'Tis a good, bluff widow, whom I shall bid keep you well hidden, and see you go to bed betimes, and do not run off to kill Roundheads till I give the word. When you have back your strength again, you shall join me in Yorkshire, and we'll go a-soldiering together again."

For the next week Hugh felt he had something to look forward to, though expectation made the days even more tedious. With long intervals of rest, he furbished up his sword and spurs, and, when that interest failed, spent much time in devising a name to assume till his peace was made with his Majesty. Strangwayes had announced early that he meant to go by the name of Henry Ramsden, and there was an end of it; but Hugh had an unaccountable feeling that he did not wish to take any one of the common names that men he knew had borne, and bestow it on a hunted duellist. He finally ended by calling himself Edmund Burley, but it was a long process of selection, and the choice was made only on the day he left the "Sceptre."

They made their start about midnight, when the road was quiet, and the houses in the fields beyond the alehouse were all black. Two horses were fetched them at the side door, the drawer held a lantern half screened with his hand as they mounted, and the host wished them God-speed in a guarded, low voice. Then they paced softly into the highway and headed northward under the starlight. At first Hugh sat straight, and would gladly have talked with Dick to tell him how easy, after all, he found the exercise. But Dick would have no speaking till almost cock-crow, when they were riding through a stretch of lonely fields, and by then no jauntiness was left in Hugh, only dull pain and faintness, so he had no will to say anything except, "Thank Heaven!" when Strangwayes, fairly lifting him off his horse, half carried him into a dwelling-place.

There he spent the day, sleeping some and for the rest lying still as he was bidden, till twilight came on and once more they got to saddle. A little fine rain was sifting down now, and the cold wet on his face refreshed Hugh somewhat, but even then, when they halted at last at the gate of a lonely farm enclosure, he was drooping over his saddle-bow. He noted of the house only that there was a green settle in the living room, the arm of which was of just the right height to rest his head upon, and the loud-voiced woman who had roused up to greet them held a guttering candle so he was assured the dripping wax must soon burn her fingers.

After that he remembered Dick helped him to bed in a little upper chamber; the sheets felt good, and he shut his eyes to keep out the troublesome candlelight. "Rain or no, I'm going to push on for Sir William's house in Worcestershire," Dick was saying. "You're safe here with Widow Flemyng, Hugh. And ere long I'll have you with me again. God keep you till then, old lad!" He bent down and kissed Hugh, who hugged him with a sudden childish feeling that he could not let Dick go.

So he turned over with his face in the pillow, broad awake now, and he heard Dick's boots creaking down the stairway. He lay listening alertly for more, but he heard only the spatter of rain upon the window.

CHAPTER XV

THE LIFE OF EDMUND BURLEY

At one end of the bench outside the garden door of Ashcroft, Widow Flemyng's great black cat lay sunning himself; at the other end Hugh Gwyeth sat hugging one knee, while he wondered drowsily which were the lazier, he or the cat. In the alert blue spring weather the tips of green things were bursting through the soft mould of the garden; the birds were making a great ado in the trees; and in the field beyond the hedge the widow's man, Ralph, was ploughing, and whistling as he ploughed. Only Master Hugh Gwyeth lingered idly on the garden bench and meditatively handled the flabby muscles of his arm till he grew impatient with himself. Three weeks and more he had been at Ashcroft, yet this was all the strength he had gained or was likely to gain with sitting still. He dragged the cat, heavy and reluctant, up from its nap, and was trying to coax the creature to jump over his hands, which at least required a little exertion, when Nancy, the serving-maid, came out to potter about the garden. Spying him, she called: "Don't 'ee vex poor Gib, now. Better get thee into the kitchen; the mistress is at her baking."

Hugh laughed, and, rising leisurely, made his

way down the garden to the rear door. Women were droll creatures, he reflected; his mother, of course, had always treated him with tenderness, but why these strangers should pamper him like a child, and concern themselves about his every movement, was more than he could puzzle out. From the first Nancy had made no end of commiserating him for the scar on his face, and even the widow herself, for all her sharp ways, had been melted to pity, when she came to examine his wardrobe. "Well, well, well! when did a woman put hand to these shirts?" she had cried, whereat Hugh informed her blushingly that 'twas his custom to have his shirts washed till they grew too tattered to serve even under a buff jacket, and then he threw them away. "You poor thriftless child!" sighed the widow, "sure, you're not fit to be sent to the wars." So she mended his shirts and stockings, and, when that way of showing her motherly care failed, brewed him ill-tasting concoctions of herbs, which Hugh swallowed courteously, though with inward protests against this expression of good-will. He was far more grateful when her kindness finally took the form of cooking him such food as he liked, and pressing him to eat at all times, for his illness had left him with an alarming appetite, which without such connivance could never have been decently satisfied.

He halted now, as he had often done, with his elbows on the sill of the opened window in the long kitchen, and took a sweeping survey of the dressers and the fireplace and the brick oven. Just by the window stood a table at which the

Widow Flemyng, with her sleeves tucked up and her broad face flushed, was rolling out pastry. "I marvel you've not been here before," she said gruffly, as she caught sight of him; "where have you been all this morning now?"

"Teasing the cat," Hugh answered. "Before that I was down through the meadow—"

The widow paused with her rolling-pin suspended. "That meadow again? And no doubt you wet your feet!"

"On my word, good widow," Hugh laughed, "my kinsfolk have trusted me abroad without a nurse for several years now."

"The more fools they!" she replied, smacking the pastry smartly once more.

Profiting by the pause, Hugh reached one arm in at the window and helped himself to a strip of pie-crust, all hot and newly baked, that lay there; he might repress his early fondness for honey and jam, but crisp pastry was still too great a temptation for him to resist.

"That's a right Roundhead trick to come thieving at a poor woman's window!" said the widow.

"Was there never such a thing as a Cavalier thief?" Hugh suggested.

"I never speak treason, sir. There do be some that say there is a garrison yonder at Woodstead Manor that never was known to pay for what it lives by, but I speak no ill of the king's men, you'll note."

Hugh had cause enough to note and remember the conversation a few days later. Of a dull gray afternoon he had taken himself to his chamber, dutifully to practise thrusts with his sword at a round mark on the wainscot, an exercise which proved tedious, so he was glad enough when a noise of horses stamping and men calling in the yard below gave him an excuse for running to the window. At the front of the cottage nothing was to be seen, so, flinging on his coat, he ran downstairs into the kitchen, whence came the sound of high talk. Bursting into the room, he found Nancy crouched by the fireplace, and Ralph skulking by her, while at the door stood Widow Flemyng, arms akimbo, in hot discourse with a cross-eyed trooper, who wore the king's colors.

"I tell you, it shall not be put up!" the man was blustering. "We'd scarce set foot in your stable when your rascal would be breaking a stave across Garrett's head."

"And I tell you, you shall put up with it!" retorted the widow. "Do you think to come plundering decent loyal bodies, you minching thieves? Not a step do you stir into this house. Reach me hither the kettle, you white-livered Ralph."

Hugh prudently got the kettle into his own hands, then presented himself at the door with the query, "What's amiss?"

"Here are three rogues from Woodstead who seek to plunder the very horses from my plough," replied the widow, clapping hands on the kettle. "Now come in if you dare, the pack of you!"

But Hugh stayed her arm, while he looked out and got the situation. In the open space between the rear door and the stable three horses drooped their heads, and by them lingered two dragoons, one heavy and surly, the other a thin-faced fellow, who, looking sharply at Hugh, nudged his comrade. It seemed just an ordinary small foraging band, who were going beyond their authority, so Hugh stepped out and confronted the cross-eyed man with a stern, "What's your warrant for this?"

"King's service, sir," the other replied, gazing at him a little doubtfully.

"'Tis service that will profit you little if it come to your captain's ears," Hugh answered. "There are none here but loyal people and friends to the king. Best take advice and go back empty-handed. 'Twill be for your good in the end."

Just there a hand was clapped heavily upon his collar; instinctively Hugh was ducking to wrest himself clear, when the cross-eyed man, too, caught him by the throat of his jacket, and, realizing the uselessness of a struggle, the boy held himself quiet. "We'll go back to Woodstead right enough, sir," spoke the thin-faced trooper, who had first seized him. "But you'll go with us, Master Gwyeth."

"My name is Edmund Burley," Hugh replied stoutly, though the heart seemed all at once to have gone out of his body.

"Well, you've enough the look of the other gentleman for Lord Bellasis to pay ten pound for the sight of your face. You can explain to him who you are, sir," scoffed the thin-faced man. "Fetch a horse from the stable for him, Garrett."

After that, as in an ugly dream, matters went without Hugh's agency. He felt his arm ache in the hard grip of the cross-eyed man, which he had no hope to shake off; he heard the widow in heated expostulation with the thin-faced trooper, assuring him the gentleman had dwelt with her near six months, and could not have had a hand in the mischief they charged him with; he saw Nancy come out, all blubbering, to bring him his hat, and he said, "Why, don't cry over it, wench," and wondered at the dull tone of his voice. It seemed an interminable time, but at length one of the plough horses was led out, all saddled, and, mounting as they bade him, he rode away with them in the gray of the afternoon. As they passed out from the yard he heard the door of Ashcroft slam, and by that he knew the widow was much moved.

Then, turning eastward, they trotted slowly across gray fields, a trooper on either side Hugh's horse, and he went as they guided. For he took no heed to them, as he told himself that Dick Strangwayes was far away in the North, Sir William busied at Tamworth, and in Oxford there was not a friend to aid him. Already he seemed to feel the chill of the cells in the old Castle at Oxford, and to see a room full of stern men who bullied and frightened him; after that he thought to hear the cart jolting beneath him across the stony streets, while the people ran and pointed at him; and then he felt a rope about his throat. He tried helplessly to battle off such thoughts, but they still pressed upon him till his head was stupid with turning them over, and, listening uncomprehendingly to the talk of those about him, he rode in a sort of daze.

The afternoon grew grayer and grayer, and was merging into twilight when they rode through a poor village, beyond which, upon a barren swell of highland, they came to a stockade flung around a small manor house. They crossed a rough bridge over a moat, and so, keeping to the left of the house, drew rein at length before a great stable. "Yon's the captain, now," spoke the cross-eyed man, peering into the dark of the building.

"Looking to the cocks, I'll be bound," muttered he of the sharp face.

"What dog's mischief have you been loitering about, you knaves?" came from within the stable, and the voice was one Hugh remembered.

"Captain Butler!" he cried, flinging himself from the saddle, and, stumbling through the door, near embraced the big Irishman who came to meet him.

"Good faith, 'tis not—" Butler began.

"I am Edmund Burley," Hugh interrupted feverishly. "Sure, you remember me, sir?"

Butler pulled him outside, where the light was clearer, and after that instant's pause turned upon the troopers with a violent demand as to what they meant. One replied, "'Tis he who killed Master Bellasis;" but the captain cut him short with a volley of abuse, that they durst hale thither an innocent man and a friend of his, too, and followed it with threats of a flogging to them all and bluster and oaths, till the three were cowed into a frightened silence.

"Well, I'll be easy with you this time, you rogues," Butler resumed after a moment, "for Master Burley is a merciful man, and I'm thinking would be better pleased that you went free. And, faith, he bears so little malice he wishes you all to drink his health." Thus admonished, Hugh pulled three shillings out of his pocket and tossed them to his late captors before Butler led him away to the house. "Come have a drink with me, Burley," he said, and added, with a chuckle, "I take it you need it."

"That was a narrow escape, eh, Gwyeth?" he spoke later, as Hugh was swallowing down a bumper of Spanish wine in the west parlor of the house.

"Narrow as I ever wish," Hugh replied truthfully.

"I think my fellows will hold their tongues now, betwixt threats and bribes," Butler went on. "But after this you'd best do as you should have done at the first, shelter yourself among honest soldiers, who'd die ere they'd let a comrade come to harm, just for spitting a paltry civilian."

In the end Hugh thought it best to take the advice; if he returned to Ashcroft there was no reason that Cavalier marauders should not stray thither again, and a second apprehension might not end so happily. Then, besides, he was glad, after his weeks of illness and dependence, to be once more among men, who accepted him as an equal and did not fret him with constant care. Holding this feeling rather ungrateful, he took pains to write a very civil and thankful letter to the Widow Flemyng, which George Allestree conveyed to her, when he rode to Ashcroft with one of the men to fetch away Hugh's clothes and accoutrements.

Allestree had welcomed Hugh boisterously, although he had an alarming habit of almost forgetting to call him Burley; the blue-eyed Irish volunteer, Mahone, received him with open arms; and even the lieutenant, Cartwright, unbent a little toward him. Before a fortnight was out Hugh understood, for by then he felt he could have fallen on the neck of the meanest scamp, just for joy at sight of a new face in the garrison. Woodstead lay close upon the borders of Warwickshire, where the rebels were up in strength, so none were allowed to venture forth far from the house. All day long there was nothing to do but to walk up and down the cramped enclosure, to converse with the troopers as to sick dogs and lame horses, or to watch Butler's cocks mangle each other in fight, till in sheer disgust Hugh turned away. But within the house he found still less amusement; there was not even a Gervase Markham or a Palmerin to read, so he was reduced to persuading Allestree or Mahone into fencing with him, and, that failing, could only play at cards or watch the others at dice, and listen to Cartwright's same old stories or the everlastingly same chatter of the younger men.

Once, to be sure, there came a day of excitement, when a part of the troop prepared to ride away to forage in the hostile country. They set forth bravely in the mid-afternoon, and till they were lost in dust Hugh, with neither a horse to ride nor sufficient strength for the work, watched them wistfully from the entrance gate. Then he loitered away to his lonely supper with Cartwright, who cursed the luck that left him behind to command the garrison, and drank so deeply Hugh must call a man to help him to bed. Next day Butler and his men came back, noisy and victorious, with cartloads of grain and much miscellaneous plunder that the common soldiery had taken to themselves. They brought also a Roundhead lieutenant, half-stripped, grimy, and sullen, whom Butler clapped into an obscure room on a spare diet till he could find leisure from his more serious affairs to look to him. For the captain had laid hands on a considerable amount of strong waters, so for two days there was high carousing at Woodstead, which shocked Hugh, used though he had become among these comrades to the sight of hard drinking.

While Butler and his officers shouted and smashed glasses below stairs, and the men in their turn let discipline slip, Hugh, in the hope of getting some tidings of his Oldesworth kindred, bribed his way in to speak with the Roundhead prisoner. The man was defiant at first, then more communicative when Hugh smuggled him in some bread and meat, but, being of a Northamptonshire regiment, he could give little of the information Hugh sought, save that he had heard of Captain Thomas Oldesworth and had had speech with Hugh's other uncle, Lieutenant David Millington, who was in garrison with his company of foot at Newick in Warwickshire. For his Roundhead kinsfolk's sake Hugh lent the lieutenant a coat, and, when Butler, in a shaky, white state of sobriety, packed him off under guard to prison at Oxford, gave five shillings to the corporal who had charge of the squad, and urged him to use the prisoner as civilly as he could. Considering the temper of the squad, however, and the fact that his old acquaintance, the surly Garrett, was one of them, Hugh decided those five shillings had probably been expended for nothing.

Near a week later the men came back, and, in his joy at any new sight in his monotonous life, Hugh turned out to meet them. He counted them idly, as they came pacing in at the gate, till his eyes fell upon a horse that Garrett led, a bay horse, all saddled, which put up its head and whickered. "Bayard!" Hugh cried, plunging into the press, and, getting the horse clear, fair put his arms about its neck in the face of the whole garrison. "Where did you find him?" he questioned Garrett a moment later, sharply, to preserve his dignity.

The man explained they had come home by a way that took them near Ashcroft, for he held there might be letters Master Burley would gladly pay a price for, and there they had found both a letter and the horse, which had been waiting him some days.

Hugh paid generously, the more so as he saw the letter was directed in Dick's black hand; that made the sending of Bayard no longer a mystery, for doubtless Dick would have him come northward now and so had sent him the horse. He could hardly wait to see the beast stabled before he ran up to the chamber he shared with Allestree, and tore open the letter that should summon him. Then he read:—

SWEET FRIEND:

It doth grieve me to bring you aught of disappointment, but patience perforce, lad. Sir W. hath need of ammunition and of fieldpieces, so he hath commissioned me, because of old acquaintance in those parts, to go into the Low Countries and see what may be procured. I would I could take you with me, but my time is short, for the ship only waits a prosperous wind. When my task yonder is done I shall come quietly to the place you know of to confer with Sir W. I will convey you a word, and if you will join me there we will try another bout with Fortune together. Till then you were best keep yourself close. There is a rumor that the lord you know of hath no such big voice in the king's counsels as he used. Time, then, and patience may bring all right with us. Commend me to good Mistress Flemyng, and be assured at longest I shall send for you ere the end of summer.

Your very loving friend,
HENRY RAMSDEN.

NEWCASTLE, May 20th, 1643.

That night Hugh ate no supper. Sitting on the broad window-bench he watched the sunlight wane upon the floor, and the twilight fill in the chamber, and from time to time, till it was quite dark, he re-read the letter. In those hours he came to realize how much he had lived on the expectation that any day Dick might call for him, and he sickened at the thought of the dull, hateful days of inactivity before him, for now he must school himself to endure the long three months of summer with Butler's crew. Below he could hear the officers singing over their wine, and, fearing lest Allestree might come half-drunk to urge him to the table and jeer at his sorry silence, he slipped out by the back way to the stable, where till bedtime he tried to find some comfort in petting Bayard.

Next day life was running its old round, save that the hope which before had made it tolerable was gone. That week Hugh discontinued fencing; the weather was over-hot, and besides, what use to drill himself for action, when Dick had no need of him, and his present companions were content to idle? Instead of using the rapier, he set himself to watching Allestree and Mahone at dice, and at length came to take a hand himself. It was an ill memory to him afterward, those feverish summer mornings when, sitting in their shirt-sleeves, they threw and threw, sometimes with high words and oaths, sometimes in silence, save for Allestree's half-laugh when he made a winning cast. Fortune varied, but in time there came a day when Hugh got up from the table, and, thrusting his hands into two empty pockets, slouched off with his head down. He heard Allestree say, "I hate a fellow who loses with ill grace," and Mahone call, "Hi, Ed! Come back. Don't give over, man, as long as you've a shirt to stake. Put up your horse now."

But Hugh shook his head. Though he had diced away every penny he possessed, and with it every hope of setting out by himself to seek other harborage than Woodstead, he would not risk his horse and sword. Not twenty-four hours later he had cause to rejoice at having kept his equipments, for at the mess table Butler announced briskly that next day the troop would ride a-foraying into Northamptonshire, to a little village called Northrope, where corn could be got in plenty. "And wine from a brave tavern there," Allestree whispered Hugh; "Else the captain would not be so forward in this business."

But in his joy at having a hand in active service once more, the end of the expedition mattered nothing to Hugh. Before noon next day he had his buff jacket on and his sword slung over his shoulder, then fretted away the long hours of expectation by tramping about the enclosure, settling Bayard's saddle, and listening to Allestree's proffered bets on the success of the night's work. The sun had set behind the low green hills, when at last Butler led half his troop forth from Woodstead, with Allestree to keep the rear and Mahone and Hugh to put themselves wherever they were bid. In spite of the gathering twilight the air was still heavy with the sweltering heat of the day, and the dust that was beaten up by the feet of the horses prickled and stung. Before the first mile was out Hugh had flung open his coat, and was more disturbed at Bayard's sweating than at the thought of the skirmish that was to come.

The night air was cooler and the stars were out thick, when at length the word ran through the line that Northrope lay over the next swell in the plain. Falling in with the squadron behind Butler, who was to sweep around and attack the village from the east while Allestree rode in at the west side, Hugh drew away noiselessly from the rest of the troop, and at a swift canter passed through a field into a piece of spicy-smelling woodland. Beyond that they rode softly along a stretch of sandy road, and at last halted upon the brow of a hill, beneath which the dark roofs of cottages could be seen. At a whispered command from Butler Hugh ranged himself among the corporal's guard who were to keep the hill and stop whoever fled that way, while the rest of the dragoons fell into place behind the captain. Then the leader turned to a trooper, who, swinging his dragon to his shoulder, fired into the air. An instant, and far to the west another shot replied, Butler shouted to charge, and with his men at his heels galloped away down the hill.

Below in the village Hugh heard the sound of clattering hoofs, of shouts of attack, and shriller cries. A moment later, and, as he gazed, he saw over to the west a reddish gleam that broadened and brightened. "They've fired the village," muttered one trooper, and the rest grumbled subduedly that all within the scurvy place would be burned ere they came to share the plunder.

The moments ran on, while the fire rose and sunk again, till Hugh judged the night more than half spent. Still none had fled in their direction; the men were restless at their useless stay, and Hugh himself had grown to hate this waiting, for it left him time to reflect, and to compare this raid with the daylight fighting he had had under Turner. For all the ugly sights of plunder to be seen he felt it a relief when the corporal gave the word to descend into the village, and gladly as the rest he trotted forward.

Once in among the houses his comrades scattered to plunder, but Hugh, left alone, rode on down the street, which grew lighter with the flare of the burning houses. He had sight of household stuff that littered the roadway; in the lee of a wall he saw a man sitting with his hand pressed to his breast; and down toward the blaze, where was a great yelling and confusion, he made out against the glare the black shapes of men running to and fro. He saw, too, nearer at hand, a flapping sign-board before what seemed an inn, where a noisy crew had possession, and he halted a moment, while he wondered grimly if Butler were not there and if he should report to him. As he hesitated he heard some one shout from an upper window of the cottage on his right, and he let his eyes travel thither. The place looked dark and blank, but as he gazed the door was kicked open and a man came forth, holding by the arm a girl, who dragged back with all her slender strength. "What devil's trade are you about?" Hugh called angrily. "Bring the wench hither."

The man hesitated, then unwillingly slouched nearer. As the firelight flared along the street Hugh saw it was his old enemy, the cross-eyed trooper; then his gaze dropped lower to the pallid face of the girl. At that Hugh sprang from his saddle with a cry, "Lois, Lois!"

CHAPTER XVI

ROUNDHEADS AND CAVALIERS

He had thrust the trooper aside and drawn the girl close to him. "Sure, you do not fear me, Lois?" he urged, for she stood with her hands to her face and her body braced tensely against the pressure of his arm. "I'm Hugh Gwyeth. You've not forgot—"

At that she uncovered her face and stared at him with so piteous a look of fright that Hugh hated himself and all who had had a share in that night's work. "Be off with you." He swung round upon the cross-eyed trooper with some of Allestree's favorite oaths. "The gentlewoman is kin to me. Get you hence and be thankful I let you go with a whole skin."

Then he looked again to Lois, and, noting now that she had no outer covering upon her shoulders, unstrapped his cloak from the front of his saddle and wrapped it about her, drawing the folds up to hide her face somewhat. He felt her hands clutch tremulously at his wrist, and her voice broke into a choking sob: "O, Hugh! In sober truth, 'tis you? You will take care of me?"

"To be sure I will," he said, and, slipping

Bayard's bridle over one arm, put the other about the girl. "Just come with me now."

They walked toward where the cottages were burning, slowly, for Lois staggered as she went, and Hugh, for all his brave speech, was dazed with the necessity of thinking what he was to do for her protection. Woodstead was no place to which to fetch a girl, nor was any other harbor open to him. He halted short in his perplexity, then turned to her with a sudden idea: "Look you here, Lois; would you wish me to convey you unto Newick, to Lieutenant Millington?"

"'Tis thither I was going," she answered faintly.

"Well, you shall be safe there ere to-morrow noon," he assured her. "Just a little time here, and be not afraid."

Thereupon he faced across the street to the house with the sign-board, where he guessed might be wine and Captain Butler. Within were lights and men stamping to and fro, while without at the entrance door lingered others, among whom Hugh caught sight of Garrett, still sober, and seized on him. "I want your help," he said brusquely; "I'll pay you for it ere I die. Procure some sort of white flag, and find me out a pillion for this gentlewoman. Put it on my horse and be ready to ride with me when I bid."

Leaving the man with mouth and eyes open in astonishment, he led Lois into the tavern. Across the corridor a trooper was sprawling, drunk, Hugh saw, as he thrust him aside with his foot to give the girl passage. Inside the common room the floor crackled with broken glass, on the chimney-piece two candles sputtered unevenly, and by the table, a bottle in one hand, a great mug in the other, stood Butler. Hugh felt Lois press closer to him, but he resolutely left her on a settle by the wall and went up to the captain. "I pray you, sir, give me a safe-conduct to pass through the lines with one of your dragoons," he blurted out his business.

Butler cursed him roundly, and Hugh, standing stiffly, heard him out without reply, while in his heart he prayed the ugly fit of drunkenness might speedily give place to the maudlin fit. A heavy stamping made him turn in sudden hope as Allestree reeled in from superintending the seizure of the tavern stores. But one look at the guidon told Hugh he was too far gone to aid him now, so he could only fall back beside Lois, and, taking hold of her hand, bid her wait a little longer and not fear.

Presently, after Allestree had pitched into a chair with his head on the table, Hugh once more made his request to Butler, and once more was gruffly refused. But then, chancing to spy ink and paper on a shelf, he blotted off a safe-conduct, and, again presenting himself to the captain, begged him sign. There were refusals of varying sternness, but with all the obstinacy of his square chin Hugh followed the man up and down the chamber, pen in hand, and, holding his temper well in check for the girl's sake, bore the other's abuse and only prayed him sign. At last Butler, snatching the pen from his hand, splashed a great signature across the sheet. "Take it, in the devil's name, you hell babe!" he cursed.

Hugh thrust the paper inside his coat, and, running to Lois, jostled a way for her out to the open air. By the tavern door Garrett, holding a pike with a white napkin bound to it, was sitting his horse, and by him stood Bayard with a cushion fixed behind the saddle. Hugh helped Lois to her place, then, leaping up before her, rode briskly out from the village.

Not till the sight of the fire and the noise of the shouts of the plunderers were quite lost to them did Hugh let Bayard's eager trot subside to an amble. He turned a little to ask Lois how she fared, and bid her keep the cloak close about her against the damp of the early morning; then he called to Garrett, and, in talking with him of the road they must take for Newick, time enough passed for the stars to grow few in the sky. After that they rode a long space in silence, save for the soft scuff of the horses now and again as they came upon a stretch of sandy road. The sky grew a fainter dun color, and in the east a slit of pale light showed, while in the west a white shred of moon yet lingered on the horizon line. The morning breeze, coming damp on Hugh's face, made him heavy with desire to sleep; only at a splashing sound of water did he rouse up with a jerk to find Bayard knee-deep in a ford and drinking greedily. To right and left the bushes above the stream were dusky, but flecks of lighter gray showed in the water where the road ran down to meet it. " 'Twill be sunrise soon," Hugh said, and shook himself awake.

" Think you, presently, I might have a drink of water ? " Lois asked hesitatingly.

"Why, here and now you shall have it!" he cried, and, flinging his bridle to Garrett, lifted Lois from her place and led her a little upstream within the shadow of the bushes.

As she knelt on the brink and drank slowly from her hand, Hugh had space to note how white her face was and how weary her every gesture. So when she rose he drew her back a little to the roots of an oak tree, where he bade her sit and rest a time. Garrett shrugged his shoulders, when the word was passed to him, then tied the horses and went to stretch himself on the bank farther down-stream. Hugh returned to Lois, and, seating himself beside her, persuaded her to lean against him, till her eyes closed and he hoped that she might sleep. He sat very still and looked sometimes at her brown head against his shoulder, and sometimes at the branches of the oak above him and the clear sky beyond that was growing brighter and taking on a bluish tinge. He listened to the hurry of the brook and the restless stamp of the horses; then, shutting his eyes, he seemed only to see Everscombe manor house and the sunlight upon the eastern terrace.

"Are you asleep, too?" The words were spoken softly, but they startled him through all his body.

"I am awake now, in any case," he replied, and laughed a little with a foolish sort of satisfaction as he looked down at Lois. For the tense look of the night before had left her eyes, and she had again the face of his old comrade at Everscombe.

"Your poor arm will sleep next, Hugh. I am leaning too heavily against it."

"I had not felt it, — if you are content."

Lois smiled slightly and tremulously, then, slipping out one hand, drew her fingers through the wet grass. "There has been a heavy dew," she said irrelevantly, "and it has soaked my shoes, — my shoe, I mean." She let her feet just show beneath her petticoat, and Hugh had sight of one stout shoe and the toe of a small gray stocking.

"You've been tramping with one foot half bare?" he broke out.

"Nay, nay, I have been riding. I knew it not till this morning, so I did not mind. I must have left that other shoe in the closet where I hid away."

"Tell me, Lois, how came you there at Northrope?" he asked, after an instant.

The girl's face lost its flash of gayety. "Why, 'tis only — " she began, and, pulling some blades of grass, twisted them between her fingers without looking at him. "Làst October 'twas, Aunt Delia said perchance I were best now go visit my mother's kinsfolk in Northamptonshire. And last week they said I had best visit her again. O me, I know not why they will not have me! I do not eat so much, Hugh, and I am ready to be of service." She pushed aside his arm and leaned forward with her head upon her knee; by the movement of her shoulders he knew that she was crying.

He realized well why she wept, and he knew, too, there was no help that he could offer; so he only bent forward, and, speaking her name gently, patted her shoulder. He heard her swallow a sob, then, with her head still bowed, she went on defiantly, "So there is nothing to tell, Hugh. A neighbor was riding to Northrope for the day, so they sent me with him and he left me at that cottage. They thought perhaps some carrier might be going to Newick, and would convey me thither; then Lieutenant Millington would find means to despatch me to Everscombe. That is all."

Hugh bit his nails and made no reply. If his own father rejected him, how could he reproach the uncles and aunts who grudged shelter to an orphan girl? Only she was a girl and weak, and somehow they seemed worse than Alan Gwyeth. He fell back on his stock piece of comfort: "You should ha' been a boy, Lois, and then it had all been easy."

"But I have no wish to be a boy," Lois said sorrowfully, as she turned away her face to wipe her eyes.

"Perhaps 'twould not be so pleasant," Hugh admitted, and added, with a thought of Frank, "Young boys are sometimes vexatious."

Lois gave a laugh that was a bit hysterical. "You have grown very arrogant. Prithee, now, tell me all about yourself and how you got that sorry scar."

Hugh hesitated, to collect himself, then set forth at great length what pertained to Strangwayes, and very hastily told her that his father had disowned him. At that her face grew so grave he hurried back to Strangwayes again, and forbore to tell her of the duel. So they talked on till a shaft of sunlight dazzled upon the brook, and the trees cast clean dark shadows on the pathway. "We must ride for Newick," said Hugh, jumping to his feet. "You're not so weary, Lois? Wait till the next village and you shall have wine to hearten you. Perchance you could eat, too?"

"Perchance, if 'twere offered," Lois replied demurely, as she smoothed her hair with her hands.

"It shall be looked to, I promise you," he answered gayly, and walked away. Before he had gone ten paces, however, his gayety was at an end, for he tucked his hands into a brace of bare pockets. He fidgeted a moment by the horses; then, taking his only course, walked over to the surly trooper. "Garrett," he began, in a low tone, "have you money about you?"

"Ay, sir."

"Will you lend unto me?"

"You swore the giving should lie all on your side," the other answered suspiciously.

"I tell you I'll pay," Hugh said angrily; and, seizing on the two shillings the other reluctantly proffered, walked away with his face burning.

It had been a petty incident, but the ill taste of it lingered with him, and took all pleasure from the getting to horse once more. Even the sight of Lois's half-smiling face, and her droll efforts to spare her stockinged foot, could not restore him to his old contented mood. He led her in silence to where Bayard stood, and there she halted suddenly with eyes upon the horse. "Why, 'tis indeed the same," she cried. "'Tis Peregrine's steed they said you —"

"Stole?" Hugh asked sharply. "Ay, 'tis the same."

Then he lifted her to her place, and without a word more set forward.

An hour later, in the full heat of the morning sun, they rode into a little hamlet, where the people stared at the Royalist red sashes, and shouted saucy comments on the strangers. Hugh made his way scowlingly to the village inn, and, helping Lois dismount, led her into the common room, where he called on the hostess to bring wine and white bread for the girl. "Are you going with these ruffians of your own will, sweetheart?" he heard the good woman whisper Lois.

He was turning away impatiently, when, just at the door, he ran upon the tapster. "Draw two mugs of ale for my man and me," he ordered curtly.

"Will I, sir? Who's to pay?" retorted the other. "An you pay, 'twill be the first of your color—"

"Will you talk?" Hugh cried, with an oath; and struck the fellow so he staggered. "Fetch what I bid now," he swore. Then he turned to go back into the common room; and there Lois sat, not eating, but gazing at him with blank, dismayed face.

Without staying to drink his ale, Hugh went out and loitered at Bayard's head, where he kicked up spiteful little spurts of dust and would not stroke the horse. When Lois hobbled out at last in a pair of over-large shoes, he helped her to mount; she did not speak, and he only looked sharply at her, but said nothing. As the roofs of the village sank behind the hill in their rear, however, he turned in the saddle and addressed her almost roughly, " So you are not pleased with me ? "

" Sure, Hugh, I must be pleased; you have used me so kindly — "

" That's a right woman's trick to bungle at a plain 'no,'" he said, with a curt laugh; then started, for tone and laugh sounded to him as an echo of Allestree, whom he had left drunk at Northrope. Putting spurs to Bayard, he pressed on at a reckless pace, so the dust rose thick and white, and turned his throat dry, and sifted in between his collar and his neck. He was hot and weary and wretchedly angry against all the world, especially against Lois Campion, why, he could not tell himself.

In such a mood he cantered into the shadow of the first of a straggling line of cottages, where a sentinel in a yellow sash, springing to the middle of the road, bade him pull up. " Conduct me to Lieutenant Millington," Hugh ordered, showing his safe-conduct; so in a few moments he was riding down the street at an easy pace, with a Roundhead corporal walking at his bridle.

They drew up without the gate of a large, half-timbered house, which set back from the road in a garden of red roses that dazzled drearily before Hugh's eyes. " If you will accept of my aid — " he said brusquely to Lois, and had just swung her down from the horse's back, when he heard the gate clatter open behind him. He turned about, and came face to face with Peregrine Oldesworth.

For an instant they confronted each other without speaking, time enough for Hugh to take note that his cousin wore a pompous great pair of boots and a long sword, and had grown a scrap of dark mustache that made him look older than his years. Then said Peregrine, "Well, have you come to fetch back that stolen horse, Master Thief?"

"The horse is best off with him who has the wit to keep him," Hugh replied quickly. "Be assured I had not come to you beneath a white flag, if it had not been to bring Lois hither."

"And a brave convoy you have had, Cousin Lois," Peregrine said, with a dull flush on his face. "The next time you must roam the country-side, pray you, seek another protector than a scape-gallows like this."

"You know well, Cornet Oldesworth," Hugh retorted, "that I would pay it back to you, if you durst put that term to me in any other place."

"So you'd like to murder me as you murdered Bellasis?"

"Murdered! What do you mean?" The words came faintly from Lois, and to Hugh's fancy she seemed to draw a little from him.

"Maybe he will set it forth to you himself," sneered Peregrine.

"I killed a man in a fair duel," Hugh replied shortly. "I leave you to your cousin's care, Lois." With that he seized Bayard's bridle and turned away, he cared not whither, only he did not wish to see the horror in Lois's eyes.

"Perhaps you'll give your horse a rest here at the stable, sir?" the Roundhead corporal at his elbow suggested civilly. Hugh slouched down the road after him, and scarcely heeded Garrett beside him, chuckling, "Well, sir, I knew from the start you were Master Gwyeth."

"Now you're sure of it, you'd best carry the news to Oxford," Hugh replied; "I cannot buy silence."

After they were into the cool of the black stable and he had seen Bayard cared for, he sat down on a truss of straw and stared at the motes that swam in the sunlight by the open door. His eyes ached with the light and the dust, and his throat was all choked; he crushed the straws between his fingers as he sat, and in this destruction found his only ease.

He roused up as a petty officer entered the stable, who prayed him, from Lieutenant Millington, to come back to the house and dine with the officers of the company. Hugh hesitated a moment, then came, rather sullen and defiant, and after washing the dust from his face entered the dining room. Millington, a heavy, slow man of near forty, greeted him courteously, and presented him to his brother officers, who were distant and suspicious. "You are of Woodstead, are you not, sir?" one asked him, with an implication that made Hugh guess the other held him to have come from a den of all iniquities.

Then they conversed of matters that concerned them, while Hugh swallowed his dinner in silence, with an occasional pause to stare defiantly at Peregrine, who scowled at him from the opposite corner of the table. It was a relief when the meal was ended and he could rise, bent on setting out from the place at once; but Millington bade him step apart with him into an empty parlor. "'Tis an ill report we have had of you this winter, Hugh Gwyeth," he began judicially, as he seated himself by the open window; "can you give me nothing better to bear to Everscombe?"

Hugh stood erect, with a feeling that he was a culprit brought to sentence, and replied that he had only slain a man in a fair fight, and he held that no wrong.

"Perhaps not;" Millington waived the question; "but I tell you, nephew, 'tis not the part of an honest gentleman to be herding with such drunken libertines and cowardly bullies as those that hold Woodstead."

"Mayhap 'tis not the company I would keep of my own will," Hugh admitted, "though they have been kind to me. But 'tis best I lie close just now."

"If you have done no wrong why need you hide yourself?" Millington retorted, with a flicker of a triumphant smile.

"Have me a murderer and a thief, if you will," Hugh flung back.

"Nay, 'tis that I held you a lad of good parts, in spite of your running after these strange gods. That you have dealt so courteously by little Mistress Campion shows you are not all lost yet. But take heed to the associates you keep."

Hugh felt a guilty hotness in his face, but, bracing himself, he listened with respect to all his uncle had to say farther in the same strain, and, when he had done, he replied honestly, "I thank you, sir; methinks you mean all kindly."

So he took his leave, and turned away to summon Garrett; then remembered, and with a downcast look hesitated back to Millington. "An't like you, uncle," he faltered, "I am ashamed to ask it, but I have had to borrow money to provide for Lois, and I promised this fellow of mine reward for aiding me. And I have no money."

"Eh? How do you live, then, sir?"

"I had some. I lost it at dice," Hugh admitted shamefacedly. "On my honor, I never will again."

There was an instant's pause, then Millington said more coldly, "I'll pay the man," and led the way from the house. Hugh, following behind like a chidden child, saw his uncle go to Garrett, who waited with the horses just outside the gate, and saw him fee the trooper; by the man's face he guessed it was done liberally, but he knew the fact that the money came from another's hand must always lower him in the fellow's eyes.

Dreading to meet the trooper's curious look, he was lingering an instant on the garden walk, feigning to adjust his boot-tops, when he heard behind him some one call his name. He would not look up till there came a touch on his arm, and he must raise his eyes to meet Lois's gaze.

"I wanted to thank you, Hugh," she said gently.

"You need not."

"And I wanted to ask your pardon, if I hurt you. Truly, I will never believe you have done anything that is base, whatever they say. Prithee, forgive me, Hugh."

"I should ask you to forgive it that I was so

surly," he hesitated. "And — and next time I meet you, Lois, I'll have mended my manners, so you need not be dismayed. Farewell now." He looked her frankly in the eyes as he spoke, then bent a little and kissed her hand.

He came out at the gate more briskly than he had hoped, and there, by the horses, found Peregrine and Lieutenant Millington in talk. "When you go back to Thomas Oldesworth tell him from me he should have taught you that a white flag protects the bearer," he heard Millington say, and he noted Peregrine had fixed covetous eyes on Bayard. Indeed, as Hugh swung into the saddle, his cousin broke out, "You'll pay me for that horse one day, sirrah."

But Hugh deliberately turned his back upon his bluster, while he bade his uncle a second farewell, then waved his hat to Lois, who still stood among the roses in the garden, and so headed his horse away from Newick.

The shadows of the two horsemen showed long in the late afternoon sun, and lengthened and blended at last into the gray of the twilight. Frogs piped to them in the dusk as they threaded their way through a bit of bog land, and after that they went a long piece in silence under the wakeful stars. Hugh suffered Bayard go slowly, while he felt the pleasant night air upon his face and harked to the hoof-beats, muffled by the yielding road, till at length a light upon a distant hill showed where Woodstead lay. At that the horses freshened their pace, and, with a good flourish, they cantered in at the gate of the manor house and pulled up at the stables.

Bayard once made comfortable, Hugh went slowly back to the house, where he found the officers, with their coats off and the table well stored with glasses, loitering in the west parlor.

"So you're back, are you, sir?" Butler greeted him. "Well, now you've had a safe-conduct and all at your disposal, is there anything else you'd command of me?"

"Nothing, sir," Hugh replied, as he threw off his buff coat. "I'll not need your good offices, for — In short, sir, I'm wearied of hiding, and I want back my own name again. So 'tis in my mind to ride for Oxford to-morrow."

CHAPTER XVII

THE STRANGER BY THE WAY

"You've a gray day for a start and a gallows at the end," Allestree spoke encouragingly, as he lounged in the doorway of the manor house.

"'Twill be profitable to you, Master Gwyeth, to turn your thoughts as you go to composing your last good-night," Mahone paused in lighting his pipe to add cheerfully.

Hugh put his attention to drawing on his gauntlets and made no reply; in the last twelve hours there had been threats and expostulations and jeers enough to teach him that his only course was to be silent and keep to his determination.

"I'll lay you five shillings, George, he loses courage and sneaks back in time for dinner," Mahone resumed.

The blood shot up to Hugh's face; he knew that was what Mahone wanted, and he was the angrier that he had gratified him. He turned sharp away and fumbled at Bayard's headstall till he felt surer of his self-control, then asked stiffly: "Can you tell me if the captain is in the west parlor? I must take my leave of him."

"I don't begrudge you the task," Allestree hinted. "The captain lost his temper at Northrope, because the scurvy little tavern was so ill supplied, and he has not found it again yet. So look to yourself, Hugh."

It did not need Allestree's warning to bring the heart down into Hugh's boots; the mere inhospitality of the closely shut door of the west parlor and the grim tone in which Butler bade him come in were enough to daunt him. The captain had been writing ponderously at the table in the centre of the room, but at Hugh's coming he flung down his pen, and, after surveying him scowlingly, burst out: "You're still set in your folly, then? Well, for Dick Strangwayes' sake I'd fain have saved you, in spite of your cursed sullen ways."

"I have not meant to be discourteous to you, Captain Butler," Hugh protested; "I thank you for sheltering me and saving me that first time, I do thank you heartily. But now I think it better—"

"To seek other company," Butler retorted. "If you were a bit older, I'd be angry with you, sir; and if you were a small bit younger, by the Lord, I'd cuff some wit into you; as 'tis—Well, I'll shake hands, if you wish. On my soul, 'tis pity so decent a lad should not have the sense to keep his head on his shoulders." Thereupon he turned his back, and, with great show of being occupied, fell to his writing, so Hugh, feeling miserably rebuked, had no course but to go quietly from the room.

Perhaps his downcast state touched Allestree a little, for he met him more kindly and spared farther jests while Hugh was mounting Bayard. "Better go to Tamworth if you are ill at ease here," he counselled wisely. "But in any case God speed you and protect you for the sake of the innocence of you."

At this Mahone went into a fit of laughter, from which he recovered only in time to bawl a farewell that reached Hugh but faintly, as he rode out by the sentinel at the gate of Woodstead.

Travelling slowly, to spare Bayard after his heavy work of the preceding day, he came about noon to a cross-road, where for a moment he hesitated: should it be north to seek Sir William's help, or south to put himself into the provost's hands and trust to his own innocence of ill intent to bring him clear? But he soon told himself that, if Sir William had had the power to aid, he would long ago have helped Dick Strangwayes; and, in any case, he had no will to live longer in holes and corners, as if he were indeed the murderer Peregrine had called him. Perhaps he would find friends if he went on boldly. So he jogged southward at an easy pace, so easy, indeed, that he gave up all idea of reaching Oxford that day. "And we don't care to lie in the fields, Bayard," he talked softly to the horse. "And we've not a penny to our names to hire lodgings. What say you if we swerve off to Ashcroft? Perhaps they'll shelter us this night."

At heart he knew they would, yet, remembering how carelessly he had departed thence, he felt a little backward about presenting himself to the Widow Flemyng. His pace lagged more and more as he drew near the farm, and he might have halted short to reconsider, had not the spat of rain upon the white roadway warned him to look to the sky. There the clouds were black with storm and thunder, so, having no wish to come at last to Oxford all bedraggled, he spurred forward hastily and galloped Bayard into Ashcroft stable just as the rain began pelting down.

Storm or no storm, so soon as he had delivered over the horse to Ralph's care, he put his head down and ran for the house, where he pitched blindly in at the kitchen door. He heard a shriek from Nancy, "Preserve us! mistress, 'tis Master Burley come back," and then the widow's peremptory tones: "Take those boots off right where you stand, sir, else you'll track mud over my new-sanded floor."

Hugh balanced uneasily on one foot as he obeyed, then asked meekly if he mightn't be permitted to sit down now?

"Oh, at table, is it?" questioned the widow, bustling to the nearest cupboard. "Hungry as ever, I take it?"

"Always," Hugh replied, and fetched a stool to the table against the kitchen wall, where he was presently busy with a cold capon.

In the midst the widow paused at his side and laid a folded paper by his trencher. "'Tis well you came hither now, Master Burley," she said. "This was fetched from Tamworth for you by a close-mouthed trooper three days agone. I was almost resolving me to get upon the old mare and ride to seek you at Woodstead. I am no chit of a girl to fear those saucy knaves."

Hugh laughed, and with frank curiosity unfolded the paper; within were two gold sovereigns, but not a sign of writing, though he turned the sheet over and over. "What does this mean?" he asked blankly.

"I've told all I know," replied the widow. "I did my best to learn more of the fellow who brought it."

Hugh finished his dinner in silence, while he turned over various solutions. Dick was out of the kingdom, and in any case he would never have sent the coins and no word; but Sir William had supplied them with money while they lay hid at the "Sceptre"; or perhaps Frank, with his well-filled pockets and his boyish fondness for mystery, had had to do with this. At any rate the money was there in his hands and made his journey easier, so much so that he felt, had he been superstitious, he would have hailed it as a sign that he was to go on to Oxford as he had started.

Yet when the twilight shut in, gray with drizzling rain, there came on him a heavy feeling of uncertainty; his own determination, though he felt so sure of it, weakened a little before the memory of the opposition of all his friends. In such a mood he loitered into the cottage parlor, where, finding the Widow Flemyng sitting idle in the dusk, he drew up a stool and blurted out to her his true name and how matters stood with him. "I fear you'd not have cared to harbor me, had you known what a charge I lay under," he concluded humbly.

"Why, child, I suspected all along," the good woman hastened to reply, and Hugh, staring dutifully at the gray rain outside the lattice, thought it wise not to contradict her. It gratified him, too, as she continued speaking, to find she did not hold him a fool for his resolution. Indeed, she said emphatically no worse harm could befall a decent lad at Oxford than at Woodstead, and in any case she was well assured no one would ever have the heart to hang him. "You were best cast yourself on the king's mercy," she ended. "Now had you great friends at court, or could get to have audience with his Majesty."

"Did you ever hear the ballad of 'Johnny Armstrong'?" Hugh asked. "Dick used to sing it. There was a man sought the king for pardon and he got little good by it."

All the same her assurances made him more confident in himself, so he slept that night untroubled and woke ready for whatever the day might bring. Perhaps it was the widow's continued encouragements, perhaps it was the good breakfast he made, or perhaps the sight of the sun struggling through the watery clouds, that served still farther to put him in high spirits. Be as that may, he took a gay farewell of Widow Flemyng and of Nancy, and cantered out by the pasture lane at a hopeful pace, as if he were eager to cover the distance to Oxford and whatever waited him there.

The rain of the preceding day had laid the dust well, and left in the air a lingering fragrance of moist earth and beaten grasses that made it a temptation to slacken speed along the country road. In the hedges by the wayside the honeysuckle was still dripping with wet; Hugh pulled a tuft of blossoms as he passed, and crushed them slowly in his bare hand. How sweet and good was life in summer time, he reflected, and then he flung the blossoms away and, whistling persistently, thought no more, for his mind was all made up.

At the first tavern he came to he bought him a draught of ale, bravely, now there was money in his pocket, then trotted on without halt till past noon. By that the sun had burnt away the clouds, and the still heat made the journey less pleasant; so, coming upon a sleepy village with a small neat inn, the "Bear and Ragged Staff," Hugh thought well to rest the midday hours and get food for himself and his horse. The fear of being recognized and apprehended before he should have a chance to give himself up made him call for a private room, where he ate alone, except that the host bustled in to serve him and retail a variety of gossip. Oxford was near enough for the daily news to pass to the village, so Hugh heard a deal of authentic information of how the king was said to lean now to the counsels of the hot-heads and to the army, and how the royal troops might any day set forth to take in Bristol. He scarcely heeded more, for the talk of Oxford had turned his thoughts again to what was before him. Where should he eat his next meal, he wondered, with a remembrance of the grim Castle; and then, impatient at his own faltering, he jumped up hastily, and, paying his reckoning, went down to the little court of the inn, where he bade them saddle Bayard at once.

The horse had been led out into the shade of an open shed, and Hugh was lingering by the stirrup to fee the hostler, when outside the gateway sounded a great clattering of hoofs, and a gentleman came spurring in upon a white horse, that stumbled on three legs. "Have me hither a fresh mount, briskly, you knaves!" he shouted, flinging a handful of loose coin among the stable-boys and loiterers. Then, as he put eyes on Bayard, he swung himself from his saddle. "This beast will serve my turn," he called to the host, who had just showed himself at the door of the inn.

"By the Lord, this beast will not serve your turn!" Hugh cried hotly, and, catching hold on Bayard's bridle, flung himself before the horse in time to confront the stranger. "This is no post-horse, sir, but mine own."

The other turned sharp away with a shrug of the shoulders; they were broad shoulders, Hugh noted, and the rough gray coat fitted them ill. "Put saddle to another horse at once," the man bade.

"There is no other at hand, your Honor," the host apologized, as he ventured out into the court. "All are at the smith's. Belike in a half-hour, your Worship —"

"Enough," the other interrupted him, and strode back to Hugh. "What will you sell this beast for?" he asked curtly.

"Not again for all the gold in England," Hugh replied, tightening his grasp on the bridle.

"My faith, sir, I've no intent to knock you down and steal the horse," the other answered, with a short laugh.

His cool tone allayed the heat of Hugh's anger sufficiently for him to note the man more closely now, and he perceived he was not above three or four and twenty, of a tall strong build, with sharp eyes. Hugh caught his breath and stared frankly, while his mind jumped back to his first day at Oxford, when he and Allestree, standing upon the steps, had watched the king and his retinue ride by. The stranger had turned his back upon him now, and drawn over to the centre of the court, but his voice was loud, and Hugh could hear him bidding the hostler run out and procure him a farm-horse or aught that went upon four legs. With a sudden desperate impulse Hugh thrust forward and spoke boldly, "If it like you, sir, you may have my horse now."

"Your price?"

"No price. I'll lend him unto you."

"You've changed your tune quickly, sir," said the man, coming back to Bayard's side.

"I'm thinking 'tis likely your business is of more weight than mine, your Highness," Hugh answered, in a tone that sank to a whisper.

"So you know me?" asked the stranger, with his foot already in the stirrup.

"I can guess, sir."

"Spare guessing, then, for taxing the brain," retorted the other, as he settled himself in the saddle. "Give me your name, though, sir; I'll not forget your service."

Hugh hesitated an instant, then replied, "Hugh Gwyeth."

"I've heard that name. Perhaps you're kinsman to him that killed Bellasis' son?"

"I — I am the man that killed him, sir."

"You? The deuce you are!" the stranger

broke out; and, to Hugh's amazement, he did not look horrified, but more as if he were inclined to laugh. "Come seek me to-morrow morning at my quarters," he said abruptly, then, gathering up the reins, went out of the inn yard at a gallop.

Hugh stood gazing blankly after him, and could not decide whether to be elated or dismayed, for he knew the stranger was Prince Rupert, and he was to have audience with him next morning. Carry his cause to the king, the widow had counselled him, Hugh reflected, and he tried to smile at the remembrance, though his heart was sober and anxious.

Just there the host interrupted him; what was his pleasure now? Surely he would not attempt to make his journey with the lame horse? "No, let him rest," Hugh ordered; "I'll venture him in the morning. For now give me a chamber; I'll lie here this night."

He was early astir next day, for, though the way to Oxford was short, he was not sure of his mount, and, in any case, he was burning with desire to present himself before the Prince and know the worst that was destined for him. The white horse still went lame with a strained foreleg, but, sparing him as much as he could, Hugh contrived about eleven of the clock to pace slowly into the city. Before he entered the suburbs he had flung on his cloak, in spite of the heat, and pulled his hat low on his forehead; but still he was nervously alert to avoid the fixed gaze of those he met, and he dreaded any delay in the street. By dint of such precautions, perhaps, he came at last unchallenged to Christ Church, where he remembered Prince Rupert had his quarters.

The groom who took his bridle eyed him sharply, and, once across the quadrangle and within the broad hall, a trig gentleman usher looked askance at his worn boots and shabby buff coat. Hugh had too much upon his mind, however, to trouble for his poor attire. He sat uneasily in the great chair to which he had been motioned, and studied the sunlight that fell from a long window high up toward the roof of the hall, till the usher came at last to bid him follow. Hugh trudged obediently up a great flight of stairs that creaked alarmingly, and, as he went, wondered why there was an emptiness where his heart ought to be, and his throat felt all choked up.

A great door was swung open, he remembered; then he was within a long sunshiny chamber, with heavy table and big dark chairs, the usher had gone, and he was left face to face with his Highness, the Prince, and another youngish gentleman, who sat at opposite sides of the table with a jumble of papers betwixt them. "You keep your time well, Master Gwyeth," spoke the Prince, and put by a paper like a map he had been studying.

"Your Highness bade me," Hugh stammered.

"So 'twas you killed Bellasis' son," the other repeated, still amusedly. "Lay down that order, Grandison. I want you to have a look at this desperate duellist."

"That boy, your Highness?" drawled the man at the table.

The blood came hot into Hugh's cheeks. " I pray your Highness, hang me, if you will, but do not mock me," he blurted out.

"Who speaks of hanging you here, lad?" Prince Rupert answered, in so kindly a fashion that Hugh gazed at him in surprise. "Nay, had I my way, I'd give a captaincy to every man who has the goodness to take off one of these cursed civilians who are always holding our hands. You are of the army, sir?"

"I hope to be, your Highness. I am only a volunteer now."

"'Tis near enough for all soldiers to aid you as a fellow-soldier. — And how think you, Grandison, my Lord Bellasis would take it, if this gentleman received a free pardon?"

"He would deem himself most notably affronted," the other answered soberly.

Hugh made a step forward and let his words come fast: "If it be your Highness's will, if 'tis in your thought to aid me, I do entreat you, let my case go, so far as it concerns me. But there is my friend that went to the field with me, for my sake, and cared for me when I was ill with my hurt afterward. He lost a commission because of me. If there is only one can be pardoned, I beseech your Highness let it be he."

"And how do they call this notable friend of yours?"

"Richard Strangwayes, your Highness. He was lieutenant in the regiment of Sir William Pleydall."

"Pleydall? Ah, your case was brought unto our notice two months back. Ay, surely.

Gwyeth and Strangwayes. Sir William Pleydall was urging your pardon through a certain Captain Gwyeth who came to me."

Hugh dropped his hand down on the back of a chair close by and griped it hard, while he gazed blankly at the Prince, yet scarcely saw him. Captain Gwyeth had been urging his pardon, he repeated over and over to himself, yet could not make it comprehensible. Then he realized that his Highness was speaking again, and he roused himself up to listen. "Two months back that was. Well, there is time for many matters to change in two months. Perchance your business can be settled for you, Master Gwyeth. Only you must promise to fight no more duels," the Prince added, with a laugh in his sharp eyes.

"I will promise, your Highness," Hugh answered soberly.

"And break it, I'll wager. You were ready to draw your sword on a poor dismounted traveller yesterday. Maybe you'd like to have back that horse you'd not take all the gold in England for?"

"If it does please your Highness," Hugh said politely; then added honestly, "I should be loath to part with him."

His Highness laughed outright. "Go to my stable and call for the horse," he bade. "Come hither again in a week or so, and there may be tidings for you. Only see you do not come to court too often, Master Gwyeth; 'twould be a pity to spoil the honest blunt soldier you are like to be with a slippery courtier polish."

Then he turned again to his map in sign of

dismissal, and Hugh somehow contrived to bow himself safely through the door. He was out in the green quadrangle before he got it through his head that Prince Rupert himself would move for his pardon to the king, and then he recollected he had not even said "thank you," and he flushed hot with the consciousness of his own churlishness.

It changed his thoughts a trifle to seek out his way to the stable and claim Bayard, whom he had been ready to give up for lost and was proportionately glad to recover. Once upon the horse's back, he took himself unostentatiously through the streets to the lodgings of his fencing-master, de Sévérac, who received him warmly, when Hugh assured him he was fairly sure of pardon and sought only to have quiet harborage for the week. Those seven days he passed in the dingy sleeping-room behind the fencing-hall, where he studied the pictures in a great French folio, "L'Academie de l'Espee," or entertained de Sévérac in his leisure moments with a full account of the duel with Bellasis. The fencing-master, who took a professional pride in his pupil's success, entreated Hugh not to persist in saying the victory was due solely to Bellasis' carelessness; 'twas just as easy to give credit to himself and those who taught him the use of the rapier.

Thus the week dragged to an end, while Hugh counted the days impatiently, and heard with terror that troops were setting out for Bristol, for in the confusion the great men might well forget his business. At last the seventh day came, and, having put on a clean shirt and brushed his coat, he set out for Christ Church. As he went he tried to steel himself against possible disappointment by telling over the many cases of the ingratitude of kings; but at heart he knew he did not believe so ill of the Prince, and in the end his trust was justified. He had not been kept waiting many minutes in the great hall, when a trim officer came from above-stairs, and, asking him if he were not named Gwyeth, delivered to him a fair great piece of parchment all sealed up. "'Tis my pardon?" Hugh burst out.

The other smiled, not unkindly. "The king of his clemency has been pleased, at his Highness's entreaty, to grant a full pardon to those who had a hand in the death of Philip Bellasis," he explained formally; then added, "Suffer me congratulate you, Master Gwyeth."

In a dazed fashion Hugh shook the other's hand, then came forth from the hall into the open air. There he paused, and pushed his hat well back on his head so all could see his face, then, walking out into the South Street, tramped half across the city. For he need not skulk nor shrink now, he was a free man again; and how stoutly he meant to fight for Prince Rupert, since he could show his gratitude in no other way. Then it came over him that he were best post off at once to Tamworth and thank Sir William Pleydall, who had first begun the movement to relieve him, and thank Alan Gwyeth, who had been Sir William's instrument. Hugh scowled and walked a little slower.

But still all his friends lay at Tamworth, and he would speed a letter thence to tell Dick the good news; so in the end he made briskly for his

XVII THE STRANGER BY THE WAY

quarters. Taking time first to hale out de Sévérac to a fine dinner at an ordinary, where they ate under the full gaze of the town, he got to horse, and, ere mid-afternoon, trotted forth from the city. He calculated he would make the "Bear and Ragged Staff" just about dusk, and, true enough, he rode down the village street while the red flush of the sunset still lingered in the west.

Inside the court of the inn he saw five horses standing, stripped of accoutrements and already half rubbed down by the hostler and his groom. "Take this beast of mine in to make the half-dozen," Hugh bade, and, dismounting, walked leisurely across the court to the side door. His eyes travelled above the door to an open lattice, and, as he gazed, like the flash of a face in a dream, he had sight of Dick Strangwayes.

For an instant Hugh stood petrified while he took in each detail, — Strangwayes' clean-shaven jaw, the sweep of mustache, the bandage about his forehead, even the way in which he leaned heavily at the window, resting one hand against the casement; then he sprang forward, crying, "Dick!"

Right on that Strangwayes flung himself forward half out at the casement, and shouted, "Into the saddle and off with you, off with you!"

CHAPTER XVIII

THE CALL OUT OF KINGSFORD

JUST inside the door of the inn was a steep flight of steps; Hugh tripped over the first, but, almost ere his outstretched hand touched the floor, was on his feet again and rushing up the stairway. As he ran he pulled his sword clear from the scabbard; if matters were so ill Dick wished him thence, he would have need of it. But in the corridor above-stairs all was quiet, he noted in the instant in which he paused, holding his breath, and gazed at the closed doors along the gallery. "Dick!" he called again, so there came a little echo from the end of the corridor. Then he ran headlong for the nearest door, and, dashing it open with his foot, flung himself well into the centre of the chamber. By his very impetus he thrust out of his way a man in a blue livery coat, and, clearing free passage thus, pushed up to the wall and set his back against it. There were three blue-coated serving men in the room, he perceived now, and a gross, short-necked man in a fine riding-suit, who was deliberately bolting the entrance door. Then his eyes rested on Dick, who, seated well away from the window, was leaning back indolently in his chair and tugging at his mustache; only Dick's white face was tense, Hugh saw, and he noted, too, that his friend wore no sword.

It was the short-necked man who broke the instant's expectant hush: "Master Hugh Gwyeth, the tall swordsman? On my soul, I be rejoiced to meet with you. Put down that sword. You are my prisoner."

"What knaves are these, Dick?" cried Hugh, with his sword-hand alert on the hilt.

"Of the old Bellasis breed," Strangwayes answered, and let his hand fall from his mustache with the merest gesture toward the open window, and just a look which bade Hugh take his chance.

"Ay, we apprehend you for the foul murder of my kinsman, Philip Bellasis," spoke the man by the door.

"Is that all?" Hugh asked, with a sudden nervous laugh of relief. He clapped his sword back into the sheath and tore open his coat.

"Seize his arms!" cried the short-necked man.

One of the serving fellows had sprung at him, when Hugh, striving to throw him off, saw Dick come to his feet at a jump and hit out. Somebody bellowed with pain; he found his arm free, and Dick's shoulder pressing against his as they stood to the wall. "Have done, have done!" Hugh cried. "Read you there, Dick."

He thrust the parchment into his friend's hands, and Dick, with a smothered exclamation, broke the seals. An instant of silence came upon the room, as if all had half guessed; only the rustle of the parchment and the heavy movement of the fallen serving man dragging himself to his feet broke the quiet, till Strangwayes spoke with ominous civility, " Will you deign, Master Bellasis, to bestow one glance upon his Majesty's seal and signature ? "

" You'll not deceive me — " said the gross man with much bluster, yet he came hastily, and, gazing upon the paper, read with dropping jaw.

" Now have you any farther business with me, Master Bellasis ? " Strangwayes asked easily. "Speak quickly, ere I go across the corridor to sup with Master Gwyeth."

The other said something that was choked with inarticulateness in his short throat.

" I am ordering my supper now," Strangwayes finished, as he went with much dignity to the door; "and hark you, sir, I want my sword brought back to me ere supper be on the table. For I'll be wishing to fetch it along with me when next I come to seek you."

Then he made Master Bellasis a very low bow, and, catching Hugh by the arm, brought him out into the corridor. Right across the way was a vacant chamber, but almost before they were inside the door Hugh's arms were about Dick, and Strangwayes, with his voice half smothered in the roughness of the embrace, was jerking out: " Heaven forgive Bellasis his other sins for the good turn he did in bringing us together. But 'twould have been a sorry companionship, had you not come so furnished." Thereat he got Hugh by the scruff of the neck and set him down hard on the nearest stool. " Now, you thick-witted rogue," he ordered, "why in the name of reason did you not call out to me from the inn yard and say you had that piece of parchment inside your coat? Here I sat a good half-hour and schooled myself into seeing you laid by the heels along with me. Faith, I'll look to find white hairs in my head to-morrow."

Hugh laughed, because the world was so good now he could do nothing else, then poured out his story thick and fast, — Prince Rupert at the "Bear and Ragged Staff," and behind that Newick, and Woodstead, and Ashcroft, all huddled together. "Lord save us! We must have food to help down such a lump," cried Dick, and, summoning the host thereupon, ordered supper to be ready in quick time.

A drawer came speedily to fetch them candles, and barely had he gone when one of the bluecoats, bowing his way in, handed over to Strangwayes his sword. Dick gave him money, and bade him and his fellows go drink. "A pleasant company I've been keeping, eh, Hugh?" he asked, with a dry smile, as the man backed out. "How came I by it? Alas, a man cannot always choose. I was about my business at The Hague, like a decent gentleman. And that fat calf, Herbert Bellasis, — 'tis a cousin to the whole scurvy connection, — he was there on some mischief, and recognized me."

Just there came supper, but across the table Strangwayes drawled on: "My friend Bellasis feared a young man like myself might come to harm in foreign parts. So he fetched me home."

"Fetched you, Dick?"

"Very simply. He and his bluecoats met me of a dark night in a byway. He was urgent, but

I refused his invitations. Then they picked me up and conveyed me aboard an English ship."

"I don't believe they could," Hugh said bluntly.

"To be sure, they had knocked the senses out of me, else I had not come so meekly. 'Twas there I got this souse in the head; 'tis near healed now. But there were four bluecoats once; one of them is still at The Hague, cherishing a punctured lung; I gave it to him. We had a merry passage over, Hugh; Bellasis and I must share the cabin and eat together. He used to tell me over the wine — 'twas ship's beer and flat at that — how I ought to be hanged, and he hoped to live to see it done. And I used to compliment him on his mad dare-devil courage. For if at five and thirty he durst attack a single man when he had only four to back him, no doubt at seventy he would dare come on with only two to aid. Nay, if he lived long enough, he might yet arrive at fighting man to man. Methinks the length of years he had to wait discouraged him, by the vile temper that put him in. Every pleasure has an end, so at last we made the Welsh coast and posted hither, in the very nick of time, it seems. For, Hugh, after this last exploit of yours, I'd be loath to leave you fending for yourself. Man alive, where do you think you'd be lying now, if you hadn't chanced to take the Prince's fancy?"

Hugh answered submissively that he didn't know.

"Neither do I," Strangwayes retorted grimly. "Nay, nay, don't look conscience-stricken now, for you found the one good chance in a hundred, and it has all come well. But 'tis a blessing for us that his Highness delights to fly about noisily in disguise, instead of plodding soberly about his business. It has been more of a blessing to us, perhaps, than to the kingdom."

"You shall not speak slurringly of Prince Rupert in my presence!" Hugh flared up.

Strangwayes said, with a laugh, that he would make honorable amends by drinking his Highness's health, on his knees, if Hugh desired; so they ended amicably by drinking the health together as they stood by their chairs, then religiously smashed their glasses, and went away to bed.

The early sunrise roused them up to repeat and re-repeat all that had befallen in the months of their separation, a subject which lasted them through breakfast till they quitted the table and went down to the inn yard. "Why, Herbert Bellasis has taken himself and his people hence," Hugh cried, after one glance into the vacant stable.

"I respect wisdom in any man," Strangwayes commented, as he loitered at Hugh's side in among the stalls. "You say the Prince said something to you about not fighting any more? Tut, tut! 'Tis a pity." There he broke off suddenly, "Why, lad, how came old Bayard back to you?"

"Why should you ask?" Hugh replied wisely. "If you don't know, I don't."

"I'd take it kindly if you'd talk reason," Strangwayes said pathetically. "What have I to do with your horse? I don't know even who bought the beast, or whither he was taken from Oxford."

Hugh whistled a stave. "It must ha' been the

same who sent me the two sovereign from Tamworth. Maybe 'twas Sir William, or perhaps Captain Turner."

"Or perhaps Captain Gwyeth," Dick said, after an instant.

Hugh stared blankly a moment, then stamped his foot down on the stable floor. "I won't believe it," he cried fiercely. "I tell you, I'd fling away the money and turn the horse loose, if I believed it."

"Captain Gwyeth had a hand in that first movement to gain your pardon," Strangwayes spoke impartially.

"He was only Sir William's instrument," Hugh insisted, and, without staying to caress the horse, strode out of the stable.

Strangwayes followed in silence; indeed, that instant's jar ended conversation between them till they were back in their chamber, and Dick was busied in writing the news of his whereabouts and the outcome of the Bellasis affair to Sir William. "What use?" urged Hugh, wearied of gazing out of the window with no one to talk to. "We'll be at Tamworth soon."

"Not for a little time," Strangwayes answered, with his eyes intent on the sheet; "I've business here at Oxford."

He did not tell his companion what the business might be, but to all appearances it was furthered by taking a room in Oxford, by dining with various gentlemen and officers, and by devoting some days to a happy and care-free time of which Hugh enjoyed every moment. Not till the morning succeeding the day on which the king left the city to take possession of Bristol did Strangwayes make mention of the northward journey; then he routed Hugh early from his bed with the announcement that they would set out at once. "But first we must eat a meal at the 'Sceptre,'" he concluded. "Fit yourself for the road, Hugh, and gallop thither to order dinner. If I'm not with you ere noon I'll have been called north by the other way, so do you post after as fast as you can. Remember."

An hour later Hugh was gayly riding out by the western road, which he had last travelled with such different feelings, and, coming in the mid-morning to the "Sceptre," ordered dinner grandly. Afterward he loitered down to the bowling green, now all short velvety grass, where he had inveigled Martin, the friendly drawer, into giving him a lesson in bowls, when Strangwayes hailed him noisily from the doorway. "My business is despatched," he said smilingly, as Hugh came to meet him. "After all, we'd best bribe Martin here to eat the dinner for us. We must be off."

They went out from the "Sceptre" at a rattling pace, but the first hill slackened their speed so conversation was possible. Then Strangwayes drawled pleasantly, "I've no wish to deceive you into any danger, Hugh, so you should know I have just fought with Herbert Bellasis."

"Dick!" Hugh cried.

"I was most circumspect," Strangwayes apologized. "I waited till the king was well away, so I might not do it in the very teeth of him. And I did not hurt the fat lump, though I'd fain have done so. I only knocked the sword out of his fist, and then the poor knave was very ready to kneel down and crave my pardon, and swear never so to abuse a gentleman again. Don't put on your Puritan face, Hughie. The fellow had so treated me I could do nothing else."

"Why did you not let me come to the field with you?" Hugh protested. "I take it most unkindly of you."

"I was not going to let my folly spoil your new fortunes," Strangwayes answered. "I think 'twas done so quietly 'twill all blow over, since we have got away to Tamworth. But if not, no charge can come against you."

"Why will you always be sparing me as if I were a child?" Hugh cried, with an angry break in his voice.

"Because some ways you are still just a long-legged, innocent bairn," Dick replied, with a chuckle, whereat Hugh tried to sulk, but that was impossible with Dick talking fast of their comrades at Tamworth. In the end he must talk, too, and laugh with Dick, till he forgot the hurt to his dignity.

By hard riding they contrived before moonrise to reach Ashcroft and rouse up the Widow Flemyng. She fair hugged Hugh, and said of course she knew he'd get his pardon; then fell to cooking their supper, while she talked loudly and contentedly to either of them or both. Next morning they set out in dubious weather, and, going a short stage out of their direct road, passed that night with Butler and his officers, who made much of Strangwayes, though they looked askance at Hugh, and were half loath to forgive him for not getting hanged as they had prophesied. Next evening brought them to Sir William Pleydall's great house in Worcestershire, where his widowed daughter, Mistress Cresswell, gave them a hearty welcome, and, riding thence at sunrise, they came at last unto Tamworth.

It was about four of the afternoon, hot and moist with slow rain, when they rode across the King's Dyke down the narrow High Street of the town. At the door of a tavern Hugh caught sight of a trooper loitering, a shiftless fellow of Turner's company, but he longed to jump down and have speech with the rascal. "Let us push on briskly, Dick," he begged, and so they went at a swinging pace down the street and across the river, where on its height Tamworth Castle towered black against the gray sky. There was a shout of greeting to the petty officer of the watch, a scurrying of grooms in the paved south court of the castle, and then the word of their coming must have travelled at high speed, for barely had they crossed to the main door of the keep when a young officer ran out to meet them, and fell on Strangwayes. "Have you forgot me, Lieutenant?" he cried.

"Sure, no, Cornet Griffith," Dick answered heartily. "Your leg's recovered?"

"A matter of a limp; it does well enough in the saddle. I have back my commission under Captain Turner now, so we'll serve in the same troop. Ay, your lieutenancy is waiting for you."

Talking boisterously, they crossed the great hall that was now a guardroom, and, passing into one of the lesser rooms that served the officers, came upon Michael Turner. It pleased Hugh more than he could show that the captain did not scoff at him, but gave him a half-embrace, saying kindly: "Faith, we're glad to have you back, Gwyeth." Though next moment he had turned away to talk with Strangwayes: "You've come in time for work, Lieutenant. They're drawing all the men they can find westward unto Gloucester, where they say there will be brisk doings. Leveson's and my troops are here in the castle; Gwyeth's has gone a-raiding into Warwickshire; the others are all prancing into the west. We're a scant hundred to defend the whole town, so we'll gladly give you the pleasure of keeping the watch to-night."

Strangwayes came away laughing, and under Griffith's guidance they went down a corridor to a snug parlor, where they had the good fortune to find Sir William, idle for the moment, and unattended save by a single hound. The dog made a dash to meet Dick, barking hilariously the while, so Hugh could only see that the baronet embraced his nephew warmly, and he stepped back a little to leave them to themselves. But Dick haled him forward, and Sir William spoke to him with a gracious sort of welcome that made Hugh stammer, when he tried to thank him for the effort to secure his pardon. "Nonsense, nonsense," spoke Sir William; "we had no need to seek it, sir. You have the wit or the good fortune to be able to maintain yourself without our help. Your father ought to be proud of you." He stopped there, then, as he turned again to Strangwayes, added with a certain diffidence: "I pray you, Master Gwyeth, do not forget to go speak to Francis; he has been in a fit of the sullens since yesternight."

Hugh left the room in some wonderment, and, seizing upon a serving man, was speedily conducted by a passageway, up a flight of stairs, and along a gallery to a closed door. Hugh knocked, and, getting no reply, knocked again, then tried the door and found it bolted within. "Frank," he called, and began shaking the door. "Open to me. 'Tis Hugh Gwyeth."

There was an instant's pause, then a slow step across the floor, and the grate of the bolt in the socket. "Come in, hang you!" Frank's voice reached him.

It was a big cheerless tower chamber, Hugh saw, with heavy scant furniture and windows high from the floor that now gave little light. He stood a moment, half expecting Frank to speak or bid him be seated, but the boy slouched back to the bed that stood in the farther corner, and, without looking at him, flung himself down upon it. "Why, what's amiss?" Hugh broke out, and went to him; now he came nearer he saw Frank had been crying much.

"Nothing," the boy answered, and kept his face bent down as if he were ashamed.

"Tell me," Hugh urged, "you'll feel the better for it. Is it anything because of Griffith?"

"Yes, it's that," Frank cried, raising his head defiantly. "They have taken away my cornetcy, Hugh. 'Tis all along of Michael Turner. And I never harmed him; I had done my best. But he comes to my father; he says he must have a man for his troop. So my father turns his anger on me; he said I was a selfish, heedless child, where 'twas time I bore me as a young man. And then Ned Griffith comes back all cured, and they stripped me of my cornetcy to give it to him." Frank dropped down with his face buried in the pillow. "I pray you, go away," he choked; and, in the next breath, "Nay, come back, Hugh; you've always been my friend."

Hugh sat down obediently by the bed, scarcely knowing what to say, when Frank with his face still hidden suddenly broke out, "Hugh, did you look to have that cornetcy last winter?"

Hugh hesitated: "Yes, I did hope. But I had no reason, 'twas no fault of yours."

"My faith, I had not taken it of you, had I known. I'd not have used a man as Ned has used me, as they all have used me. I have been playing the fool, and they all have been scoffing at me, and I did not know it."

"Sure, you must not take it so grievously, Frank," Hugh urged. "Get up and wash your face and show you care not. You'll have another commission soon, when they see you are in earnest."

Between coaxing and encouraging he got Frank to his feet at last, and even persuaded him to eat supper, which he ventured to order sent to the chamber. Throughout Hugh did his best to talk to the boy of any and all matters that had befallen him, till he roused him to a certain dull interest. "So you've had back your horse all safe?" Frank asked listlessly. "'Twas I procured Captain Gwyeth the name of the place where you were hiding.

He bought the horse when 'twas sold at Oxford, and he wished you to have it, that time when he was working for your pardon. Yes, I know your father well; he is always kind to me, and does not mock me as the others have been doing. I used to tell him all about you, and then he asked me find where you were lodging. I had influence with my father then, so I could learn it," he added bitterly.

All thought of comforting Frank had left Hugh; he tried to listen with sympathy to his piteous complaints, but it was useless; so he rose, and, bidding him as cheery a good night as possible, and promising to come back in the morning, went out from the chamber. At the end of the gallery was a deep window-seat, where he sat down and stared out at the roofs of the town that huddled gray in the twilight, so intent on his own thoughts that he started when Dick touched his shoulder. "How did you leave the poor popinjay?" Strangwayes asked, with a trace of a laugh in his voice.

"Better, I think," Hugh replied.

"Poor lad! Sir William might remember there is a mean betwixt over-indulgence and severity. But Frank has brought it on himself. When he forgot to do his duty in the troop he would be trying to cajole Captain Turner into good humor, just as he has always cajoled Sir William. And Michael Turner is not the man to coax that way. He has influence with Sir William, too, and so— Well, 'twill be for Frank's good in the end," Dick concluded philosophically, as he settled himself on the window-bench.

Hugh made room for him, then went on staring at the gray sky. Suddenly he broke out, "Dick, it was Captain Gwyeth sent me Bayard."

"Ay?" the other answered, without surprise. "And I have it of Sir William, he was main urger, and drew him on to what seemed a hopeless attempt to gain our pardon."

Hugh scowled at his boots. "I take it I must wait on him and tell him 'thank you,' when he comes back out of Warwickshire. I wish he had let me alone!" he cried.

"You *are* like your father," Strangwayes said judicially, leaning back on the window-bench. "See to it, Hugh, you do not make the resemblance too complete."

"How that?" Hugh asked guiltily.

"By giving way to your ugly pride, so you do what it may take months of repentance to undo."

Hugh made no answer, and the silence between them lasted till the gallery was quite dark, when, slipping off the window-seat, they tramped away to their comrades below.

Next day Hugh gave himself up to Frank, who, truth to tell, in his present half-subdued state was pleasanter company than he had been at Oxford. He persuaded Master Pleydall to come out and view the town, which took them till mid-afternoon; and then they loitered back to the castle, with discreet turnings to avoid meeting any of the other officers. Frank dodged into a tavern to keep out of sight of Griffith, but he dragged Hugh half a mile down a blind lane to avoid a suspected encounter with Captain Turner. "Mayhap I was impudent and forward, so he got at last to ask my advice about conducting the troop, when others of the men were by. And I thought he meant it all in sober earnest." Frank made a brave attempt at nonchalance, but his lips quivered so Hugh had an improper desire to chastise Michael Turner; for all his swagger and affectation, Frank had been too innocent and childish a lad to be scathed with the captain's pitiless sarcasms.

Luckily they had no more encounters with men from the garrison till they were nearly at the gate of the castle, and then it was only Strangwayes, riding forth in full armor, with some twenty men behind him, to post the watch about the town for the evening hours. Hugh made him a formal salute, which Dick returned gayly before he rode on.

"Dick is right fond of you," Frank said, with a shade of envy; and after that they sauntered in a moody silence, till, the sight of the stables cheering Frank a bit, he prayed Hugh come in and look at The Jade. "I've not seen the old lass since day before yesterday," he explained.

They were still lingering to admire the mare, when two grooms came hurrying a lathered horse into the stable. "Who's been riding so hard?" Hugh asked carelessly.

"Messenger from the troop to the south, sir."

"To the south?" Hugh repeated. "Come quickly, Frank, I must see—"

He walked rapidly across the courtyard to the door of the guardroom. About it men were crowded, and more were pressing into the room itself; but at Hugh's jostling they made him a way into the thick of them. Over on a bench in the corner he had sight of a man with the sleeve cut from his coat, who sat leaning heavily against a comrade. Another, whom Hugh recognized as the surgeon of the regiment, was washing a wound in his arm, and as he moved, Hugh got a glimpse of the face of the injured man. "Cowper!" he cried, and ran forward, for he knew the fellow for one of Captain Gwyeth's old independent troop.

Men gave him place; he heard a mutter amongst them, "The captain's son," but he did not heed; just pushed his way to the wounded man, and bent over him: "Cowper, what has happened? Is anything wrong with my father? Tell me."

"They closed in on us, sir," the man roused up to speak. "Captain Oldesworth's horse, and a company of foot beside. They took our horses and they slew Cornet Foster. I came through for help. They have the colonel blocked up in Kingsford church."

CHAPTER XIX

THE RIDING OF ARROW WATER

FOR a moment the faces of the men about him went all blurry to Hugh's sight; then he was making his way fumblingly across the guardroom, and, thrusting out one arm before him, found the door to the inner part of the castle. Now that he was hurrying at a surer pace down the corridor within, he realized that his breath was coming in short gasps and he was shaking with a nervous tremor. Kingsford, Kingsford, the word kept singing through his head; the Oldesworths, who had so hated Alan Gwyeth, held him at their mercy now at Kingsford. Only to Hugh it was no longer Alan Gwyeth, but his father, the father whom his mother had taught him to respect, who had tried to win him a pardon. And he had begrudged the man even a grateful thought.

Hugh dashed open the door of his chamber, and, kicking off his shoes, began tugging on his boots. He heard a step behind him, as he struggled with his head bent; then came Frank's voice: " Hugh, you've heard? They have cut him off; he has cried for help; my father is taking counsel with the captains — "

" Counsel? " cried Hugh, springing to his feet. " Why don't they send him aid? " He tore his buff coat down from the wall.

"Faith, 'tis a question if there is aid to send," Frank cried, in equal excitement, as he made a hindering effort to help Hugh into the coat; "they have taken away so many of our regiment; we are scant a hundred men all told; they say 'tis doubtful if we can send—"

"Then I'll go to Kingsford alone. Run bid them saddle Bayard, Frank, quick." With that Hugh caught up his sword, and, going full speed out of the chamber, drowned in the clatter of his boots the protests Frank sent after him.

Below, in the tower room that served for conferences, Sir William would be with his officers, and he hoped there to learn farther news. Almost at the door he ran upon a man from Turner's troop, all accoutred, who drew back and saluted him. "What seek you? Know you what they are planning?" Hugh asked excitedly.

"Nay, sir; only I was bid have my horse ready, and stand at their service."

Hugh could guess the service. Pushing by the trooper to the door of the chamber, he knocked a rattling, peremptory knock, and another right upon it. At that the door was wrenched open, and Leveson, grim and dignified, had begun, "What brings you, sirrah?" when Turner's voice interrupted: "Hugh Gwyeth, is it? Let him come in."

After that Hugh had a confused sight of the high-studded room, with the sunlight far up on the walls and the corners dusky, and of the men by the table, who had faced toward him. Then he found himself over by Sir William's armchair, his hand resting hard upon the table, and he was speaking rapidly: "I am going to Kingsford, Sir William, to my father. If you are seeking a messenger for anything, I'll bear it safely. For I am going straightway."

"Nay, I shall not suffer it, Hugh Gwyeth," the baronet cut him short. "Do you understand? The roads are close beset; the trooper who brought us the tidings was shot in the arm and the side."

"But I know the Kingsford roads. I can make it," Hugh protested, and looked from one to another of the three dubious faces. "Sure, you'll let me go," he burst out. "I must. If he be — harmed and I not there. I must go." His eyes dropped to his hands that were clinching his hat fast, and rested there; he dared not glance again at those about him lest he find refusal in their looks, and he hoped they might not be gazing at him, for he knew his mouth was working.

Then Turner's voice sounded quick and decided: "Let him go, Sir William."

"Ay, he is a light rider and he knows the roads. A good messenger, after all," Leveson added in a matter-of-fact tone.

Hugh looked up hopefully and saw a glance exchanged between Sir William and his captains that meant his case was won. "We'll not endanger you with a written message," the baronet spoke at once; "for I tell you frankly, sir, you run a hundred chances of capture. If you do contrive to bring yourself through the rebel lines, bid Captain Gwyeth from me to hold out but two days, till Saturday, and he shall have help. 'Tis so you have determined, gentlemen?"

"If the Lord aid us, we can recall enough troops to make the town good and ride for the rescue by then," Turner answered.

"That's all your message, Gwyeth," Sir William resumed; "and remember, if the rebels knew the time when relief could be looked for, 'twould aid them mightily, so if you be taken —"

"I'll not be taken, sir, I do assure you," cried Hugh, with his hand on the latch of the door; "I'll come through safe to Kingsford."

"Heaven grant it!" the other said, with a trace of a smile, and then soberly, "I can warn you, the captain will be glad at heart to see you."

Turner said something kindly, too, Hugh remembered afterward, but for the present it was just people speaking and wishing him God speed, and he was glad when he clapped on his hat outside the door and could run for his horse.

Outside, the whole castle seemed emptied into the south court; Leveson's and Turner's men, some in coats and more in shirt-sleeves, who shouted questions and the tidings back and forth, and swore and scuffled at the jostlings of the crowd. The sun was down, but the early twilight still was clear between the gray walls, enough to bring out every detail of the swarming courtyard, and to enable Hugh to distinguish the faces of the men. Down in the thick of the throng he caught sight of Frank, with a groom holding The Jade, and he ran down from the doorway to him. At that, some of the men set up a cheering, under cover of which Frank, putting his arm round Hugh's shoulders, said in a low tone: "I want you to take the mare, Hugh;

XIX THE RIDING OF ARROW WATER

she's faster than Bayard, and she's not been used these two days; and I did not know it was your cornetcy I was taking, and I want you to ride her. Into the saddle with you!"

Without wit or time to reply, Hugh found himself on the mare's back, felt her quiver beneath him, and had opened his mouth to bid the groom let go her head, when the shouting swarm between him and the great gateway was suddenly cleft apart. Up the lane Black Boy came swinging with Strangwayes pulling taut on the bridle so he eased up at Hugh's side. "Get you down," Dick cried without question, and, springing to the ground himself, began tearing off his cuirass.

"What will you have? Be brisk," Hugh shouted, coming out of his saddle.

Strangwayes flung his cuirass about him, and began very deliberately taking in the straps to fit Hugh's body. "Did you think you were going on a pleasure ride?" he asked. Frank burst into a nervous laugh, which others caught up, and some began cheering for the lieutenant. Hugh heard The Jade prancing with impatience at the sound, and he himself fairly squirmed under Dick's touch. "Let me be off!" he cried.

"You've all night before you," Strangwayes drawled. "Hold up your arm so I can get at the strap."

Just then, through the clatter of The Jade's restless hoofs and the hum of the eager crowd about him, Hugh heard his name called. Looking over his shoulder he saw Cowper, with his face the color of ashes, limp up between two comrades. "They said 'twas you should go to Kingsford, sir," the man addressed him.

"I'm to venture it," Hugh answered. "How left you matters there, Cowper?"

"The captain has the church and the graveyard, sir. The rebels hold the village and the bridge over the Arrow. I got across two mile up at the Blackwater ford. The river ran high, and they had set no guard. 'Twas breaking through the village they shot at me."

"Go tend your hurt now," Hugh found thought to urge. "I'll remember the ford, be sure. Are you done now, Dick?"

"Done with that," replied Strangwayes. "Are your pistols in order? And the word for the night is 'Gloucester'; you'll need it at the gates."

"Yes, yes," Hugh cried, and made a dash for The Jade, who, dragging her groom at her head, had fretted herself a good ten feet away. A trooper jumped forward and caught her bit to stay her; but it was Dick, Hugh remembered, who held the stirrup so he could swing himself easily into the saddle. "God speed!" he heard Strangwayes say in the instant that followed. "We'll be at your heels soon. God speed!"

That was all the farewell between them; for the men stood back from The Jade's head, and, with a shrill squeal, she darted forward across the court. Hugh heard the click of her hoofs on the cobblestones, then lost the sound in the cheer upon cheer that broke from those about him. His arms ached with the tense grip he was holding on the bridle, and then he found the mare had the bit in her teeth. "Go, if you will," he cried, letting the reins looser. The shadow of the gateway fell upon him; he saw the flicker of the torch beneath it and the white faces of the men on guard. Then he had jammed his hat on hard, and, bending his head, was striving to hold The Jade straight as she tore down the slope and sped through the town.

Houses and shops rushed by; he heard a woman shriek abuse after him for his mad riding; the crash of opening casements, as the townsfolk leaned out to see him pass; once, too, his heart gave a jump as a boy, like a black streak, shot across the road just clear of The Jade's nose. Then the bulk of the town gate blocked his way; he saw the sentinels spring forth to stay him, and, contriving to check the mare an instant, he leaned from the saddle to say "Gloucester" to the corporal in charge.

"Pass free," came the word; the men stood from his path, and, giving loose rein to The Jade, he flew by them out into the twilight stretch of open country road.

For a time it was just breathless riding, with his full weight on the reins to slacken the mare's speed; for the road was all ruts, and he feared for her slender legs. The mud spattered up even into his eyes, and once, at a dip in the road, he felt his mount make a half-slip in the mire, which sobered her somewhat, so he could ease her down to a slow, careful trot that promised to carry him well through the night. Now he was first able to look about at the broad, dusky fields and back over his shoulder, where Tamworth town and castle were merged into the night. The first exhilaration of the setting forth went from him in the stillness and dark; it was steady, grim work he had before him, yet he felt assured he would come safely into Kingsford, and, spite of the gravity of it all, he found himself smiling a little at the way in which, at last, he was going to his father. He wondered perplexedly how he should greet Captain Gwyeth, and how phrase his message; a formal tone would perhaps be best till he was sure of his welcome. But Sir William had said his father would be glad at his coming; at that thought Hugh pricked on The Jade a little faster.

Once clear of the first village beyond Tamworth he entered a stretch of woodland, where the black tips of the trees showed vivid against the starless gray sky. Below, the undergrowth was all dense darkness and Hugh thought it well to keep a hand on his pistol, for he was drawing into Puritan country where a Cavalier was fair game for an ambuscade. Out beyond he trotted again through fields, only blacker and lonelier now than those by Tamworth. Such cottages as he passed were silent and dark; at one farmstead he heard a dog howl, and once, in a tangled hollow, a bat whizzed by his head, but he saw or heard no other living thing. Though once, as he gazed across the fields on his left, he made out in the distance a gleam of light; a farm must lie yonder, and he pictured to himself the low cottage chamber, where the goodwife would be watching with a restless child. Such shelter and companionship was betokened by the light that he turned in the saddle to gaze at it till a clump of trees shut it from him.

It must have been something after midnight,

though under that starless sky he could not tell the time surely, when he clattered into a considerable town. An officious watchman with a bobbing torch ran from a byway, calling on him to stand, so Hugh clapped spurs to The Jade and shot through the street at such a pace that the next watchman could only get out of his course without trying to stay him. But after that he grew wary and, when the outlying houses of the next town came out of the black, turned off into the fields and picked his way about it. The roundabout course saved him from interference, but it took much time; by a dull, unbraced feeling, that was not sleepiness nor yet quite weariness alone, he knew he had been many hours in the saddle, and he began to look to the east, in dread lest he catch the first signs of daybreak.

Presently he must give his whole attention to The Jade, for they spattered into a ford where the going was treacherous. While she halted to drink he gazed about at the bushes and the field before him, and, spite of the dark, knew the place. It was home country he was drawing toward now, so he trotted on slowly, with his senses alert and his eyes peering into the dusk for the landmarks that should guide him. So it was that at last on his right hand he caught sight of a big leafless oak, beneath which he pulled up short. True enough, he remembered the way in which the tree stood up bare and alone with scragged common at its back; he could not see well for the dark, but he knew that at the farther edge of the open land was a belt of young oaks that hid the ford of Blackwater.

He lingered beneath the blasted oak, time enough to look to his pistols, and time enough, too, for him to recall the ghostly reputation of the lonely tree, so his nerves were crisping as he rode by it into the common. But he quieted The Jade's fretty step, and, in the action and the thought of what might be before him, steadied himself till, though his body was trembling with eagerness, his head was cool. He took the precaution of making the mare keep a slow trot that was half muffled in the turf, though he urged her as much as he dared on the uneven ground; for to the east, as he looked over his shoulder, the dark was beginning to pale. The early summer morning must be near at hand, for when he had crossed the open there was light enough for him to make out the break in the trees where the bridle path wound down to the ford.

Hugh went in cautiously, with the reins taut in his left hand and his right on his pistol; but for all that The Jade's feet splashed in the sloughs of the pathway with a loudness that startled him. He pulled up a moment and listened; ahead he could hear the lap, lap of swift water, but for the rest the wood was silent. He was about to press the mare forward with a touch of the spur, when, flinging up her head, she whickered shrilly. Right upon that, somewhere to the front by the water's edge, a horse neighed.

Next moment Hugh felt the lash of low boughs across his neck, as he pulled The Jade round with her haunches in among the bushes by the path. Spite of the crash of the branches, and the pounding of the blood in his temples that near deafened him, he caught the sound of hoof-beats on his left, coming down on him from the common as well as up from the river. At that he urged The Jade forward, straight into the bushes at the other side of the path, where the limbs grew so low that he bent down with his bare head pressed against her mane. For all the hurry and tumult, his ears were alert, and presently he heard their horses crashing behind him among the trees at the right. Then, cautiously as he could pick his way in the gray dimness, he turned The Jade's head to the common. Brushing out through the last of the oaks he faced southward, and, as he did so, cast a glance behind him. Out of the shadows of the trees in his rear he saw the dim form of a horseman take shape, and a command, loud in the hush of morning, reached him: "Halt, there!"

Hugh laid the spurs to The Jade's sides and, as she ran, instinctively bent himself forward. Behind him he heard a shot, then the patter of many hoofs upon the turf, and a second shot. Right upon it he felt a dull shock above the shoulder blade; the ball must have rebounded from his cuirass. After that he was in among the trees once more; through the wood behind him men were crashing and shouting; and even such scant shelter as the oaks gave was ending, as they grew sparser and sparser, till he dashed into an open stretch that sloped to the Arrow. To the front he had a dizzy sight of more horsemen straggling from cover; there were two patrols closing in on him, he realized, and with that, jerking the mare to the right, he headed for the river.

Before him he could see the slope of hillside, the dark water under the bank beyond, even the dusky sedge of the low opposite shore. He saw, too, a horseman, bursting out from the trees, halt across his path, but he neither stayed nor swerved, just drove the spurs into The Jade and braced himself for the shock. He must have struck the other horse on the chest; he had an instant's sight of a trooper's tense face and a horse's sleek shoulders, then only black water was before him and men behind him were shouting to pull up. There came a sickening sense of being hurled from the earth; a great splashing noise and spray in his face. After that was a time of struggling to free his feet from the stirrups, to clear himself from the frightened mare; all this with water choking and strangling him and filling his ears and beating down his head. He had no thought nor hope nor conscious plan of action, only with all the strength of his body he battled clear till he found himself in mid-stream, with the current tugging at his legs, and his boots and cuirass dragging him down. Once his head went under, and he rose gasping to a dizzy sight of gray sky. He struck out despairingly while he tried in vain to kick free from his boots. The current was twisting and tossing him helplessly; he turned on his back a moment, and still the sky was rushing past above him and whirling as it went. Above the din of the water he heard faint shouts of men and crack of musket-shot. A base end for a soldier, to drown like a rat! he reflected, and at the thought struck out blindly. The water swept him down-stream, but he fought his way obliquely shoreward till of a sudden he found the tug of the current had abated. He could rest an instant and look to his bearings; quite near him lay the shore, a dark sweep of field with a hedge that ran down to the water, and on the farther side the hedge he saw horsemen following down the stream.

Hugh struck out with renewed strength, till, finding the bottom beneath his feet at last, he splashed shoreward on the run, and, stumbling through the sedge and mire of the margin, panted upward into the field. Off to the left were the roofs of Kingsford, so far the current had swept him, but near at hand there was no hiding-place, nor even a tree to set his back against, and, with his boots heavy with water and his breath exhausted with the past struggle, he had no hope to run. He halted where he was, in the midst of the bare field, and pulled out his sword, just as the foremost horseman cleared the hedge at a leap. It was not so dark but Hugh recognized the square young figure, even before the man charged right upon him. "Good morrow, Cousin Peregrine," he cried out, and dodged aside so the horse might not trample him. "Get down and fight."

As he spoke he made a cut at the horse's flank; then Peregrine, crying out his name, sprang down and faced him. They were blade to blade at last, and at the first blow the older lad flinched, stumbling back in the long grass of the field, and Hugh, with eyes on his set, angry face, pressed after him. Horses were galloping nearer and nearer, men calling louder, but Hugh did not heed; for Peregrine, mistaking a feint he made, laid himself open, and he lunged forward at him.

Then his sword-arm was caught and held fast, and he was flung backward into the grasp of a couple of troopers. The man who had first seized him, a grim corporal in a yellow sash, wrenched the sword out of his hand, and he heard him speak to Peregrine: "Has the knave done you hurt, sir?"

Hugh pulled himself together, though his whole body was still a-quiver with the action of the last moments, and looked about him. Yellow-sashed troopers surrounded him, six or seven, he judged, and a few paces distant stood Peregrine, with his hand pressed to his right forearm. "He slashed me in the wrist," young Oldesworth broke out; "I tripped, else he had not done it."

"You had not tripped if you had stood your ground," Hugh flung back, with an involuntary effort to loosen his arms from the grasp of those who had seized him.

"Hold your tongue, you cur!" snapped Peregrine, and might have said more, had there not come from across the river a prolonged hail. One ran down to the brink to catch the words; but Hugh had no chance to listen, for at Peregrine's curt order he was hustled upon one of the troop horses. They tied his hands behind him, too; whereat Hugh set his teeth and scowled in silence. What would Peregrine do with him before he were done, he was wondering dumbly, when the man from the river came up with the report that the captain bade to convey the prisoner to Everscombe, and see to it that he did not escape. "I'll see to it," Peregrine said grimly, and got to his saddle, awkwardly, because of his wounded arm, that was already staining a rough bandage red.

The morning was breaking grayly as the little squad turned westward through the fields, and by a hollow to the Kingsford road. As they descended into the highway, Hugh faced a little about in his saddle, and gazed down it toward the village; a rise in the land shut the spot from sight, but he knew that yonder Captain Gwyeth lay, awaiting the message that he was not to bring. The trooper who rode at his stirrup took him roughly by the shoulder then, and made him face round to the front. "You don't go to Kingsford to-day, sir," he jeered.

Hugh had not spirit even to look at the fellow, but fixed his eyes on the pommel of the saddle. Trees and road he had known slipped by, he was aware; he heard the horses stamp upon the roadway; and he felt his wet clothes press against his body, and felt the strap about his wrists cut into the flesh. But nothing of all that mattered as his numbed wits came to the full realization that this was the end of the boasting confidence with which he had set forth, and the end of his hope of meeting with his father. The last fight would be fought without him, or even now Captain Gwyeth, ignorant of the aid that should hurry to him, might be putting himself into his enemies' hands. At that, Hugh tugged hopelessly at the strap, and found a certain relief in the fierce smarting of his chafed wrists.

Like an echo of his thoughts Peregrine's voice came at his elbow: "So you were thinking to reach Kingsford, were you?"

"I should not be riding here just for my pleasure," Hugh replied, with a piteous effort to force a light tone.

"'Twould be as well for you if you were less saucy," his cousin said sternly. "You know me."

"I know you carry one mark of my sword on you," Hugh answered, looking his tormentor in the face, "and if you'd not let your troop come aid you, you'd carry more."

For a moment he expected Peregrine to strike him; then the elder lad merely laughed exasperatingly. "You'll not talk so high by to-night," he said, "when you're fetched out to see that dog Gwyeth hanged up in Everscombe Park."

"You'd best catch him before you hang him," Hugh answered stoutly, though the heart within him was heavy almost beyond endurance. What might the Oldesworths not do if once they laid hands on Captain Gwyeth? A prisoner of war had no rights, Hugh was well aware, and so many accidents could befall. He felt his face must show something of his fear, and he dreaded lest Peregrine goad him into farther speech, and his words betray his wretchedness.

But happily just there they turned in between the stone pillars of Everscombe Park, and Peregrine paced to the front of his squad. Hugh listlessly watched the well-remembered trees and turnings of the avenue, which were clear to see now in the breaking dawn. The roofs of the manor house showed in even outlines against the dull sky, all as he remembered it, only now the lawn beneath the terrace was scarred with hoof-prints, and over in the old west wing the door was open, and a musketeer paced up and down the flagstones before it. Heading thither, the squad drew up before the entrance, and Hugh, haled unceremoniously from the horse's back, was jostled into the large old hall of the west wing, that seemed now a guardroom.

"How do you like this for a home-coming, cousin?" Peregrine asked, and Hugh looked him in the eyes but answered nothing. His captor laughed and turned to his troopers. "Search him thoroughly now," he ordered; "then hold him securely till Captain Oldesworth comes.— And I can tell you, sirrah," he addressed Hugh once more, "you'll relish his conversation even less than you relish mine."

CHAPTER XX

BENEATH THE ROOF OF EVERSCOMBE

THEY had searched Hugh, thoroughly and with more than necessary roughness, and now he was permitted to drag on his dripping clothes again. It was in a long, narrow room at the end of the old hall, where the ceiling was high and dark and the three tall windows set well up from the floor. A year ago it had been a closed and disused apartment, but now a couple of tables and some stools were placed there; Hugh noted the furniture in listless outer fashion as he sat wrestling on his sodden boots. For once his captors had taken their hands off him; one trooper was guarding the door and another was pacing up and down beneath the windows, but the corporal and the third man stood within arm's reach of him. When Hugh rose to his feet the corporal made a little movement, and he realized they were all alert for his least suspicious action. " My faith, I'm not like to get away from the four of you," Hugh broke out in a despairing sort of sullenness. " 'Tis only that I'd fain put on my coat, unless you claim that along with my cuirass and buff jacket."

One bade him put on and be hanged, and Hugh, having drawn on the wet garment, sat down again on the stool by the table, too utterly weary and hopeless to note more than that the room was damp and the chill of his soaked clothes was striking to his marrow. With a thought of tramping some warmth into his body he rose again, but the corporal sharply bade him sit down quietly or be tied down. Hugh resumed his place on the stool with his shoulders against the edge of the table and one ankle resting on the other knee; he would gladly have swung round and rested his head upon the table, so worn-out and faint he felt, only he knew if he did his captors would think him childish and frightened.

Of a sudden he heard the sentinel at the door advance a step and announce to the corporal: "Captain Oldesworth has just come into the guardroom, sir."

A queer tingling went through Hugh's veins, and upon it followed a sickening faintness. Bringing both feet down to the ground, he faced about with his clinched hand on the table and his eyes fastened upon the door. He knew now why he had not been able to think, those last moments, why every humiliation had been scarcely heeded, in the expectation of this that was before him. He saw the corporal draw up stiff in salute, the sentinel stand back from the door, and then, clean-shaven, set-mouthed as ever, he saw Tom Oldesworth stride in.

It had been in Hugh's mind to stand up to meet his uncle, but at the last he dared not trust his knees to such a test. For the moment the old boyish fear of the elder man, whose raillery had cut him, whose blows had made him flinch, came back on him, and he could only stare at him dumbly.

"'Tis not the place I had looked to find you, nephew," Oldesworth greeted him, in a tone that though brusque was kindly enough. Only in the hurriedness of his bearing and the eagerness in his eyes Hugh read no friendly presage, so he let his gaze fall to the table and studied the grain of the wood, while he listened to the beating of his heart that vibrated through all his body.

Oldesworth spoke a word aside to the corporal, and as the troopers drew to the farther end of the room came and set himself down opposite Hugh. "Now attend me, sir," he began rapidly. "By your trappings you seem to have learned something of war; then you know how the case stands with you now we have you fast. So I trust you will not suffer any childish stubbornness to vex me or harm you."

Hugh watched the man's hard face with fascinated eyes and lips half-opened, but found no tongue to reply.

"You were riding to Kingsford," Oldesworth continued, gazing at him fixedly. "You came from Tamworth, whither a messenger was posted yesterday. You brought an answering message. What was it?"

Hugh flung back his head. "If there be a message, think you I'd be such a fool as to tell it?" he cried, in a voice that was so firm it made him glad. After all, he had no need to fear, for this was only a man like the rest, and he was now a man, too.

"You brought a message from Sir William Pleydall," Oldesworth repeated, unmoved. "He is going to send aid to this man, is he not? Why, I can read that in your face, Hugh. Aid is coming, then. Is it to-day? To-morrow? Answer me."

Hugh met his uncle's gaze fairly, with his head held a little upward and his lips tight-set now. There was nothing for him to say, but he knew they fought the battle out betwixt them while their glances met.

"So you're stubborn, are you?" Oldesworth said, rising to his feet. "You young fool! Do you think you can set your will against mine?"

"I think I will not tell what you ask," Hugh replied without a tremor.

Oldesworth leaned a little forward with his fist upon the table. "I have been waiting all my manhood to take satisfaction from Alan Gwyeth," he said slowly. "Now the opportunity is given me do you think I shall suffer a boy's obstinacy to hinder me? I will have that message. If you'll not yield it for the asking, why — Come, come, speak. I'd be loath to hurt you, Hugh."

"I'd be loath to have you, sir," Hugh replied soberly, though his whole inclination was to laugh; for now the worst had come he was braced to meet it, and quite unafraid.

Captain Oldesworth's jaws were set ominously at that. "Corporal," he ordered sharply, "send a man to fetch rope and a piece of match."

With an involuntary start Hugh came to his feet, for his mind had jumped back to something Butler had once hinted, — that a length of burning match tied between the fingers was the surest way to make a dumb knave find his tongue.

"'Tis no laughing matter, you'll perceive," the captain said, with a trace of satisfaction. "Now you'll tell?"

Hugh shook his head, not looking at his uncle but with eyes upon the door. He saw it pushed open, and then came in the trooper with a length of rope in his hand, but Hugh scarcely heeded, for behind him, with an eager step, walked Peregrine Oldesworth. After that it did not need the tramp of the men crossing from the other end of the room to set every fibre of Hugh's body tense for the coming struggle. With a quick movement he swung about to catch up the stool he had just quitted; Oldesworth must have stepped round the table behind him, for he blocked his way now, and catching him by the shoulders made him stand, for all Hugh's effort to wrench clear. "'Twill be no use fighting, my lad," he said, with something oddly like pity in his face. "Do as I ask straightway. You've done all a gentleman need do. Tell me now when Pleydall is coming. Else you go into the hands of Cornet Oldesworth and his squad here. And Peregrine is keen for this work. But tell, and no one shall lay hand on you, nor—"

"I care not if you kill me!" Hugh cried hoarsely.

"Have it your way, then!" Oldesworth retorted, and, flinging him off, turned his back. "Tie him up, lads," he ordered.

Some one griped his collar, Hugh felt; there was a rip of cloth, and for a moment he had torn himself free and struck out blindly at the mass of them. They must have tripped him, for he felt the floor beneath his shoulders; but he still had hold on one of them, and he heard a shirt tear beneath his hands. There came a dull pain between his eyes, as if the bones of the forehead were bursting outward, and he made a feeble effort to strike up as he lay. Then the struggling was over; he could not even kick, for one that sat upon his legs; a man's knee was grinding down on his back, and his arms were forced behind him. His face was pressed to the floor, and he could see nothing for a blackness before his eyes, but he heard Peregrine's voice, cool and well-satisfied: "He'll be quiet enough now. Here's the rope."

Some one else had entered the room, Hugh realized; a slow step, a pause, and then a stern voice that rang loud: "Thomas Oldesworth! Bid your ruffians take their hands from your sister's son."

"Father!" the captain's voice spoke, then after an instant's blank pause ran on: "You do not understand, good sir. He—"

"Will you stand arguing?" There came a noise as of a staff's being struck upon the floor. "Do I command in this house, son Thomas, or do you? You ruffianly knaves, up with you all!"

They had left him free, Hugh found, and dragging one arm up to his head he lay panting desperately, without strength or heart to move. "Help him to his feet," the stern voice spoke again. "Or have you done him serious hurt?"

They lifted him up, with gentler handling than

they had yet given him, and staggering a pace to the table he leaned against it. He drew his hand across his eyes unsteadily to rub away the black spots that danced before them; he had a blurry sight, then, of the troopers drawn back to the windows, and of the captain and Peregrine, who stood together with half-abashed faces, for in the doorway, leaning on his staff, was Master Gilbert Oldesworth. "Get you back to Kingsford and fight out your fight with the scoundrel who wronged your sister," he spoke again. "At such a time can you find no better task than to maltreat a boy?"

"If you would only pause to hear how matters stand, sir," the captain urged, with a visible effort to maintain a respectful tone. "The lad holds the information that shall make us masters of that villain Gwyeth. If he will not speak, though he were twenty times my nephew, I'll —"

"If he were twenty times the meanest horse-boy in the king's camp, he should not be put to torture beneath my roof," Master Oldesworth answered grimly. "Come here to me, Hugh Gwyeth."

Wondering dully why all the strength had gone out of his body, Hugh stumbled across the room and pitched up against the wall beside his grandfather. He noted now that his shirt was torn open, and drawing his coat together he tried to fasten it; his fingers shook unsteadily, and the buttons were hard to find. He felt his grandfather's hand placed firmly on his shoulder. "I think you have mishandled this gentleman enough to satisfy you," the old man spoke contemptu-

XX BENEATH THE ROOF OF EVERSCOMBE

ously. "Henceforth you will merely hold him as a prisoner taken in honorable war. And I shall myself be responsible for his custody."

"My good father," Captain Oldesworth broke out, "I cannot suffer him to pass from my keeping. My responsibility to the state—"

"Will you school me, Thomas?" Master Oldesworth cut him short. "I am neither bed-ridden nor brain-sick that you should try to dictate to me now. But I will advise you, sir, that there are decencies to be observed even in war, and there are those in authority would make you to smart if ever they got knowledge of this you purposed. Lift your hand against my grandson, and this day's work comes to their ears."

Then the grasp on Hugh's shoulder tightened, and submissively he walked at his grandfather's side out into the guardroom. Those loitering there drew back to make way for them, he judged by the sound of footsteps, but he had not spirit even to look up. By the difference of the oak planking of the floors he perceived they were entering the passage that led to the main building, when he felt a firmer grip close on his arm and heard the voice of the Roundhead corporal: "I crave your pardon, sir. The captain bade me see the prisoner safely locked up."

"No need," Master Oldesworth spoke curtly, and then addressed Hugh: "You will give me your parole not to attempt an escape."

Hugh looked up helplessly into his grandfather's stern face, and felt the grasp of the corporal press upon his arm. His breath came hard like a sob, but he managed to force out his answer: "I cannot, sir, I cannot. You'd better thrust me back into my uncle's hands. I cannot promise."

He was trying to nerve himself to be dragged back to the chamber behind the guardroom, but though Master Oldesworth's face grew harder, he only said, "Bring him along after me," and led the way down the passage.

Hugh followed unsteadily, glad of the grasp on his arm that helped to keep him erect. They had entered the east wing, he noted listlessly; then he was trudging up the long staircase and stumbling down the corridor. At the first window recess he saw Master Oldesworth halt and heard him speak less curtly: "I have indeed to thank you, mistress." Raising his eyes as he passed, Hugh saw that by the window, with hands wrung tight together, Lois Campion was standing.

Instinctively he tried to halt, but the grip on his arm never relaxed, and he must come on at his captor's side, down to the end of the corridor. There Master Oldesworth had flung open a door into a tiny chamber, with one high, narrow slit of a window, bare of furniture save for a couple of chests and a broken chair, over which the dust lay thick. "Since you will have no better lodging, you shall stay here," he said coldly.

Dragging his way in, Hugh flung himself down on a chest with his head in his hands. "Could you let me have a drink of water, sir?" he asked faintly.

"Go to my chamber and fetch the flask of Spanish wine, Lois," Master Oldesworth bade, and Hugh heard the girl's footsteps die away in the corridor, then heard or heeded nothing, just sat with his face hidden.

A touch on the shoulder roused him at last; he took the glass of wine his grandfather offered him and slowly drank it down. They were alone in the room now, he noted as he drank, the door was drawn to, and Lois was gone. He set down the empty glass and leaned forward with his elbows on his knees. "I thank you, sir, for this, for all you have saved me from," he said slowly.

"You might thank me for more, if you were less self-willed."

"'Tis not from self-will, sir, I did as I have done, that I refused my parole," Hugh broke out, "'tis for my father. I cannot bind myself. I must go to him. I —"

"No more words of that man," Master Oldesworth silenced him. "You shall never go to him again. A year ago I dealt not wisely with you. I gave you choice where you were too young to choose. For all your folly there are parts in you too good for me to suffer you destroy yourself. Now where I let you walk at your will I shall see to it that you keep the right path, by force, if you drive me to it. For the present I shall hold you in safe custody at Everscombe. Later, as you conduct yourself, I shall determine what course to take."

"But my father!" Hugh cried.

"Captain Oldesworth will deal with Alan Gwyeth," Master Oldesworth replied. "Do you forget him."

"I can never forget him, sir. Sure, I'd liefer

be hanged with him than be saved apart from him thus. I — "

The door closed jarringly behind Master Oldesworth, the key grated in the lock, and the bolt was shot creakingly.

For a time Hugh sat staring stupidly at the door of his prison, then, getting slowly to his feet, he began dragging and shoving the chest beneath the window. His hands were still unsteady and he felt limp and weak, so again and again he must pause to sit down. The little room was close and hot; the perspiration prickled on the back of his neck, and stung above his eyebrows. The movement of the chest cleared a white space on the gray floor, and the dust that rose thick sifted into his mouth and nostrils till he was coughing painfully with a miserable feeling that it needed but little for the coughing to end in sobbing. He hated himself for his weakness, and, gritting his teeth, shoved the chest the more vigorously till at last it was in position beneath the window. Lifting the one chair upon it, he mounted up precariously; the sill of the window came level with his collar bone while the top grazed his forehead. He stretched up his arms and measured the length and breadth of the opening twice over, but he knew it was quite hopeless; there was no getting through that narrow window, and, had it been possible, he must risk a sheer fall of two stories to the flagged walk below. For a moment he stood blinking out at the green branches of the elms that swayed before his window, then he dropped to the floor again and sat down on the chest with his face in his hands.

So he was still sitting, when the door was unlocked and one of the serving men of the household came in to fetch him dinner. Hugh looked up, and, recognizing the fellow, would have spoken, but the man only shook his head and backed out hastily. Hugh noted that it was no trooper's rations they had sent him, but food from his grandfather's table; still he had no heart to eat, though he drank eagerly, till presently he reasoned this was weak conduct, for he must keep up strength if he were ever to come out of his captors' hands, so, drawing the plate to him, he resolutely swallowed down a tolerable meal.

Then he set himself to watch the motes dance in a sunbeam that ran well up toward the ceiling, but presently it went out altogether. He leaned back then on the chest where he sat, and perhaps had lost himself a time in a numb, half-waking sleep, when of a sudden he caught a distant sound that brought him to his feet. He could not mistake it; off to the east where Kingsford lay he could hear the faint crack of musketry fired in volleys. Hugh cried out something in a hoarse voice he did not recognize; then he was wrenching at the latch and hammering on the door with his clinched hands, while he shrieked to them to let him go. He saw the blood smearing out from his knuckles, but he beat on against the unshaken panels till the strength left him and he dropped down on the floor. Still, as he lay, he could hear the distant firing, and then he ground his face down between his hands and cried as he had never cried before with great sobs that seemed to tear him.

Afterward there came a long time when he had not strength even to sob, when the slackening fire meant nothing to him, and, lying motionless and stupid, he realized only that the light was paling in the chamber. The door was pushed open, and mechanically he rolled a little out of the way of it. The serving man he remembered came in with supper, and at sight of him Hugh lifted up his head and entreated brokenly: "Tell me, what has happened? Have they taken my father? For the love of Heaven, tell me."

The man hesitated, then, as he passed to the doorway, bent down and whispered: "They've beat the Cavaliers into the church, sir, but they've not taken the captain yet. Lord bless you, don't cry so, sir."

For the sheer nervous relief had set Hugh choking and sobbing again without pride or strength enough left to hold himself in check. As the darkness closed in, however, he grew a little calmer, though sheer exhaustion more than inner comfort held him quiet. His eyes were hot and smarting, and his throat ached, so he crept over to the chest where the food was placed, and laying hands on a jug of water gulped down a good deal and splashed some over his face. After that he stretched himself again upon the floor, where for pure weariness he dropped at length into a heavy sleep.

He awoke in darkness, his blood tingling and his pulses a-jump in a childish momentary fear at the strangeness of the place and a something else he could not define. He had recollected his position and laid down his head again, with a little effort to place himself more comfortably upon the floor, when there came a second time the noise that must have wakened him, — a stealthy faint click of the latch, as if the door were being softly opened. Hugh sprang to his feet and set his back to the wall, in the best position for defence, if it were some enemy, if it were Captain Oldesworth came seeking him. The door was opening, he perceived, as his eyes grew accustomed to the darkness. "Who is it?" he asked in a guarded tone.

"Hush! 'Tis I, Lois."

Hugh caught his breath in a gasp of relief. "Lois, you've come to free me?" he whispered, and, stepping softly to her, fumbled in the dark and found her hand.

"Yes, yes. I was afraid for you. I told Master Oldesworth that Peregrine was bragging how the captain would serve you. He saved you that time. But 'tis possible the captain will lay hands on you again. I slipped into Master Oldesworth's chamber and took the key. I know 'tis wicked; I care not. Pull off your boots and come away, quick."

Noiselessly as he could, Hugh got his boots in his hand and in his stockinged feet stole out of the chamber. In the corridor it was all black and still, just as it had been that other time when he ran from Everscombe, only now Lois was with him, and when the stairs creaked they pressed close together. Then she went forward boldly, and he, still half-blinded with sleep, was content to follow the guidance of her hand. "In here," she whispered at length, and so led him into the east parlor, where the great clock still ticked, solemn and unperturbed. "Go out at the window," Lois spoke softly; "I dare not open the door. There are a few men in the house, but they lie in the west wing and the stables. The bulk are at Kingsford. Northward you will find the way clear."

"I am not going northward," Hugh answered, as he warily pushed open the casement. "I go to my father now."

"Hugh!" The girl's voice came in a frightened gasp. "I had not released you— If you come unto them at last— They wish it not— You may be killed! You shall not do this thing."

Leaning from the casement Hugh dropped his boots carefully where the dark showed an edge of grass bordered the flagged walk; as he set himself astride the window ledge he spoke: "'Tis just the thing I shall do, Lois, and the only thing. If you be sorry for what you did, call, if you will, but I shall jump and run for it."

"I shall not call," she answered. "Oh, I care not who has the right and wrong of the war. I cannot bear they should hurt you."

She was kneeling on the window-bench with her face close to his; he suddenly bent forward and kissed her. "God bless you for this, Lois," he said.

Then he swung himself over the window ledge, and letting his weight come on his hands dropped noiselessly to the walk below. He dragged on his boots, and taking a cautious step across the flagstones slid down the terrace to the lawn. Once more he glanced back, not at Everscombe manor house, but at the opened window of the east parlor. It was too dark more than to distinguish the outline of the casement, but he knew that at the lattice Lois was still standing to wish him God speed to his father.

CHAPTER XXI

THE FATHERHOOD OF ALAN GWYETH

THE sky was bluish black with heavy masses of clouds, but through a rift in the west showed a bright star, by which Hugh guessed roughly it must be within two hours of dawn. Quickening his pace to a run at that, he came into the shelter of the park, where it was all black, and he went forward blindly, with one arm thrust up to guard his face. Now and again he had through the tree-tops a distant sight of the sky, and by it took his directions; but for the most part he stumbled on haphazard, though at a brisk pace, for the night was passing rapidly. When at length he crushed his way through a thicket to the edge of the brook that marked the bounds of the park, the bright western star had sunk out of sight behind the trees.

Beyond the brook he hurried through a tract of woodland, where he bore to the southward to keep clear of the Kingsford highway and a farmstead that lay back from it. He came out in a cornfield, where the blades felt damp against his face as he forced a rustling passage through, and after that climbed over a wall into the open fields. There were no more houses to avoid before he reached the village, so with less caution he pressed on at a good jog-trot. For the night was waning, and Kingsford was still to come.

An ominous pale streak showed in the east before him as he climbed the swell of land that cut off sight of the village. Fearing lest his figure show up too distinctly against the sky line, he made for a clump of bushes at the summit, and had just got within their shadow when he caught the sound of hoof-beats. Dropping flat he dragged himself in under the bushes, where, peering out between the leaves, he saw the black bulk of a horseman ride along the slope below him. A little to Hugh's left he pulled up and called to another rider a challenge that reached the boy's ears quite clearly, then turned and came pacing back.

They had set a mounted guard about the town, then; and with that Hugh told himself he must slip past it and quickly, too, or the dawn would be upon him. But first he waited for the horseman's return, to know what was the time between his passing and repassing, and while he waited he strained his eyes into the dark to get the lay of the land. At the foot of the rising ground was a hollow, he remembered, and across it, on the higher land, stood an irregular line of three cottages, beyond which ran a lane that led by the side wall of the churchyard. Very likely troops were lodged about the cottages now, perhaps even more patrols in the hollow, but all he could see was the black depths beneath him and the outline of the nearest cottage. Then he heard the sound of hoofs loud again, as once more the horseman on guard rode by below. Hugh could make out his form far too clearly; dawn was coming, and he durst stay no longer.

So soon as the man had turned and paced a rod on his journey back, Hugh crawled from beneath the bushes and, rolling noiselessly, creeping on hands and knees, made his way down the hillside. He remembered afterward the feel of the moist grass in his hands, the look of the mottled dark sky and the faint stars, and how at a distant hail in the village he pressed flat on the cold ground. But at last he crawled across a more level space he judged the bridle path, and scrambled down into the depth of the hollow, where a chilly mist set him shivering. As he lay outstretched, resting his weary arms a moment, he heard up above him the horseman ride by.

Now that he was within the lines of the patrol only caution and quickness were necessary. Still on hands and knees, he dragged himself slowly up the hillside, bearing ever to the south to get behind the cottages, yet not daring to venture too far, lest he come upon another line of guards. As he approached the first cottage he rose half erect and tried a short run, but the bark of a dog made him drop flat in the grass, where he lay trembling. Next instant, realizing that it was better to push on, whatever befell, he sprang up and made a dash to the cover of a hedge behind the second cottage. For now the protection of the night had nearly left him; he could see clearly the lattices of the cottage, the whitish line of highway beyond it, and others might see him as well. But as he crept forward, keeping to the shelter of the hedge, he looked up, and against the gray sky saw what gave him courage. Above the farther cottage rose the church tower, and from it stood up a staff on which fluttered a red flag with a splotch of gold upon it; Captain Gwyeth and his men still were holding out.

With renewed hope Hugh worked his way past the hedge to the shelter of an outbuilding, not a rod from the lane that ran white beneath the lich wall. He could see the church clearly now, the scowling small windows, the close side door, and the gravestones on the slope below. There was little prospect of welcome, he was reckoning anxiously, as he lay crouched against the outbuilding, when suddenly he heard a cry: "Stand, there!" Off to his right in the lane he beheld a Roundhead sentinel halted with his piece levelled.

Springing to his feet Hugh dashed across the grass plot to the lane. On the left he heard hoof-beats, then a cry: "Shoot him down!" A bullet struck the sand at his feet; he heard men running, and another shot. He heard, too, the crunch of crisp weeds beneath his boots as he crashed into the overgrown tangle beyond the lane. He felt the rough stones on the top of the wall, then he had flung himself clear across it, and was struggling up the slope among the graves. His boots were heavy and hampered him, and his breath seemed gone. He looked up to the dead windows of the church and tried to cry: "King's men! To the rescue!" but what sound he could make was lost in the din behind him. A bullet struck on a headstone just to one side; then of a sudden came a numbing pain in his left arm. He staggered, stumbled blindly a pace; then the sky was rolled up like a gray scroll, the stars were dancing before his eyes, and he was down flat upon the ground. Lifting his head dizzily he had a dim sight of the lane below, men swarming from the cottages, and one he saw leap the wall and come running toward him. Hugh's head dropped back on the ground; he saw the sky pale above and waited for the butt of his pursuer's musket to crash down upon him, and prayed it might not be long to wait.

They were still firing, he heard; and he heard, too, quick footsteps behind him and a man breathing fast. He was swung up bodily from the ground, and there came a voice he knew: "Your arm round my neck, so. Have no fear, Hugh; I've got you safe."

There was firing still and faint cheering; the rest darkness; but before it closed in on him Hugh had one blurred glimpse of a strong, blue-eyed face above him, and he knew it was his father who held him.

The light returned to Hugh in a dim and unfamiliar place; high above him, as he lay on his back, he had sight of a vaulted roof full of shadows. His head felt heavy and dazed, so he did not care to stir or speak, just closed his eyes again. There had been faces about him, he remembered vaguely, and he felt no surprise when he heard a voice that was unmistakably Ridydale's: "He's coming round, sir."

They were pressing a wet cloth to his forehead, Hugh judged, and his head was aching so he tried to thrust up his arm to stop them. "Let — me — alone," he forced the words out faintly, and opened his eyes. It was his father who was bathing his head, he saw, and remembering what brought him thither his mind went back to the formal message he had framed on the way from Tamworth. "Captain Gwyeth, Sir William Pleydall bade me deliver word, he will send you relief; it shall come to-morrow."

"Saxon, take that word to Lieutenant von Holzberg," Captain Gwyeth's voice came curtly. "Spread it through the troop that help is coming. — Spare farther speaking now, Hugh; I understand."

Hugh closed his eyes heavily and lay quiet. He felt a wet cloth tied round his head, and then he winced through all his body as a knife ripped halfway up his sleeve. "Thank Heaven, 'tis only a clean flesh wound," he heard the captain say. "Nay, Jack, I'll hold him. Do you bandage it."

Hugh felt himself lifted up till his head rested against the captain's shoulder. Half opening his eyes he had a confused sight down the nave of the church, only now it seemed unfamiliar, for the pews were torn from their places and piled up against the great entrance door. Up and down by the walls men were pacing, and some lay silent on the floor of the choir, and some he heard groaning as they lay. Then he closed his eyes and clinched his teeth, for his arm was aching rarely, so the lightest touch made him shrink. He wondered if the bandages they were putting on would never end, and if he could keep on biting down all sign of pain, when at last Ridydale spoke: "There, sir, 'tis done the best I could. If we only had water to wash the hurt properly!"

That suggested to Hugh that his mouth was dry, so he said under his breath: "I am thirsty."

"If there be a drop of water in the place, fetch it," Captain Gwyeth bade; and a moment later Hugh's head was lifted up and a cup set to his lips. It was brackish water, and very little at that; he swallowed it with one gulp, and opened his eyes to look for more. "Nay, that's the last," the captain spoke out. "'Tis an ill lodging you have taken with us. I would to God you were elsewhere!"

With the scant power of his returning strength, Hugh tried to move clear of the arm that was about him. "I had hoped, this time, you would not be sorry to see me," he broke out, in a voice that quavered in spite of himself.

He heard the captain give a sharp order to Ridydale to be off, and he felt it was to save the dignity which had almost slipped from him. He put his head down on the captain's shoulder again. "Father, you are glad to have me, after all," he said softly.

He felt the sudden tension of the arm that drew him closer, though when Captain Gwyeth spoke, his tone was of the driest: "After the trouble I've had to get hold of you, do you not think 'tis reasonable I should be glad?" Then he cut short all response with a hasty: "Lie you down here now and be quiet. You've been knocked just enough for you to make a fool of yourself if you try to talk."

Hugh grinned weakly, and suffered his father to

XXI THE FATHERHOOD OF ALAN GWYETH

put him down with his head upon a folded cloak. "I'll send Ridydale to have an eye to you," the captain said in a low tone, "and if anything happens, I'll be near." Then he rose and tramped away down the nave of the church, but Hugh, watching him through half-shut eyes, saw him halt to glance back.

After that Hugh lay a long time in a heavy, half-waking state, where he listened to the slow pacing up and down of those about him who kept guard, and to the quicker step of men who, on other errands, hastened across the reëchoing church; he heard men shout orders across the aisles or nearer to him speak in curt monosyllables; and he heard, too, all the time, the labored groaning of one who must lie somewhere near. Then there were moments when, losing all sounds, he drifted off into an unknown world, where he lived over again the happenings of the last hours, and struggled in the water of the Arrow, and fought Oldesworth's troopers, and made the last run through the churchyard under the Roundhead fire.

It was a relief to come back to consciousness and find himself lying comfortably on the floor of the choir with the dark roof far above him. A glint of purple sunlight from a broken window wavered on the ground beside him, and, forcing his mind to follow one train of thought, he contrived at last to reason out that it must be past noon. Pulling himself up on his sound arm, he tried to look about the church, but the effort made his head ache so he was glad to lie down. But he had got sight of Ridydale, who stood on a bench beneath one of the tall windows in speech with a trooper, and after a moment's rest he called the corporal by name.

Ridydale stepped down, carabine in hand, and came to Hugh's side. "Is there anything you'll be wanting, sir?" he began.

"Yes," Hugh replied, "I'd take it kindly of you if you'd just tell me what hit me that time."

Ridydale grinned and settled himself close by on the steps of the altar with his carabine across his knees. "'Tis all very simple, Master Hugh," he explained. "They wasted a deal of lead trying to wing you,—they're clumsy marksmen, those Roundhead cowherds. Somehow, by good luck, they contrived to shoot you in the arm. I take it you stumbled on one of those sunken stones, then, for you went down and broke your head against another gravestone."

"Was that it?" Hugh asked, in some mortification.

"And then the colonel stepped out and fetched you in. We had sight of you, those that were keeping the west windows, as you came down to the lane. 'It's Hugh,' says the colonel, sharp-like; 'unbar the door.' Soon as we had the barrier tore down, and we made short work of it, he out after you. 'Twas a most improper thing, too," Ridydale grumbled; "captain of a troop to risk himself under a fire like that for a mere volunteer. When there were others ready enough to go out. Maybe you were too flustered, sir, to note what a pretty shot I had at the knave who followed you over the wall?"

Hugh confessed he had missed that sight.

XXI THE FATHERHOOD OF ALAN GWYETH

"Ay, 'twas not a shot to be ashamed of," the corporal resumed, pulling his mustache with much satisfaction. "'Twas brisk give and take we were having then, sir. The colonel had a bullet through the skirts of his coat ere he got you within the church. Ay, 'twas improper conduct of him. What would have become of us all, tell me now, had he been hurt?"

"Why, just the same that will become of you now he is not hurt," the captain struck in crisply as he came up. "Tell me, Hugh, did it commend itself to the sapience of Sir William Pleydall to say what time Saturday we might look for relief?"

"No, sir."

"Perhaps it does not matter to him whether it gets here at sunrise or sunset," the captain remarked dispassionately. "It makes a mighty deal of difference to us, though." He stuck his hands in his pockets and stood staring up at the broken window where the sun came through. In the strong light Hugh noted how haggard his face looked about the eyes, and how three days of neglect showed in the red-gold beard. But when the captain turned from the window there was a laugh in his eyes. "Jack," he addressed Ridydale, who was standing at attention, "what devilry do you suppose Tommy Oldesworth is at now that he keeps so quiet?"

"Shall I try a shot to stir him up, sir?" the corporal proffered.

"Not for your life, Jack. Go rest you, while they let us."

As Ridydale strode off, Captain Gwyeth, with a soberer look, set himself down in his place.

"You ought to know, Hugh, that we're in a bad way," he spoke out in a brusque, low tone.

"There's help coming," Hugh answered stoutly, and dragged himself up on one elbow so he could rest against the steps beside his father.

"Ay, but it must be quick," the captain replied, "for Oldesworth is hot upon us. He came hither this morning under the white flag to advise us surrender to his mercy ere he batter down our walls."

"Ordnance?" Hugh asked blankly.

"He may bring it from Warwick. Our only hope is that he may be so long in the bringing it— Well, he's bravely worried that you got in to us, else he'd not have offered us terms. He's troubled about that relief; and, faith, I'm troubled, too. The men will hold out another twenty-four hours in the hope, but we've had neither food nor drink since yesterday afternoon. And we are scant thirty men now, and there are six with disabling wounds besides."

"Couldn't I make one in the fighting?" Hugh ventured hesitatingly. "I might not be able to steady a carabine with one hand, but I could load—"

"Then we could not use you long," the captain said, with a dry laugh. "That's the crowning curse of it all, Hugh; there's not above three bullets left to a man."

Hugh gazed down the dismantled church, where the pews were all turned to sorry defences and the windows were shattered with the rebel balls. He noted, too, the set, weary faces of the nearest men on guard, and something of the hopelessness

of the whole position came home to him. His
face must have shown his thought, for the captain
suddenly put a hand on his shoulder. "That's
why I'm sorry you are here," he said briefly.

"I care not for that," Hugh choked, "but if
they do not bring aid in time, — Peregrine said
they would hang you."

"Peregrine?" the captain queried. "Tut, tut!
He should be old enough by now to know a gentleman does not let himself be taken and hanged
while he has weapons in his hands. Though I
knew from the start 'twould be a fight to the
death if ever I came sword to sword with the
Oldesworths." There was a space of silence, then
he broke out: "I suppose they taught you I was
a scoundrel, did they not?"

"At the last, yes, my grandfather said it,"
Hugh admitted, "but while my mother lived she
told me only good of you."

"Then, she had forgiven me?" the captain
asked in a low tone.

Hugh's eyes were not on him, but straying
across the church to where the great Oldesworth
pew had stood; even at that distance he seemed
to read on the tablet set in the wall the name,
"Ruth Gwyeth." "She did not hold there was
anything to forgive; she said the wrong had all
been hers," he broke out; "she said you were the
best and noblest gentleman that ever lived, and
far too good for her."

"Poor lass, poor lass!" the captain said under
his breath; he was sitting with one hand shield-
ing his eyes, Hugh noted, but of a sudden he
looked down at the boy and spoke curtly: "So

you came seeking me, believing all that, and then I thrust you out of doors?"

Hugh nodded without looking at his father; he was conscious of a queer, shamed feeling, as if he had been himself at fault.

"Yet you stood up before that hound Bellasis and took that hack in the face for me. I used you like a villain, Hugh," the captain blurted out; "even Ruth could not forgive me for it. But, lad, if we come alive from this, I'll strive to make you forget it."

"I am forgetting now," Hugh said honestly. "And if you'd looked as if you wanted me, I'd ha' come to you before."

"I did want you. And you waited for me to look it, did you? I'm thinking we're something alike, lad." He put his arm about the boy's neck with a sudden, half rough caress. "Turner said you had as decent a courage as most lads and a bit more sense," he broke out. "Faith, I believe him. And if we come through here you shall have a chance to show it to every man in the troop, yes, to the same fellows that flogged you."

Hugh edged a little nearer his father. "I'd do my best to show them; I'd like the chance," he answered; then added thoughtfully, "Though, after all, I am not sorry for that flogging. If I'd not known some hard knocks already, they might have been able to frighten me yesterday."

There he stopped, unavailingly, for the captain pounced down on him and did not rest till he got the whole history of the last hours. Hugh put all the emphasis he could on Master Oldesworth and on Lois, but Peregrine and Thomas Oldesworth were dragged in at the captain's urgence, and the captain's face grew ominous. "'Twas not clean dealings on Tom Oldesworth's part," he said betwixt his teeth. "Well, when it comes to the last we'll remember it against him."

With that he got up to go about his business, but presently strode back with a cushion. "Put that under your head, Hugh," he bade, and taking up the cloak helped the boy wrap it round him. "You'll find it cold here in the church as soon as the sun goes down," he explained. "Try to sleep, though; get what strength you can against to-morrow."

After he had gone, Hugh settled himself to sleep, but it took a time, for his arm ached relentlessly, and his head was hot and his mouth dry. Moment after moment he lay staring down the dusky church, where the twilight was filling in, and harked to the slow step of those on guard. The shades had gathered dark, and his eyes were closing, when he realized that the man who had been groaning in the transept was quiet now. He guessed what that meant, and something of the ugliness of death came home to him. He sat up eagerly to look for some companionship, then felt ashamed and lay down again to listen and listen once more, and think on Peregrine's threats and Thomas Oldesworth's set, implacable face. When he went to sleep at last his kinsmen followed him, even through his dreams.

Dreams, recollections, of a sudden all were blotted out. He was sitting up, he knew, in a place that save for two feeble flickers of light was pitchy black, he heard men running and shouting, and, over all and subduing all, he heard a crash, crash which he judged bewilderedly to be of cannonading. The roof must fall soon, he feared, and scrambling to his feet he ran forward into the darkness and tumult. Above the uproar he caught Captain Gwyeth's voice, steady and distinct: "Lieutenant von Holzberg, your squadron to their stations at the windows. Corporal Ridydale, take six men and bear the wounded down into the crypt."

Following the voice, Hugh stumbled into the transept and, getting used to the dark, had a vague sight of his father, who, with his hands behind him, stood giving orders to right and left. Hugh leaned against the wall close by and kept his hand to his head that throbbed and beat with each stroke of the cannon and shake of the building. During a lull in the firing he caught the captain's voice in a lower key: "You here, Hugh?"

"I — I take it I was frightened up," he stammered. "You'll help me to a sword before the end?"

"No need for that yet," Captain Gwyeth answered. "They'll not be able to batter in these walls for hours. And by then — " His voice took a curious change of tone: "You are sure, Hugh, they made no mention of what time Saturday the aid would come?"

"No, none," Hugh replied; "but 'twill surely come, sir. Dick promised."

"Well, well, we've much to hope," said the captain, "and, faith, that's all we can do now. Sit down here, Hugh," he went on, leading him over to the pulpit stairs. "I've a notion 'twould be pleasing if I could lay hands on you when I want you."

Then he went back into the din and confusion of the nave, and Hugh, leaning his head against the balustrade, harked dazedly to the successive boom of cannon. Through it all he found space in his heart to be glad that his father had not suggested sending him down into the crypt with the other wounded.

Out through a shattered window to the east he had sight of a strip of sky, uneven with clouds, and some small stars. Little by little they paled while he sat there, and still the guns kept up their clamor. Once, after the shot, came a great rattling, and a piece of stone crashed down from the western wall; Hugh heard a confused running in that direction, and the captain's voice that checked it. Once again, when oddly he had fallen into a numb sort of doze, came another shattering crash, and right upon it a man screamed out in a way that made Hugh shudder and choke. After that he dozed no more, but rigid and upright sat listening.

It was light enough to distinguish faces when at length Captain Gwyeth, with his brows drawn and his teeth tugging at one end of his mustache, came up to him. "I've a sling here for that arm of yours," he said brusquely, beginning to fasten the bandage. "'Twould be in your way for any fighting purposes. And here's a sword. You may have to use it, unless our friends come quickly." Then he paused a time by Hugh, not speaking, but scowling upon the floor, and at last strode moodily away.

The light broadened and brightened within the church; a patch of sunshine gleamed upon the floor, and through an east window Hugh could catch the rays of yellow light glinting across the sombre leaves of the yew tree. It was a rare, warm, August day, a strange time for a life and death struggle, he told himself, as he drew the sword clumsily from its scabbard. Then he looked to the western wall of the church, where the light was smiting in now at a great gap and the crumbled stones lay scattered across the floor. Up above he saw a broken fragment of the roof that hung and swayed so its motion fascinated him. Of a sudden, as he gazed stupidly, he became aware the cannonading had ceased, and he wondered that he had not marked it before. Then he heard again his father's curt, quick tones, and saw the troopers quit their stations to gather opposite the gap in the wall.

Getting to his feet, Hugh went down to join the others. At the west door he perceived Von Holzberg standing with six men, but he passed on into the nave of the church. There at the gap the men had fallen into double line, a battered, haggard little company, some in their breastpieces, some in their shirt-sleeves. There were bandaged arms and bandaged heads among them, Hugh noted, but the carabines were all in hand, and each had his sword, too, ready at his side. Captain Gwyeth was with Ridydale, peering out at the gap in the wall, but now he turned to his men. "As you see, they have made a practicable breach in our walls," he began. "Now they have it in mind to storm us, and afterward knock us o' the head. So it behooves you fight for your worthless skins. And in any case, if they destroy us, see to it a good crew of these cursed rebels go to hell before us."

Then he looked about till his eyes fell on Hugh, and, coming to him, he took him by the shoulder and brought him over to front the troop. Hugh faced the men he had once served, and he saw Unger on the farther end of the front line, and Saxon, with his head tied up, and Jeff Hardwyn, who looked at him and fumbled with his carabine. Somehow his eyes rested on Hardwyn, as the captain began speaking briskly: "I'm thinking some of you know this gentleman, my son. He has risked his neck twice to break through the lines and share this fight with us. So I set him in Cornet Foster's place, and you will follow him as your officer. Cornet Gwyeth, you will take six men and make good the north door."

Right on that, some one, Hugh guessed it was Saxon, broke into a cheer, which the others took up. Under cover of the noise, Captain Gwyeth, still holding Hugh by the shoulder, whispered him hurriedly: "When they come in, and we have the last fight, try to get to me. We'll fight it out back to back, if it be God's will."

Just there Ridydale, standing by the breach in the wall, spoke: "Captain Gwyeth, the rebels are advancing up the hill."

CHAPTER XXII

AFTER THE VICTORY

In the moments while the besieged held their fire, a hush came upon the church. Hugh could hear the footfalls startlingly loud as he led his squadron briskly to the main door, but it did not seem it was himself who went forward. He saw the floor slip by him and heard his own tread, but it was in an impersonal way, as if it were another man who was to fight that last fight, while he stood by, unmoved and unaffected, and watched and passed judgment. Before him now he saw the entrance door, with the broken pews heaped in a stiff barricade; to the right, beneath the window, the ends of the barrier furnished some foothold, so he started to scramble up and reconnoitre. His injured arm made him awkward; at the first step he tottered, and was glad that one of his followers caught him about the body to steady him. Glancing down he saw that it was Hardwyn, but he felt no surprise; everything now was beyond wonder. "Keep hold on me, Corporal," he said, as if Hardwyn had never been any but his obedient underling, and made a move to step to the next projection.

Just there the heavy stillness of the church was broken by a jarring rattle of carabine fire that sent a cracking echo through the high roof. Looking over his shoulder Hugh saw gray smoke belch across the nave, and saw the ordered movement of the men as the second line, with their carabines raised, stepped forward to the breach. Right as he looked the second volley rolled out, and there came a cracked and dry-throated cheering from the men. "Four volleys left," he heard Hardwyn beside him mutter. "Best cheer while we can."

Once more there was a lull, and Hugh, getting his sound hand on the window ledge, pulled himself up, balancing precariously upon the broken boards, and peered out. He could see the white walk that ran up to the porch, and on either hand the untroubled graves, but he beheld no enemy astir. Venturing to lean a little from the window, he saw the roadway beyond the church wall, the arch of the bridge, the water beneath, bright in the sun, and across it the slope of hillside road. There Hugh's eyes rested, and then his voice came high and shrill so he scarcely knew it: "Hardwyn, look, look you there! What is coming?"

Hardwyn was elbowing him at the window; through the crash of the fourth volley he heard the barrier creak under the weight of the rest of the little squadron as they pressed up about him. But he did not take his eyes from the hilltop till, black and clear against the sky, a moving line of horse swung into view.

"Cavalry, sir," spoke Hardwyn, imperturbably, but Hugh had already turned from the window. "Run to the captain, Saxon," he cried. "Tell him they are coming. Relief, relief!" His voice rose to a shout that carried through the church, and his squadron took up the cry, and ended with a cheer that spread even to the fighters at the breach.

Through the uproar sounded Captain Gwyeth's voice: "If they will have it, out at them!"

The besieged swarmed forth at the breach, and Hugh, plunging headlong down off the barrier, ran to join them. The stones slipped noisily beneath his feet, and as he stumbled over the crest of the debris he turned his ankle. Outside the hot blur of sunshine dazzled him; he was conscious of light, light all around him, and men, grappling, clubbing, stabbing, in a tumult that bewildered his brain. Loud amidst the shrieks and oaths and cries for quarter rattled the crack, crack of carabines and small arms, but through it all he could hear the hollow thud, thud of horses thundering across the bridge. Some one struck at him, and instinctively he defended himself, though it was hard to swing a sword in the press. Then, getting sight of his father's red head, clear from the breach in the thick of the fight, he forced his way down to his side. At the foot of the fallen stones he stumbled over a man and, as he recovered himself, came one who tried to strike him with a clubbed musket. Hugh ducked, and, as he bent, saw the trampled grass beneath his feet, then, thrusting low, came away unscathed. Still he heard the thud, thud of coming horses, and now, too, he caught clearly from the undistinguishable shouts and yells the cry: "For a king! God and the king!"

Hugh had one glimpse of horsemen leaping the low wall; then he was guarding himself from the slashes of a Roundhead trooper, and only just saved his head. He gave the man back an undercut, when suddenly the fellow cast the sword from his hand. "I yield me, sir. Quarter!" he cried.

Hugh paused, and, glancing about him now, saw the battle was indeed over. Down in the road troopers in red sashes were guarding the way, and men of the same color were swarming up through the churchyard, but there was no resistance, save here and there where single conflicts were still contested to the end. Then Hugh spied Alan Gwyeth, picking himself up from the grass at the foot of the shattered wall, and he ran thither, just as the captain dragged to his feet the man with whom he had been grappling. It was Thomas Oldesworth, Hugh saw, with the dirt grimed into his coat and his face streaming blood; he stood unsteadily with one hand pressed to his side, but his lips were hard set as ever. "Take him within the church and look to him," the captain bade Ridydale, and then there was no room for thought of the vanquished, for Captain Turner came riding comfortably up the slope and hailed them: "Good day to you, Captain Gwyeth. Is there enough of the troop left to pay us for posting hither to rescue you?"

"Rescue be hanged!" said the captain, ungraciously, as he stood wiping the sweat from his forehead with his sleeve. "We could a held out three hours longer."

"Vour hours und more," put in the stolid Von Holzberg, and such of the troop as had gathered thither murmured a resentful assent.

"Well, well, I crave all your pardons for coming so inopportunely," Turner answered dryly, and then: "So that lad of yours got through in safety? Better go look for Lieutenant Strangwayes, Master Gwyeth; I think he's troubled about you. He has ridden on the trail of the rebels a piece."

Hugh started down the slope, but, chancing to glance back, saw Michael Turner had dismounted, and he and Captain Gwyeth were embracing each other amicably. Then he went on down the sunny hillside, and across one mound saw a man lying motionless on his back, and down by the wall one who, pulling himself up on his elbow, called for water. But Hugh could give him no heed, for up the white, hot roadway he saw a squadron coming, and at its head a black horse that he knew. He scrambled up on the low wall and stood staring and meaning to call, but could not find voice till the black horse had shot out from the bulk of the squadron, and Dick Strangwayes had reined up by the wall. "Hugh! And safe?" he asked in a low tone.

Hugh came down off the wall and reached up to grasp Dick's hand. "Safe, I think; I'm not sure yet. And, Dick, 'tis all well now between my father and me." Then he stood a moment with his head leaning against Black Boy's neck, and gazed up into Dick's face and the dazzle of blue sky beyond, but found nothing he could say.

"So you're alive, old Hugh?" came Frank's voice behind him. "Faith, you're a lucky lad. Here's your bay horse I borrowed, turn and turn about. You can ride him back, for we'll have enough and to spare."

There they must break off speech, for Turner, leading his horse carefully, came down from the church and with him Captain Gwyeth. "Call the troop to saddle again, Lieutenant," Turner ordered; "we'll ride for Everscombe and entreat these people give the captain back his horses."

"I'll ride with you," spoke Alan Gwyeth; "I want to see the house again." Then he turned to Hugh and asked in a low tone: "You say 'twas your grandfather took you out of Captain Oldesworth's hands?"

"Yes, sir. He sent me dinner, too, though I was not feeling hungry then."

The captain smiled a bit. "I'll remember it to his credit," he said. "Now keep you quiet at the church and save your hurt arm." He walked off to mount upon a spare horse, and Hugh watched him till he rode away with Turner's troop.

As he was clambering back over the wall into the graveyard, Frank came panting in his trail. "Captain Turner bade me stay with you," he announced; "sure, he has less liking to me as a volunteer than as an officer."

"Nonsense! 'Tis only that he does not wish to take you home wounded. And if they find The Jade at Everscombe they'll bring her—"

"Oh, I have The Jade safe already," Frank answered cheerfully, as he kept step with Hugh up into the churchyard; "they found her grazing in the fields beyond Tamworth yesterday morning with her stirrups flapping loose. Dick shut his mouth then as he does on occasion, and before nightfall Turner's and Leveson's men got off to bring help. I know not how they'll do without us," he went on, "for Captain Marston's troop was the only one recalled to Tamworth. But we are to make a forced march back to-night, if 'tis in our horses. And that reminds me, Hugh, you're not fit to be trusted with a good piece of horse-flesh. The Jade has strained the tendons of her near foreleg, and her coat is rough as a last year's stubble-field. Not but I'm glad she could serve you," Frank corrected himself with tardily remembered courtesy. "And, faith, I am glad as Dick that you are still alive."

Up in the church, whither the wounded and prisoners were being brought, Hugh reported himself to Von Holzberg, who despatched him with a squad to forage out food in the village. The Roundheads had already stripped it pretty clean, but in an hour's time Hugh secured enough for his father's hungry troop, and, leaving Frank idling in the village street, led his men back to the church. In the shade outside several of Gwyeth's troop, battered and weary, were easing themselves with grumbling that they had not been suffered to come share in the plunder of Everscombe. The word put it in Hugh's head that now he had eaten and felt a bit like himself he would gladly ride to the manor house and, if he could, thank his grandfather for the kindness he had thought to show him. With that intention he passed into the church to seek Von Holzberg and get his permission for the journey.

At first, as he came from the bright sunlight, the shadows within the church blinded him, but he could hear the sorry groaning of injured men, and presently made out that the wounded were laid in the transept before him. It was an ugly, pitiful sight, and knowing his helplessness to aid he passed on quickly into the choir, where he had caught sight of Ridydale. Once more the corporal was seated with his carabine on the altar stairs, but he now had on his grimmest look, for down in Hugh's old place lay Captain Oldesworth. They must have looked to his hurts somewhat, for the blood had been washed from his face, and his coat was flung open as if his side had been bandaged; he lay quiet now, with his eyes closed and his lips white, but Hugh, remembering how mercilessly the man had dealt by him, told himself he did not pity him. Without heeding the captain he stepped over to Ridydale and asked him where Lieutenant von Holzberg might be found. " He has just passed down into the nave, Master Hugh," said Ridydale relaxing his grimness a trifle. " Crave your pardon, sir, I should have called you Cornet Gwyeth now."

" Perhaps not yet," Hugh answered discreetly; " Sir William Pleydall will have a word to say in the matter."

" Humph!" Ridydale retorted conclusively. " Hasn't Colonel Gwyeth said you were his cornet? What more would you have?"

Hugh laughed, and was turning away, when he perceived that Captain Oldesworth had opened his eyes and was watching him; he halted short and waited, for he would not be the first to speak. "So it's your day now," Oldesworth began, in an even tone that might be construed a dozen ways.

" Fortune of war, sir," Hugh answered coldly.

" You got in, after all," the captain pursued, with something like a groan. " That comes of letting a civilian meddle with military matters. If you had remained in my hands —" There he broke off. "I crave your forgiveness, sir," he finished, with a bitterness that angered Hugh, yet moved him to something faintly like compassion, "I had forgot; a prisoner should be circumspect in speech."

It was on Hugh's tongue to retort that Cavalier gentlemen were not wont to mishandle their prisoners, but he thought on Dennis Butler, and that speech was silenced. He merely said: "My father will not abuse you, sir," and had half a mind to pass on, when Oldesworth struggled up on his elbow. "Tell me one thing, Hugh," he broke out as if against his will, "has Peregrine been taken?"

"No, sir, not here at Kingsford."

Oldesworth sank down again with his head on his arm. "He ran away, then," he said in a constrained voice. "He should have come in with the other squadron. We need not have been so cut to pieces had the whole troop been there. Lieutenant Ingram came in with me; he was killed at the breach. And Peregrine ran away." He paused a moment, then spoke half to himself, "If I come free again I'll strip him out of his commission for this."

Hugh dropped on one knee beside his uncle. "I pray you, sir, take it not so to heart," he urged, "mayhap 'twas not that he ran away —"

"Nay, I know Peregrine," Captain Oldesworth answered. "I would 'twere he had turned Cavalier and you had stayed Roundhead; you'd not have slunk off to save your skin." But next moment he spoke in his bitterest tone: "Nay, get you hence, lad. I don't want your pity; I'd liefer have your hate." Then he turned his face to the wall, still with his mouth hard set, and closed his eyes.

There was nothing more to be said, Hugh saw, so he came to his feet slowly, with a feeling that after all he was sorry for Oldesworth, in his pain and bitter humiliation, much though he had deserved it. He turned again to Ridydale and said under his breath: "Corporal, if you love me put on a less appalling face and use the gentleman more civilly. After all, he is my kinsman."

Then he walked away to seek Von Holzberg, and, getting his permission to ride to Everscombe, routed out Saxon to make ready Bayard and two other horses, while he went in search of Frank, for whom he had a feeling of responsibility. Not finding him at first, he was a bit worried till, chancing to step into one of the deserted cottages, he came upon the lad, curled up snugly on a settle and fast asleep. He jumped to his feet in a hurry as Hugh's hand was laid on his forehead, and after a first bewildered stare put on a great assumption of alertness and came stumbling out into the roadway. "You see, we were in the saddle all yesternight," he found tongue to explain, as the two boys, with Saxon in their wake, rode out from Kingsford. "So perhaps 'tis no great blame I just shut my eyes a moment. But, Hugh, I'd take it kindly if you did not tell Dick I went to sleep for so little. And by no means let Captain Turner know."

Hugh promised soberly, then, as they trotted along the highway, relapsed into heavy silence.

But Frank still chattered on gayly, insisting on a rejoinder: "How does it seem to come home thus? Sure, you're a dutiful lad to ride this distance to see your grandfather."

Hugh blinked at Bayard's erect ears, and told himself in dull fashion that while he was at Everscombe he would see Lois again and thank her, but he did not hold it necessary to speak it all to Frank.

A little patrol of horse guarded the park gate, but knowing Hugh they suffered him pass through with his companions. For all the roadway was cut with horse hoofs they ventured a brisk trot, and so came speedily out into the open, and following the track across the lawn drew up by the west wing. The rest of the house was silent, but here were stationed two sentinels of Turner's troop, a wagon had just been brought lumbering to the door, and from within the long guardroom Strangwayes himself hailed them: "Get off your horse, and come in, Master Cornet. I've recovered my cuirass from the plunder of these crop-eared thieves, and I'm thinking I've lighted on your buff coat and sword."

Sliding off his horse, Hugh strode briskly into the big room. At one side a long table had been hastily set forth, at which a squad of Turner's men were making a nondescript meal, but the rest of the hall was littered with arms and accoutrements that the troopers were still fetching in noisily; they must have stripped the manor house of every warlike furnishing. "Yes, the work is near done, and we can be off," Strangwayes said low to Hugh. "Sure, I'm not the man will be sorry. Did you know, my lad, there's a harder thing than storming a town, and that's to keep your troop from stealing the town after you've taken it? As 'tis a sort of family matter Captain Gwyeth is loath to have this house plundered, so we've done our best. But it's well Leveson's thieves have been used in clearing the stable; our own men have held the house, and they are the best and most obedient in the regiment. I've knocked down one or two of them, and put three under arrest, and promised a few floggings, but barring that they've been good as lambs and not stole from the house more than each man can hide in his pockets. Trust them? I'd trust my troop anywhere, that I had my eyes on it," he concluded lugubriously. "But now I'm going to risk taking one eye off them and leave Griffith to see the spoils loaded in the wagons, while I tie up your hurts again."

Accordingly, Strangwayes sent men running for water and bandages, and, putting Hugh on a bench against the wall, was dressing his head and arm, when Captain Gwyeth came in. Hugh caught sight of him as he paused an instant in the doorway, and at the changed expression of the man's face a sudden fear struck him, for it came home to him that, though the captain forgave the son who had defied him, he might never forgive the son's friend who had threatened to bar the door upon him. It was a new thought, and it checked Hugh's first impulsive movement to rise to meet his father; instead he moved a bit nearer Dick. There was an instant's dangerous silence, then Master Frank, nodding half-asleep at Hugh's side, perceived Captain Gwyeth and ran to him. "Why, this is a lucky meeting," he cried, leading the captain over to the bench. "And did I not tell you, sir, when once you were acquainted with Hugh, he was a right friendly, generous fellow for all his stubborn face?"

That made Dick turn and come to his feet, stiff and respectful. "Maybe 'twill please you look to Hugh's hurt now, sir," he said, with a slight bow.

"Nay, you've looked to his hurts before this, Lieutenant," the captain said slowly. "You've the right to do so now." He hesitated, then held out his hand, and Strangwayes took it.

Next moment Strangwayes was tying the bandage about Hugh's arm again, while he talked briskly with Captain Gwyeth of the ill ride they had had from Tamworth, and the worse ride they were like to have back, to which the captain replied with a satisfied account of the good spoil of horses and arms they had made in compensation for those lost at the first overthrow of his troop. "So soon as the carts are laden, you are to quit the house, so Captain Turner bids," Captain Gwyeth finished in an everyday tone. "We must be out of the village before sunset."

Then as Strangwayes, ending his surgery, jumped to his feet to aid Griffith in superintending the loading, the captain turned to Hugh: "I bade you stay rest at the church, but since you've taken your way and come hither you can do me service." He dropped his voice a little, though they were screened well enough under the racket of the men who were carrying forth the captured arms: "Get you to the east wing of the house, where the family have withdrawn, and, if you can, procure access to Master Oldesworth. He denied it unto me. Tell him from me that it is for the sake of his daughter and his daughter's son that I have saved his house from utter spoil to-day. And tell him that I will use Tom Oldesworth better than he deserves, and exert my influence to have him speedily exchanged. That's all."

Hugh passed out through the confusion to the front of the house, where the carts were loading, and with a rather dubious foreboding crossed the terrace to the east wing. Within, the hall was cool and dark with long afternoon shadows; the din of the western quarter drifted hither only faintly, so his mind went back with a vaguely homesick feeling to the peaceful, humdrum days at Everscombe a year ago. It seemed like a bit of the old life to go to the door of the east parlor and knock and hear his grandfather's voice bidding him enter.

But once inside, Hugh knew a year had passed since last he faced Master Oldesworth there. Not only did a glance at his own buff coat and high boots, his sword and bandaged arm recall the change, but he could see his grandfather bent a little in his chair, and his head looked whiter even than it had looked two days before. The old man was sitting by the window, but at Hugh's step he turned toward him with a cold, angry face that made the boy hesitate at first; then taking courage he repeated his father's message respectfully. Master Oldesworth's face relaxed a little at the word of Captain Oldesworth, and at that Hugh ventured to add in his own behalf: "And, aside from my father's message, sir, I wished to come hither and thank you that you used me so kindly the other day."

"I would use you still better if your stiff-necked childishness did not prevent," the old man answered sternly. "So you will yet refuse what I would offer and follow this man because he is your father?"

"Nay, 'tis not for that now, sir," Hugh replied happily, "'tis because he saved my life yesterday, and he has made me his officer. 'Tis because I know him to be a valiant and a kindly gentleman, though his temper is hot. And I must go, too, because my friends all fight for the same cause as he."

"So you will play your mother's part over again," Master Oldesworth said sharply, and gazed out at the window so long that Hugh made a motion to go, when the old man rose and bade him come to him. "You are set to go your own way, and 'tis a foolish way," he began, putting his hand on the boy's shoulder. "'Twas her way, too. Yet spite of all I loved her best of all my daughters or yet of my sons. Well, well, Hugh, I would not say it the first time you went, but now if God can look on a man who fights in so unjust a cause I pray He may keep you uncorrupted and turn your heart aright while there is time. Now go your way."

He turned to the window, and Hugh murmured that he thanked him from his heart and would strive never to shame him by his conduct.

Then he passed out into the hall again, and,

with his mind on what had just been said, was stepping slowly to the door, when from the stairway he heard his name called. Before he faced about he knew it was his sharp-tongued Aunt Delia, but the sensitive boyish dread of her was all gone now. He turned back briskly to learn her bidding, and as he turned he perceived Lois Campion standing by her at the foot of the stairs. "'Tis well you have come back, Hugh Gwyeth," Mistress Oldesworth began in a cutting voice that might have made Hugh wince, only he told himself that she was Peregrine's mother, and Peregrine was a coward and a runaway; she had need of words to vent her bitter sorrow. "There is one here maybe has claim on you, if you still hold in remembrance this gentlewoman," she went on, leading Lois forward. "She has remembered you so well that she has forgotten her duty to her kindred and to—"

"Let me go, aunt!" Lois cried in a smothered tone. She had brushed by Hugh and run out at the open door before he fully comprehended, and without a glance at Mistress Oldesworth he ran after.

Out under the elms of the east terrace he overtook Lois, and catching her hand made her stay. "What is it? What does it mean?" he urged.

"Nothing," she answered, with her head erect and her cheeks blazing. "Only, I can never go under that woman's roof again. Some things even a poor weak-spirited creature like a girl will not endure."

"But if you cannot stay at Everscombe," Hugh repeated blankly, but next moment he was half laughing. "Faith, Lois, the time has come now; you shall run away with me. Come, we'll be off at once."

The most of the troop had already ridden for Kingsford, Hugh perceived, as they came to the front of the house, but by the west door Dick and Frank, with Saxon and a trooper or two, still stayed for him. Hugh led Lois up to his two friends, a bit slowly, for the girl's steps faltered shyly. "Dick," he began, "this is Mistress Campion of whom I have told you. They have cast her out from Everscombe because she set me free from them yesterday, so 'tis in my mind to take her unto Tamworth."

Dick's expressive eyebrows went up, but before Hugh had time for resentment, or even comprehension, he had swung round on the trooper who waited at Black Boy's head: "Off to the stable with you and fetch a pillion. Frank, use your impudence well and bring out a cloak for Mistress Campion from the house. 'Tis well thought on, Hugh, for surely all the regiment is indebted to the gentlewoman who aided you to bear that message. Say, by Mistress Campion's leave, we convey her to my cousin, Mistress Cresswell, in Worcestershire?"

"Did I not tell you, Lois, that Dick was the best good fellow ever lived?" Hugh broke out.

"Pshaw!" said Strangwayes. "Get to your saddle, you one-armed warrior. You'll have all you can do to manage Bayard, so I shall entreat Mistress Campion to ride behind me."

In such order they went from Everscombe in the late afternoon, and, urging the horses a trifle, for Captain Turner and Captain Gwyeth had long since ridden forth, came into Kingsford as the sun was setting. Already the troops were falling into marching order in the road, and Strangwayes, only pausing to bid Hugh look that he did not go to sleep and pitch over his saddle-bow ere he reached Tamworth, trotted ahead to take his place in the rear of Turner's men. At a word from him Frank followed at his side, but Lois, seated behind Dick, kept her face turned back to Hugh.

He watched till they passed in the rear of the troop down to the bridge of the Arrow, then drew Bayard back to the little band that represented Gwyeth's men; the troopers were all in the saddle; behind them Leveson's squads were getting to horse, and the graveyard was deserted. The slope of the hill and the church were red in the sunset but very peaceful now; Hugh looked to the church tower and saw no flag was flying. Then he heard a voice at his elbow: "The colors, sir."

He looked down at Ridydale, stiff and soldierly, who saluted and passed him up the red and gold cornet of the troop.

"Can you manage the flag, Hugh?" spoke Captain Gwyeth, getting leisurely to horse beside him. "Leave it to the corporal if your arm —"

"Sure, sir, I can manage it very well indeed," Hugh broke in, much alarmed; he braced the staff against his stirrup and, resting it in the crook of his elbow, gathered the reins into his sound hand.

"Nay, none shall take it from you, Cornet Gwyeth," the captain laughed, and turned to the trumpeter to sound the order to march forward.

They rode slowly down the slope to the bridge. The water splashed beneath the archway, and the horses' hoofs sounded hollow on the road; Hugh listened happily, while his thoughts sped back to the last time he had crossed the bridge, a friendless little runaway. On the thought he turned in his saddle and gazed back at the church that now showed black against the sunset sky. Did the mother who lay buried there, he wondered, know that at last he had found Alan Gwyeth? He faced slowly to the front again, and as he faced he met the captain's eyes; there were no words between them, but each guessed something of the other's thoughts. Hugh tightened his hold on Bayard's bridle and drew close, so he rode knee to knee with his father.

www.ingramcontent.com/pod-product-compliance
Lightning Source LLC
Chambersburg PA
CBHW030215170426
43201CB00006B/96